Supporting Students with Emotional and Behavioral Problems

Supporting Students with Emotional and Behavioral Problems

Prevention and Intervention Strategies

by

Lee Kern, Ph.D.
Lehigh University
Bethlehem, Pennsylvania

Michael P. George, Ed.D.
Centennial School of Lehigh University
Bethlehem, Pennsylvania

and

Mark D. Weist, Ph.D.
University of South Carolina
Columbia, South Carolina

·P A U L·H·
BROOKES
PUBLISHING Co.®

Baltimore • London • Sydney

· P A U L · H ·
BROOKES
PUBLISHING CO.®

Paul H. Brookes Publishing Co.
Post Office Box 10624
Baltimore, Maryland 21285-0624

www.brookespublishing.com

Typeset by Absolute Service, Baltimore, Maryland.
Manufactured in the United States of America by
Sheridan Books, Inc., Chelsea, Michigan.

The individuals described in this book are composites or real people whose situations are masked and are based on the authors' experiences. In all instances, names and identifying details have been changed to protect confidentiality.

Library of Congress Cataloging-in-Publication Data

The Library of Congress has cataloged the print edition as follows:
Kern, Lee, author.
Supporting students with emotional and behavioral problems : prevention and intervention strategies / by Lee Kern, Ph.D., Lehigh University ; Dr. Michael P. George, Lehigh University ; and Dr. Mark D. Weist, University of South Carolina.
pages cm
Summary: "This book provides educators with practical, simple step-by-step strategies to address serious problem behaviors, framing interventions within a tiered approach focused on prevention and positive approaches. Although the book primarily presents intervention strategies for students with significant emotional and behavioral problems, these interventions are applicable for children with and without a diagnosis of emotional behavior disorder and also can be used to target less severe behavior problems. This cost-efficient, proactive framework helps prevent the development of more severe behavioral issues and sets the stage for an assessment-based, proactive, and functional approach to addressing serious behavior problems. The book includes case stories, teacher reflections, forms, and ready-to-implement intervention approaches and strategies for both the classroom and school setting"—Provided by publisher.
Includes bibliographical references and index.
ISBN 978-1-59857-806-5 (paperback)
1. Mentally ill children—Education. 2. Problem children—Behavior modification. 3. Behavior therapy for children. I. George, Michael P., author. II. Weist, Mark D., author. III. Title.

LC4165.K47 2015
371.94—dc23 2015023730
British Library Cataloguing in Publication data are available from the British Library.

2019 2018 2017 2016 2015

10 9 8 7 6 5 4 3 2 1

Contents

About the Forms

Purchasers of this book may download, print, and/or photocopy for educational use these blank forms: Figures 2.2, 3.1, 3.2, 3.3, 3.4, 3.5, 3.6, 3.7, 4.5, 8.2, 8.3, 8.4, 8.5, 8.9, 9.3, 10.1, 10.2, 10.3, and 10.4. These materials are included with the print book and are also available to print and e-book buyers at **www.brookespublishing.com/kern/materials**.

About the Authors

Lee Kern, Ph.D., received her doctorate in special education from the University of South Florida. She is currently Associate Chair of the College of Education and Professor of Special Education at Lehigh University. Dr. Kern has worked in the field of special education for more than 35 years as a classroom teacher, behavior specialist, professor, and consultant. Her research interests are in the area of interventions to reduce challenging behavior. She has published numerous articles, book chapters, and two books on topics related to problem behavior. Dr. Kern has received more than $20 million in grant support from the U.S. Department of Education and National Institute of Mental Health to pursue research in behavior problems. She is currently Co-editor of *Journal of Positive Behavior Interventions* and Associate Editor of *School Mental Health.*

Michael P. George, Ed.D., received his doctorate in special education from the University of Missouri–Columbia and is presently Director of Centennial School of Lehigh University. For nearly 30 years, Dr. George has been an administrator of programs for children and youth with the most severe social, emotional, and behavioral difficulties. He has served as a director of day school programs in St. Louis County, Missouri; Eugene, Oregon; and Bethlehem, Pennsylvania. His work on behalf of students and families has received numerous accolades over the years, including recognition by the U.S. Department of Education, the U.S. Department of Justice, the American Institutes for Research, CNN, and ABC's *Nightline.*

Mark D. Weist, Ph.D., received his Ph.D. in clinical psychology from Virginia Polytechnic Institute and State University (Virginia Tech) in 1991 and is currently the director of the clinical community program and professor of school psychology in the Department of Psychology at the University of South Carolina. He was on the faculty of the University of Maryland for 19 years, where he helped to found and direct the Center for School Mental Health (http://csmh.umaryland.edu), one of two national centers providing leadership in the advancement of school mental health policies and programs in the United States. He has edited nine books and has published and presented widely in school mental health and in the areas of positive behavioral interventions and supports, interconnecting school mental health and positive behavioral interventions and supports, trauma, violence and youth, evidence-based practice, and cognitive behavioral therapy.

Foreword

The life trajectory of children and adolescents with significant challenging behavior, especially those with disabilities, has been well documented as bleak and fraught with barriers. Alarming figures illustrate this, such as only 42% of youth with emotional/behavioral disorders (EBD) graduate with a high school diploma (Wagner, Kutash, Duchnowski, Epstein, & Sumi, 2005) and over half of students with EBD are arrested after leaving school and up to 70% of those who drop out spend their adult life in and out of prison (VanAcker, 2004). Students with EBD face higher rates of unemployment, substance abuse, and dysfunctional social networks compared to all other groups of students with and without disabilities (Wagner et al., 2005). In describing social interventions and supports for this high-risk population in the early years of IDEA, Walker and Bullis (1991) stated, "The public schools' record of effectively accommodating students with behavioral disorders...is close to abysmal.... [A] strong case can be made regarding their neglect of students experiencing serious behavior problems" (p. 78).

In response to the challenges noted above, a group of leaders in the field of EBD gathered and put forth a seminal paper outlining the evidence-based practices educators should be implementing and the necessary systems of support to ensure implementation fidelity (Peacock Hill Working Group, 1991). Unfortunately, their recommendations remained largely unheeded by the larger educational community. Around the same time, embracing the Peacock Hill Working Group's recommendations and other emerging research, advocates of early intervention and prevention of EBD began work on creating schoolwide systems of positive behavioral support (Lewis & Sugai, 1999; Walker, Horner, Sugai, Bullis, Sprague, Bricker, & Kaufman, 1996). Over 2 decades of schoolwide research has demonstrated through systemic implementation of evidence-based practices that educators can improve social and academic behavioral outcomes (see www.pbis.org). The results of these, and other research efforts, are evident throughout this text.

Kern, George, and Weist have authored a state-of-the-art volume of evidence-based practices to support students with challenging behavior. In addition to providing key elements in creating effective behavior plans for individual students, guided by the logic of functional behavioral assessment, they have described necessary strategies that will both prevent problem behavior as well as build learning environments that will increase the success of individual plans. The inclusion of chapters focusing on classroom management, effective instruction, and school connectedness is a great example of using prevention science to simultaneously reduce potential problems as well as build learning environments to increase the likelihood that students with challenging behavior are more successful. The interconnectedness of schoolwide, classroom-based, and individual plans is contextualized for the reader through their chapters on essential features of schoolwide positive behavior support, including the explicit teaching of social behavior. As they discuss, the degree to which any efforts to support individual student academic and social behavior success will be predicated on the degree to which schools build effective and comprehensive systems of support that go beyond single classrooms or intervention plans designed and implemented in isolation.

The final chapter of the book, focusing on mental health needs, further speaks to the comprehensive and systemic focus of the text. Often presented in many similar texts as an afterthought that educators might also want to make sure they "collaborate" with mental health providers, the authors once again outline how all of the elements of effective supports for high-risk students should be 1) interconnected to all facets of what happens in the child's school day, 2) designed by a school-based problem-solving team, and 3) grounded in universal supports to build in de facto generalization strategies.

Supporting Students with Emotional and Behavioral Problems: Prevention and Intervention Strategies should become an essential text for all pre- and in-service educators and related professionals who work in prekindergarten through high school settings. It captures all of the critical elements advocated in prevention science and evidence-based practices to address challenging behavior, then contextualizes both in a multi-tiered system of support framework. The authors of the text also bring a unique blend of years of experience conducting research, leading implementation efforts, and working across related agencies—all with a passion for ensuring children and youth with disabilities and those at risk, and their families, are afforded every opportunity to be successful.

Tim Lewis, Ph.D.
Professor of Special Education
University of Missouri
Co-Director of the Office of Special Education Program's
Center on Positive Interventions and Supports

REFERENCES

Lewis, T.J., & Sugai, G. (1999). Effective behavior support: A systems approach to proactive school-wide management. *Focus on Exceptional Children, 31*(6), 1–24.

Peacock Hill Working Group. (1991). Problems and promises in special education and related services for children and youth with emotional or behavioral disorders. *Behavioral Disorders, 16*, 299–313.

VanAcker, R. (2004). Current status of public education and likely future directions for students with emotional and behavioral disorders. In L.M. Bullock & R.A. Gable (Eds.), *Quality personnel preparation in emotional/behavioral disorders: Current perspectives and future directions.* Denton, TX: Institute for Behavioral and Learning Differences.

Wagner, M., Kutash, K., Duchnowski, A.J., Epstein, M.H., & Sumi, W.C. (2005). The children and youth we serve: A national picture of the characteristics of students with emotional disturbances receiving special education. *Journal of Emotional and Behavior Disorders, 13*(2), 79–96.

Walker, H.M., & Bullis, M. (1991). Behavior disorders and the social context of regular class integration: A conceptual dilemma? In J. Lloyd, N. Singh, & A. Repp (Eds.), *The regular education initiative: Alternative perspectives on concepts, issues and models* (pp. 75–94). Champaign-Urbana, IL: Sycamore.

Walker, H.M., Horner, R.H., Sugai, G., Bullis, M., Sprague, J. R., Bricker, D., & Kaufman, M.J. (1996). Integrated approaches to preventing antisocial behavior patterns among school-age children and youth. *Journal of Emotional and Behavioral Disorders, 4*, 193–256

Foreword

In this book, Lee Kern, Michael P. George, and Mark D. Weist "flip the script" on models for the prevention and early intervention of emotional and behavioral problems among children: Instead of describing how to ensure that children are ready for school, the authors provide innovative and timely strategies that show *schools* how to be ready for *children.* Brilliant in its clear messages and timely in its recognition of the importance of effective classrooms, this book puts the tools for change in the hands of the teachers.

The prevalence of emotional and behavioral problems for children and youth across North America is well established. The school mental health perspective used here promotes schools as key in the prevention and early intervention of such problems and thereby makes sense on the level of the child, family, school community, and society at large. Kern, George, and Weist are leaders in both research and practice who have established the critical importance of school mental health prevention and intervention models. With this book, they widen the circle of care to include and recognize teachers as team members who can promote mental health and intervention and leverage the relationships they develop with students and their families in planning, teaching, and assessing for student success. Their clear and unwavering message is summarized in Chapter 1: "This book is designed to help teachers remove and reduce academic and nonacademic barriers to learning and… to empower teachers and offer further skill training in work they are already doing to promote student wellness, mental health, and positive behavior."

There is no doubt about the important role teachers play in the mental health and well-being of students, but as Gibson, Stephan, Brandt, and Lever (2014) noted, "There is a discrepancy between the identified role of teachers in mental health care and their training related to mental health" (p. 270). Those who provide support for social emotional learning and needs, including teachers, must have a good understanding of child development, promotion of health and wellness (including mental health), social determinants of health, culture, and context. The development of these critical knowledges, beliefs and skills, however, has been described as limited (Gibson et al., 2014; Weston, Anderson-Butcher, & Burke, 2008) or altogether missing (Rodger et al., 2014).

In this book, the authors have provided straightforward information about the importance of tiered models of support and schoolwide positive behavioral support (SWPBS). They share current tools and practices so that educators need not spend time reinventing the wheel but can instead create opportunities to engage in critical thinking and reflection about what defines a well-functioning school and whether there is a need for change. Chapters 3, 4, and 5 offer (in order) a guided tour of Assessing the Classroom Environment, Managing Classroom Behavior, and Effective Instructional Practices. These chapters are written for teachers, communicating the value and efficacy of what teachers do and offering evidence-supported and practically grounded ways to extend their practice and further develop their teaching effectiveness. In guiding teachers to think about their classroom expectations, for example, we see the clear links between students knowing *what* is expected, teaching the skills and creating the environment so students know *how* to meet those expectations, responding to the needs of students who are struggling, and seeing students experience success. As the authors note in the Chapter 4 summary, they "described a number of classroom 'basics' that every teacher should have in place." Just as making expectations clear to students helps them prepare for success, providing this chapter on how teachers can do this helps them in ways that will influence numerous students during one teacher's career.

In the beginning of this foreword, I noted that Drs. Kern, George, and Weist have turned school readiness around in an important way, from viewing the child as arriving at school in some state of "readiness" or "not-readiness" to viewing the school as being ready to meet the needs of each child. But as I close this foreword, I realize that they are also providing the means for teacher readiness in a way that encourages the teachers who read this book to recognize that in their teaching, they have the opportunity to create safe and healthy classrooms for all children, including those who experience emotional and behavioral problems, and to the benefit of all. For this, I have profound respect and appreciation for Lee, Michael, and Mark and thank them for this unique and most valuable resource.

Susan Rodger, Ph.D.
Associate Professor
The University of Western Ontario

REFERENCES

Gibson, J.E., Stephan, S., Brandt, N.E., & Lever, N.A (2014). Supporting teachers through consultation and training in mental health. In M.D. Weist, N.A. Lever, C.P. Bradshaw, & J.S. Owens (Eds.), *Handbook of school mental health: Research, training, practice and policy: Issues in Clinical child psychology* (pp. 269–282). New York, NY: Springer Science + Business Media.

Rodger, S., Hibbert, K., Leschied, A., Pickel, L., Stepien, M., Atkins, M.-A,,...Vandermeer, M. (2014). *Mental health education in Canada: An analysis of teacher education and provincial/territorial curricula.* Prepared for Physical and Health Education Canada and available at http://www.phecanada.ca/sites/default/files/mentalhealtheducationincanada.pdf

Weston, K.J., Anderson-Butcher, D., & Burke, R.W. (2008). Developing a comprehensive curriculum framework for teacher preparation in expanded school mental health. *Advances in School Mental Health Promotion, 1*(4), 25–41.

Preface

Our collective work in schools spans over 100 years. As classroom teachers, mental health providers, and consultants, we at times have struggled to address the social, behavioral, and mental health needs of our students. We have also seen many otherwise skilled educators leave the field because of student behavior problems. As we continued in the field, we came to understand the multitude of effective interventions that can be employed to create a positive school and classroom climate, motivate learners to their best performance, and support children and youth who are struggling with personal and family issues. Unfortunately, the important strategies that need to be in place in every school and classroom do not reach the hands of educators often enough. The intent of this book is to describe the approaches that research and our own personal experiences have taught us will be most effective yet feasible for educators to implement.

This is an exciting time in the area of student behavior, with many new advances that we sought to capture in this book. One area that has long been considered important but has only recently gained practical consideration is the role of student mental health. A student struggling with mental health challenges simply cannot perform to full capacity at school. Fortunately, new approaches are emerging that place teachers in a pivotal role. Furthermore, schools are finding ways to evaluate their current practices and make sure resources are properly allocated to prevent common mental health challenges. In this book, we attempt to explicate the important role of mental health services and describe how they can be embedded into regular school practices.

Although we often hear educators talk about the important partnership between schools and mental health services, we see it far less often in practice. We believe this book is novel in that we explain in a user-friendly manner how to make it happen.

Another important development is a tiered approach to intervention. This approach focuses on prevention by providing basic support and instruction to all students. Tiered intervention is resource-efficient because when it is employed, far fewer students will engage in problem behavior, leaving resources available for those who need more intensive support. We describe the rationale and logic of this intervention model and detail how it can be delivered in a school setting. We also describe how a tiered approach can be implemented in the classroom, whether in schools where schoolwide intervention is not in place or in particularly challenging classrooms.

Research indicates that educators—including general education teachers, special education teachers, and mental health professionals—do not receive adequate training to address the social, emotional, and behavioral problems of children and youth in schools. In fact, most preservice training programs devote very few hours to instruction on interventions that in-service teachers say they desperately need. Although there are numerous books available that focus on behavior management, they generally have a single focus, such as schoolwide strategies, classroom management for general educators, or complex assessment and intervention for students with significant challenges. We believe it is important for educators to understand the full range of intervention approaches because increasingly inclusive educational practices suggest they will encounter students with all levels of need. We believe that all educators must work collectively to recognize student emotional and behavioral challenges and ensure that effective practices are in place in their schools. Thus, we saw the need to describe a compendium of practices in a single volume.

Who will benefit from this book? We believe the book will be very helpful for teacher preservice and in-service training. The book will prepare prospective educators, including aspiring administrators, to step into their first job with an understanding of interventions they can immediately implement to prevent challenging behavior, ways to reduce problem behavior of students with more serious concerns, and the range of effective practices that should be accessible in the schools where they work. Throughout the book, strategies are presented in a step-by-step fashion for ease of understanding and ready implementation. This book also will be useful for educators who are not currently struggling with behavior management but are interested in new approaches to ensure that all students have the supports needed to perform their best.

Acknowledgments

There are many people to whom we owe our deepest thanks for assisting us with this book. First and foremost, we thank Nancy George for her patient editing, insightful suggestions, and support throughout the drafting of the book. We also thank Annette Wilcox, Viviana Gonzalez, and Beth Custer for their technical assistance. In addition, we extend our thanks to David Riddle, Anna Vande Velde, and Nathan Weist for help with literature reviews.

For Alexa and Jack
—LK

To Nancy
—MPG

For Kara
—MDW

1

School Behavior Problems and Models of Prevention and Intervention

Each year, children and adolescents across the nation assemble in schools, facing new social and emotional challenges they must navigate as they adjust to life in the classroom. For some, this is their first time experiencing the contextual features of a schoolhouse and working alongside large numbers of peers. Others are experiencing the novelties of brand-new teachers, perhaps new schools, classrooms full of different peers, and expectations they may not fully understand. Educators must be prepared not only to create safe and orderly school environments, but also to offer supports that ensure all students have the opportunity to succeed in academics as well as the social, emotional, and behavioral realms. In this chapter, we discuss many of the challenges educators face today. We also introduce readers to a model of prevention and intervention that we use to structure the delivery of supports described throughout this book.

BEHAVIOR PROBLEMS IN SCHOOLS

Educators have long understood the link between academic achievement and behavior problems. There is convincing research showing that behavior problems can impede academic success and that a poor curriculum or inadequate instruction can lead to behavior problems (U.S. Department of Education, 2009; Vander Stoep, Weiss, Kuo, Cheney, & Cohen, 2003). Moreover, some children may be genetically predisposed to particular psychiatric disorders (see Norman & Malla, 2001), which at some point can interfere with their school performance.

Although most behavior problems can be prevented and psychiatric problems reduced through appropriate intervention, schools struggle to put systems in place that adequately address students with these types of needs. In fact, research indicates that for several decades, teachers have reported that student behavior problems are one of their top concerns (e.g., Bullock, Ellis, & Wilson, 1994; Elam & Rose, 1995; Fink & Janssen, 1993; Mastropieri & Scruggs, 2002). Both experienced and first-year teachers report that the training they received was inadequate to address the behavior and mental health problems their students exhibit (Koller et al., 2004; Oliver & Reschly, 2010). For example, in a survey of more than 111 teachers, Gable and colleagues (1992) found that behavior management was ranked high in importance and that teachers reported they had failed to receive training to adequately prepare them to provide effective interventions. Even teachers specifically trained to work with children and youth having emotional and behavior problems reported poor college-level preparation. In a national survey of teachers certified in the field of emotional and behavioral disorders, nearly two thirds indicated that their college coursework was poor preparation for the situations they encountered as teachers (George, George, Gersten, & Grosenick, 1995). Inadequate preparation of teachers with students having emotional and behavioral disorders continues to be a concern (Oliver & Reschly, 2010; Rosenberg, Sindelar, & Hardman, 2004).

A close look at teacher preparation programs helps explain the genesis of this problem. State, Kern, Starosta, and Mukherjee (2011) reviewed program requirements and syllabi from undergraduate elementary general education teacher certification programs around the country. They found that 15% of the teacher training programs required no courses whatsoever in behavior management. On average, across all of the programs reviewed, future educators received 115 minutes, or just under 2 hours, of course instruction about individual interventions and only 39 minutes about classwide interventions. This provides evidence that as teachers begin their careers, they have not been taught the many indispensable skills necessary not only to organize and manage students in an effective and efficient way, but also to address the difficulties of students who enter school with more substantial emotional and behavioral needs. Moreover, the research reveals that teachers do not receive instruction in these skills after they have begun teaching, either through inservice or other methods of postcertification teacher training provided by schools (Koller et al., 2004).

Just how pervasive are behavior problems in today's schools? It is not entirely clear whether problems are on the rise or whether they have always been present, but variables such as growing class size, diminished parent involvement, and failure to implement effective interventions have driven their importance to the forefront. Regardless, the presence of students with emotional and behavioral problems is clear in every school in America. There is some research that is helpful in understanding the current prevalence of school problems, although estimates vary greatly. In a comprehensive literature review, Irvin, Tobin, Sprague, Sugai, and Vincent (2004) examined whether office disciplinary referrals (ODRs) are valid indicators of school behavior problems and climate. They found convincing evidence that the level of ODRs provides a good gauge of the climate of a school in critical areas such as student misbehavior, student and teacher perceptions of safety, classroom orderliness, student social adjustment, and the prevalence of juvenile delinquency and behavior disorders. Thus, it appears educators can rely on ODRs as general indicators of problems within a school.

Models of schoolwide positive behavior support (SWPBS), replicated in schools throughout the United States, suggest that approximately 15% of students will experience moderate behavior problems and another 3%–5% will have significant behavior problems, as measured by the number of ODRs they receive. Specifically, students with moderate behavior problems will receive two to five ODRs in a school year and students with significant behavior problems will receive six or more ODRs in a school year (Irvin et al., 2004). These data offer a general understanding of the number of students who will require supports beyond those typically provided in a well-structured school.

In the area of mental health or psychiatric concerns, roughly one in five children and adolescents will experience clinically significant levels of symptoms and impairment from mental health disorders (Merikangas et al., 2010) at some point in their development. This is a much higher number than most people realize, underscoring the universality of mental health challenges and that many people experience challenges at some point in their lives (e.g., related to loss, divorce, unemployment). The most common mental health disorders in children and adolescents are anxiety and mood disorders and disruptive behavior disorders (which include attention-deficit/hyperactivity disorder [ADHD]; see Chapter 12), and as children move into adolescence and young adulthood, these problems are also increasingly connected with co-occurring behavioral problems and substance abuse (Merikangas et al., 2010). Furthermore, around one in 10 youth are affected by a severe mental illness that will significantly compromise their adaptive and school functioning and, for many students, continue into adulthood and compromise many domains of life, including familial, social, and vocational adjustment as well as physical health status (National Institute of Mental Health, 2001).

Within the educational system, students with significant social, emotional, and/or behavioral disorders are identified under the Individuals with Disabilities Education Improvement Act (IDEA) 2004 (PL 108-446) as having "emotional disturbance." Because the term *emotional disturbance* is stigmatizing and inappropriate (e.g., Walker, Geddes, Lever, Andrews, & Weist, 2010), we use the term *emotional and/or behavioral disorders (EBD)* throughout this book. This group of students has very poor educational outcomes.

For example, more than half of students identified as having EBD drop out of high school (U.S. Department of Education, 2009). Further, acting-out behaviors (e.g., problems controlling aggressive impulses), internalizing difficulties (e.g., withdrawal), and social interaction problems contribute directly to poor outcomes later in life (see Aud et al., 2011; Levin & Belfield, 2007). The failure of students with EBD to graduate high school can be viewed as one more exacerbating milestone in an already tenuous life trajectory.

These sobering findings underscore the need for early identification and effective teaching and intervention for students at risk for, starting to show, or clearly showing emotional and/or behavioral challenges, and also highlight the critical role teachers have in assisting these students.

FACTORS CONTRIBUTING TO BEHAVIOR PROBLEMS

There has been much speculation about the causes of emotional and behavioral problems. The widely accepted diathesis–stress hypothesis suggests that all people are born with some vulnerabilities to emotional and/or behavioral problems but that level of vulnerability varies (Goforth, Pham, & Carlson, 2011). Vulnerability can be viewed as a predisposition or area in a person's life where there is increased risk for negative circumstances or personal problems (see Chapter 11 for additional information about risk factors). For example, a person growing up in a home with substance abuse has enhanced vulnerability later in life when around people with substance abuse issues and is also at increased risk for abusing substances. The level of vulnerability and number of risk factors or adverse events an individual experiences influence whether EBD will manifest (Sameroff & Chandler, 1975). For example, someone with low vulnerability may still display significant EBD if he or she experiences a significant adverse circumstance (e.g., severe abuse). Alternatively, someone with relatively high vulnerability may not develop more significant EBD if he or she is raised in a very nurturing environment and experiences a range of protective factors. In general, the more risk factors children experience, the more likely they are to have problems in functioning, whereas the more protective factors they experience, the more likely they are to function well and experience success. The presence of protective or "resilience" factors can help mitigate or reduce the impact of risk factors.

In terms of risk factors, educators are beginning to understand that behaviors seen in early childhood suggest which children may be at risk for later problems. For example, evidence points to children's early self-regulation skills as important for adjustment. Self-regulation refers to a child's ability to control and modulate his or her behavior in response to various cognitive, social, and emotional environmental demands (Posner & Rothbart, 2000). A child with poor self-regulation has difficulties interacting with peers, frequently argues or aggresses toward classmates, and may have tantrums or cry excessively. Poor self-regulation in young children can be exacerbated by a number of variables, such as child temperament and exposure to punitive and coercive parenting (Caulkins & Fox, 2002). Other risk factors for problem behavior that have been identified in young children, but may be less susceptible to intervention, include being male, having medical problems, and having genetic predisposition (e.g., Lavigne & Faier-Routman, 1992; O'Connor, Deater-Deckard, Fulker, Rutter, & Plomin, 1998).

Researchers have also examined risk factors that may influence the development of behavior problems as children age. For example, in a longitudinal study, O'Connor and colleagues (1998) examined variables that predict externalizing problems in middle elementary years (up to age 10) in four domains (child, sociocultural, parenting, and peer related). They found the aforementioned child risk variables (being a boy, more resistant temperament, medical problems) predicted later externalizing problems. Additional domains that also predicted externalizing problems were sociocultural risks (lower socioeconomic status, living with a single mother, higher child-to-adult ratio in the household, teenage pregnancy, unplanned pregnancy, more stressful life events), parenting/caregiving risks (extensive nonmaternal child care, lower father involvement, higher parental conflict, exposure to violence, harsh discipline, likelihood of physical abuse, lack of positive parenting, and maternal positive attitudes toward aggression), and early peer experiences (peer rejection in kindergarten). These risk variables, along with gender (male) and ethnicity (African American in the case of their study), were very good at predicting externalizing and aggressive behavior in children during middle childhood. Further, when several risk variables were present, the odds of having externalizing problems increased.

When examining risk factors in a child's life, it is equally important to consider protective factors. Protective factors are conditions or attributes that diminish a student's risk and allow him or her to adapt to otherwise difficult circumstances or situations. A number of protective factors are malleable and can be strengthened via school support and intervention (O'Connell, Boat, & Warner, 2009; Youngstrom, Weist, & Albus, 2003). For example, academic achievement has been identified as a protective factor that can be developed through good academic instruction. Teachable protective factors that can be enhanced in children and adolescents include emotional regulation, coping and problem-solving skills, spirituality and faith involvement, helping others, participating in extracurricular activities, and reading for pleasure. Other protective factors are external to the student and can be enriched by others. These include a nurturing and warm family environment, an engaging school with a positive climate, clear expectations for behavior, regular interaction with nonfamilial positive adults, and opportunities for appropriate recreation and physical exercise (see Scales, Benson, Leffert, & Blyth, 2000). Chapter 12 delineates specific strategies to increase protective factors in schools.

Because many risk factors are difficult to alter (e.g., family economic status, single parent), it is judicious and more efficient to concentrate on protective factors. Schools are uniquely positioned to capitalize upon and strengthen student protective factors. Throughout this book, we emphasize student strengths that can be enhanced and specific skills that can be taught to increase the likelihood of optimal outcomes.

THE DETRIMENTAL OUTCOMES OF PROBLEM BEHAVIORS

Educators tend to view problem behaviors as isolated events that must be addressed through consequences. This traditional and rather narrow approach fails to offer sufficient supports to change behavior in a meaningful and durable way. A look at the long-term outcomes of problem behavior underscores the need to identify more effective solutions.

In the area of academics, problem behavior distracts from learning and interferes with student success (Barton-Arwood, Wehby, & Falk, 2005; Ruhl & Berlinghoff, 1992). For example, students identified by the school system as having EBD scored in the lowest 25th percentile as a group in pivotal areas such as reading comprehension and mathematics calculation (Bradley, Henderson, & Monfore, 2004; Lane et al., 2005), and more than 66% failed competency exams for their grade (Wagner, 1993). Academic difficulties usually lead to poor grades, which are associated with school dropout (Meadows, Neel, Scott, & Parker, 1994). The deleterious outcomes of dropout have been well documented and include continued problems with social and emotional adjustment, reduced likelihood of employment, a higher likelihood of living in poverty, poorer health, and greater rates of incarceration (Newman et al., 2011; Wagner & Davis, 2006).

Social problems resulting from problem behavior, generally seen at an early age, are also associated with poor long-term outcomes (e.g., Gresham, Lane, MacMillan, & Bocian, 1999), as we describe in Chapter 6. For example, when students exhibit behavior problems in the classroom, it adversely affects their relationships with teachers, peers, and other school personnel (Reid, Gonzalez, Nordness, Trout, & Epstein, 2004; Wehby, Symons, & Shores, 1995). Further, there also is evidence that social skill difficulties are related to other long-term difficulties, including low academic achievement, teacher and peer rejection, delinquency, vocational adjustment problems, and school dropout (Gresham et al., 1999; Ollendick, Weist, Borden, & Greene, 1992; Pope, Bierman, & Mumma, 1991; Walker et al., 1995).

One might expect that the problem would be solved by identifying students as having EBD to ensure they are provided with specialized services. However, research reveals that these services come too late, are not comprehensive, and fail to meet the needs of this population (e.g., Bradley et al., 2004). For instance, longitudinal research indicates that among all special education disability groups, students with EBD receive the highest number of school disciplinary actions, unexcused absences, and suspensions (Bradley et al.). In a given year, school suspensions or expulsions occur for more than 70% of students with EBD, compared to approximately 30% of all students with disabilities and 22% of students in general education (Skiba, Peterson, & Williams, 1997; Van Acker, 2004). Further, students with EBD are retained at a rate that is twice the national average and are placed in the most restrictive settings, which are no better equipped to meet their needs than less restrictive placements (Bradley et al.). Perhaps most alarming is the high percentage of secondary students with EBD who have arrest records (34.8%) and the extraordinarily high dropout rate of more than 50% (Bradley et al.).

In addition to the many measurable adverse outcomes described above, students with EBD experience many other daily challenges. For example, Sacks and Kern (2008) found that adolescents identified as having EBD rated their quality of life significantly lower than general education adolescents. In addition, problem behavior is associated with family stress, and family stress contributes to problem behavior in children in a cyclic manner (Mantymaa et al., 2012). Finally, the lack of appropriate and effective interventions results in enormous costs to society in terms of mental health and school-based services as well as juvenile justice and general health services (Foster, Jones, & Conduct Problems Prevention Research Group, 2005).

REASONS FOR POOR STUDENT OUTCOMES

To date, schools have been unable to provide supports for students who engage in problem behavior in a way that changes the trajectory of perpetual long-term problems. Therefore, the question is, what have schools done wrong? The problem may lie in a number of routine beliefs and practices that have been ineffective.

First, schools tend to consider problem behavior a student-centered issue. This view is aligned with a medical model in which disease is something that resides within an individual and effectual treatment involves ridding the individual of that disease. This viewpoint also can be seen in the mental health field's inappropriate use of such terms as *psychopathology*, which ascribes pathology within children and often results in marginalizing and/or stigmatizing them. Many who read this book have no doubt reviewed a psychological evaluation completed by a school-employed or community-based psychologist or psychiatrist that uses words that pathologize or stigmatize children and convey that the locus of the problem is within the child. These reports are almost never helpful, and students are being damaged by the labels assigned to them, which also result in subsequent change (usually not positive) in the way they are treated after receiving the label (e.g., Burns, 2000).

In schools, this way of thinking can also legitimize the routine use of punishment. That is, educators have long adhered to the idea that eliminating problem behavior requires changing the student, generally by delivering a punitive consequence. When a consequence does not eliminate behavior in the expected way, most educators believe they need to simply find another consequence (usually more punitive) and the problem behavior will eventually disappear. Many commonly used procedures (e.g., time-out, ODRs, suspension) exclude students from academic instruction and the opportunity to learn important social skills. These strategies also frequently exacerbate students' emotional and behavioral problems (Shores, Gunter, & Jack, 1993). Further, such approaches fail to account for the role the environment plays in problem behavior. Recent approaches acknowledge that behavior problems are a result of interactions between a student and events and expectations within his or her environment (Carr et al., 2002).

The environment–behavior interaction also highlights the need to view behavior in the context of academic expectations. Educators have long separated the two, failing to understand the significant contribution that the curriculum and instruction play in occurrences of problem behavior. In fact, this notion has even resulted in educators holding the idea that behavior must improve before academic instruction can occur. A look at some recent research underscores this point. Studies show that teacher instruction time with students who have behavior problems is relatively limited, and academic instruction is characterized by easier tasks than those provided for students without behavior problems (Partin et al., 2009; Wehby, Tally, & Falk, 2004). Thus, these students are not getting the supports needed to succeed academically, and the lack of effective instruction puts them further behind and renders them less able to succeed in the future. It is now understood that there is a close link between academics and behavior (Dunlap, Kern, & Worchester, 2001; Sutherland & Wehby, 2001). Well-designed instruction that is relevant, maintains student engagement, and results in a high rate of student success can prevent or eliminate many behavior problems. Consequently, rather than reducing academic expectations, students with a history of behavior problems need more carefully designed academic instruction.

Aligned with the view of problems being student centered is a reactive approach. That is, educators generally wait until a problem occurs, then apply a consequence in the hopes that it will eliminate similar problem behaviors in the future. This is neither effective (particularly for ongoing behavior problems) nor aligned with one of the major goals of education, to prepare students for citizenship.

COMPONENTS OF EFFECTIVE APPROACHES

Although change can be slow, particularly in systems such as schools, educators are fortunately beginning to understand what is needed for broad-scale, enduring improvements in student behavior. First, educators must focus on prevention. This means that they cannot simply wait until problem behavior occurs and apply a consequence. Rather, expectations are established prior to the time students arrive at school, and students learn what is expected as soon as they enter. This approach will prevent many behavior problems. Further, when students engage in problem behavior, strategies are implemented to prevent their behavior from becoming worse.

Second, educators must approach behavior in a positive manner. That is, most efforts must concentrate on identifying behaviors that are aligned with the expectations. When students receive praise for appropriate behavior, they will be eager to continue to engage in expected behavior. A positive approach reduces the tendency to provide attention to students only when they are engaging in problem behaviors.

A third quality of an effective behavior approach is that it is instructive. This means that students are taught exactly what is expected. Teaching comes in the form of explaining and modeling the expectations, describing how they apply to every location around the school building, and reinforcing those expectations throughout the school year. Further, when students engage in problem behavior, instruction consists of describing what they should be doing (rather than explaining what they should not be doing). For instance, when Alicia is chatting and not engaged in her classwork, instead of reprimanding her for talking, her teacher states, "Alicia, the expectation is that you are completing your work."

Finally, current approaches to emotional and behavioral wellbeing are comprehensive (Kern, Evans, & Lewis, 2011). Because behavioral concerns can be associated with a variety of issues (social interaction problems, emotional difficulties, academic deficits), intervention must be linked to assessment so that it targets areas of need. This is particularly important for students with more serious problem behaviors. Generic approaches are usually inefficient and unnecessarily delay implementation of appropriate intervention.

OVERVIEW OF A TIERED APPROACH

Educators are beginning to embrace the viewpoint that schools are well positioned to address social, emotional, and behavioral problems and, more important, are responsible for doing so. Since the late 1990s, there has been an increasing emphasis on systematic, multi-tiered prevention and intervention approaches for addressing the needs of students with behavior problems in schools. These systemic approaches hold great promise for their effectiveness and cost efficiency.

Multi-tiered approaches have recently become popular in schools in both academics and behavior. For instance, response to intervention (RTI) has been used in academic areas. SWPBS is the most commonly used preventive and tiered approach for behavior. Increasingly, SWPBS is being connected to efforts to increase the likelihood that students receive mental health services through community providers working in schools (Weist, Lever, Bradshaw, & Owens, 2014). In this approach that interconnects SWPBS and school mental health services, the goal is to increase the depth, quality, and effectiveness of prevention delivered at Tier 1, early intervention delivered at Tier 2, and intervention delivered at Tier 3 (see Barrett, Eber, & Weist, 2013). These (and other) approaches follow a similar framework for addressing the behavior and academic needs of students with various levels of challenges and provide the context for interventions we describe throughout this book. It is important to note that, in all of this work, teachers are leaders and key players based on their expertise in effective teaching, their responsibility for managing student behavior, and the significant role they play in (and time they devote to) children's lives. Thus, teachers should be active participants on SWPBS teams or other teams involving data-based decision making, implementing, refining, and continuously improving evidence-based practices delivered at all three tiers (Barrett et al., 2013).

Multi-tiered systems are comprised of layers of prevention/intervention that systematically increase in intensity, as dictated by the nature of a student's problem and how responsive the problem has been to previous intervention efforts. As previously mentioned, these systems are usually comprised of three tiers (see Figure 1.1). Tier 1 involves activities and instruction implemented with all students across the school and in the general education classroom. In the area of behavior, this involves establishing a core set of schoolwide expectations that are implemented in both classroom and nonclassroom settings. The expectations are explicitly taught, and there is an emphasis on acknowledging and reinforcing adherence to the expectations, although predetermined consequences for failing to follow the expectations are consistently applied (e.g., Sugai & Horner, 2009). In addition, these systems require regular data collection and monitoring to identify students who are not responding to Tier 1 and require more intensive intervention. Details about how to implement intervention at the schoolwide level (SWPBS) are described in Chapter 2.

Students who continue to engage in behavior problems in spite of Tier 1 intervention that is implemented as designed move to Tier 2 intervention. Support at Tier 2 is generally delivered in small groups and classrooms and relies on research-based methods to help students develop self-control strategies, enhance social relationships, or (in the case of behavior problems related to academic skill deficits) improve academic performance. For example, this might include a student checking in with a school staff member at the beginning and end of the school day, having each teacher rate the student's performance at the end of each school period, participating in a social skills group, or receiving small-group academic support in an area of deficit. Tier 2 intervention is described in Chapters 6 and 11.

A small number of students may not benefit from Tier 1 and Tier 2 intervention. For these students, intensive and individualized intervention is needed at Tier 3. Intervention at this tier relies on a functional behavioral assessment (FBA; see Chapter 8) and other assessment of the student's psychosocial functioning to identify issues that are contributing to behavior problems or are in need of attention in and of themselves, such as depression or anxiety that is compromising school performance. Based on the results of the functional behavioral and psychosocial assessment, an individualized and comprehensive intervention is developed. By matching intervention to the information obtained from these assessments, the likelihood of effectiveness is greatly increased (Chapter 8).

Figure 1.1 shows the model of SWPBS. As the model depicts, the majority of students (approximately 80%) in most schools respond to Tier 1 intervention and need no additional supports. A much smaller group of students (approximately 15%) continue to have ongoing problems and need more intensive Tier 2 intervention. This leaves less than 5% of students who require Tier 3, the most intensive level of support. Please note that these percentages are general estimates and vary in some circumstances. For example, in an inner-city school in a neighborhood plagued by violence and substance abuse, 30% or more of students could be presenting problems that would warrant Tier 2 or Tier 3 intervention. When implemented as designed, tiered support represents an efficient division of labor whereby teachers and school staff work in synchrony to provide intervention at various levels of intensity such that problem behavior is either avoided altogether or is addressed proactively to prevent it from getting worse.

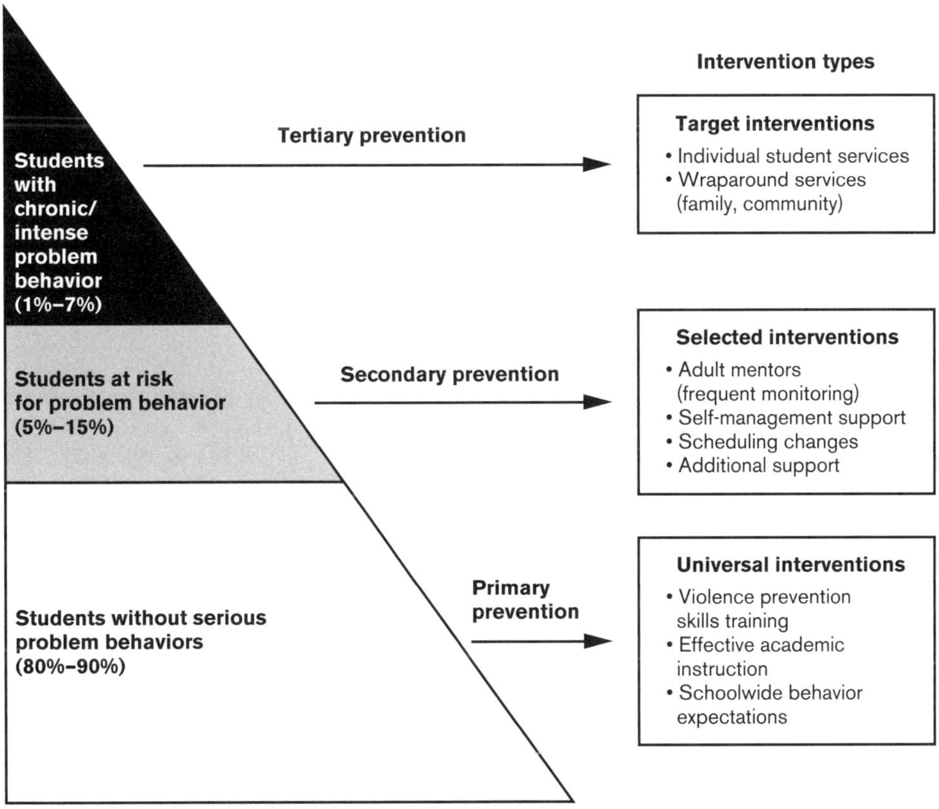

Figure 1.1. Model of tiered support.

SUMMARY

Social, emotional, and behavioral problems at school are a foremost concern among educators. There are many risk factors that increase the likelihood that a student will experience challenges. At the same time, schools are well positioned to assist students in developing assets and protective factors to overcome risk variables that are difficult to change. Perhaps most important, it is possible to construct a school environment that is positive, nurturing, and supports students in learning the social, emotional, and behavioral skills needed to succeed in school and beyond. This book is designed to help teachers remove and reduce academic and nonacademic barriers to learning and increase the likelihood of positive academic achievement as well as school (and life) success. In addition, it is designed to empower teachers and offer further skill training in work they are already doing to promote student wellness, mental health, and positive behavior.

Self-Reflection

1. Many teachers report they were unprepared to manage student behavior. How well prepared are/were you? What gaps in your own behavior management skills can you identify?
2. How pervasive are behavior problems in the school where you work or that you have visited? Where do they most frequently occur?
3. Previous approaches to behavior management focused on punishment. This assumed that behavior problems emanated from the child. Newer approaches understand that behavior problems result from interactions between a student and his or her environment. Are you more inclined to address behavior problems by punishing a student or by examining the environment?
4. To what extent do you approach behavior problems in a preventive, positive, and instructive manner?
5. Is a tiered approach to intervention in place in the school where you work or that you have visited? In what ways would the school benefit from a tiered intervention approach?

REFERENCES

Aud, S., Hussar, W., Kena, G., Bianco, K., Frohlich, L., Kemp, J., & Tahan, K. (2011). *The condition of education 2011* (NCES 2011-033). U.S. Department of Education, National Center for Education Statistics. Washington, DC: U.S. Government Printing Office.

Barrett, S., Eber, L., & Weist, M.D. (2013). *Advancing education effectiveness: An interconnected systems framework for positive behavioral interventions and supports (PBIS) and school mental health.* Center for Positive Behavioral Interventions and Supports (funded by the Office of Special Education Programs, U.S. Department of Education). Eugene: University of Oregon Press.

Barton-Arwood, S., Wehby, J.H., & Falk, K.B. (2005). Reading instruction for elementary-age students with emotional and behavioral disorders: Academic and behavioral outcomes. *Exceptional Children, 72,* 7–27.
Bradley, R., Henderson, K., & Monfore, D.A. (2004). A national perspective on children with emotional disorders. *Behavioral Disorders, 29*(3), 211–223.
Bullock, L.M., Ellis, L.L., & Wilson, M.J. (1994). Knowledge/skills needed by teachers who work with students with severe emotional/behavioral disorders: A revisitation. *Behavioral Disorders, 19*(2), 108–125.
Burns, M.K. (2000). Examining special education labels through attribution theory: A potential source for learned helplessness. *Ethical Human Sciences and Services, 2,* 101–107.
Carr, E.G., Dunlap, G., Horner, R.H., Koegel, R.L., Turnbull, A.P., Sailor, W., . . . Fox, L. (2002). Positive behavior support: Evolution of an applied science. *Journal of Positive Behavior Support, 4,* 16–20.
Caulkins, S.D., & Fox, N.A. (2002). Self-regulatory processes in early personality development: A multilevel approach to the study of childhood social withdrawal and aggression. *Development and Psychopathology, 14,* 477–498.
Dunlap, G., Kern, L., & Worchester, J. (2001). ABA and academic instruction. *Autism and Other Development Disabilities, 16,* 129–136.
Elam, S.M., & Rose, L.C. (1995). The 27th annual Phi Delta Kappa/Gallup poll of the public's attitudes toward the public schools. *Phi Delta Kappan, 77*(1), 41.
Fink, A.H., & Janssen, K.N. (1993). Competencies for teaching students with emotional-behavioral disabilities. *Preventing School Failure: Alternative Education for Children and Youth, 37*(2), 11–15.
Foster, E.M., Jones, D.E., & Conduct Problems Prevention Research Group. (2005). The high costs of aggression: Public expenditures resulting from conduct disorder. *American Journal of Public Health, 95*(10), 1767.
Gable, R.A., Hendrickson, J.M., Young, C.C., & Shokoohi-Yekta, M. (1992). Preservice preparation and classroom practices of teachers of students with emotional/behavioral disorders. *Behavioral Disorders, 17*(2), 126–134.
George, N.L., George, M.P., Gersten, R., & Grosenick, J.K. (1995). To leave or to stay? An exploratory study of teachers of students with emotional and behavioral disorders. *Remedial and Special Education, 16,* 227–236.
Goforth, A.N., Pham, A.V., & Carlson, J.S. (2011). Diathesis-stress model. In S. Goldstein & J. Naglieri (Eds.), *Encyclopedia of child behavior and development* (pp. 502–503). New York, NY: Springer.
Gresham, F.M., Lane, K.L., MacMillan, D.L., & Bocian, K.M. (1999). Social and academic profiles of externalizing and internalizing groups: Risk factors for emotional and behavioral disorders. *Behavioral Disorders, 24,* 231–245.
Individuals with Disabilities Education Improvement Act (IDEA) of 2004, PL 108-446, 20 U.S.C. §§ 1400 *et seq.*
Irvin, L.K., Tobin, T.J., Sprague, J.R., Sugai, G., & Vincent, C.G. (2004). Validity of office discipline referral measures as indices of school-wide behavioral status and effects of school-wide behavioral interventions. *Journal of Positive Behavior Interventions, 6,* 131–147.
Kern, L., Evans, S., & Lewis, T.J. (2011). Description of an iterative process for intervention development. *Education and Treatment of Children, 34,* 593–617.
Kern, L., & Wehby, J. (2014). Using data-based individualization to intensify behavioral interventions: Implementation example. *Teaching Exceptional Children, 46,* 45–53.
Koller, J.R., Osterlind, S.J., Paris, K., & Weston, K.J. (2004). Differences between novice and expert teachers' undergraduate preparation and ratings of importance in the area of children's mental health. *International Journal of Mental Health Promotion, 6,* 40–45.
Lane, K.L., Wehby, J., & Barton-Arwood, S. (2005). Students with and at-risk for emotional and behavioral disorders: Meeting their social and academic needs. *Preventing School Failure, 49,* 6–9.
Lavigne, J.V., & Faier-Routman, J. (1992). Psychological adjustment to pediatric physical disorders: A meta-analytic review. *Journal of Pediatric Psychology, 17*(2), 133–157.

Levin, H.M., & Belfield, C.R. (2007). Educational interventions to raise high school graduation rates. In C.R. Belfield & H.M. Levin (Eds.), *The price we pay: Economic and social consequences of inadequate education* (pp. 177–199). Washington, DC: Brookings Institution Press.
Mantymaa, M., Puura, K., Luoma, I., Latva, R., Salmelin, R.K., & Tamminen, T. (2012). Predicting internalizing and externalizing problems at five years by child and parental factors in infancy and toddlerhood. *Child Psychiatry and Human Development, 43,* 153–170.
Mastropieri, M.A., & Scruggs, T.E. (2002). *Effective instruction for special education* (3rd ed.). Austin, TX: PRO-ED.
Meadows, N., Neel, R., Scott, C.M., & Parker, G. (1994). Academic performance, social competence, and mainstream accommodations: A look at mainstreamed and nonmainstreamed students with serious behavioral disorders. *Behavioral Disorders, 19*(2), 170–180.
Merikangas, K., He, J., Burstein, M., Swanson, S., Avenevoli, S., Cui, L., . . . Swendsen, J. (2010). Lifetime prevalence of mental disorders in U.S. adolescents: Results from the National Comorbidity Survey replication–adolescent supplement (NCS-A). *Journal of the American Academy of Child & Adolescent Psychiatry, 49*(10), 980–989.
National Institute of Mental Health, National Advisory Mental Health Council Workgroup on Child and Adolescent Mental Health Intervention and Deployment. (2001). *Blueprint for change: Research on child and adolescent mental health.* Rockville, MD: Author.
Newman, L., Wagner, M., Knokey, A., Marder, C., Nagle, K., Shaver, D., & Wei, X. (2011). *The post-high school outcomes of young adults with disabilities up to 8 years after high school: A report from the National Longitudinal Transition Study-2 (NLTS2).* NCSER 2011–3005. Washington, DC: National Center for Special Education Research.
Norman, R.M., & Malla, A.K. (2001). Duration of untreated psychosis: A critical examination of the concept and its importance. *Psychological Medicine, 31,* 381–400.
O'Connell, M.E., Boat, T., & Warner, K.E. (2009). *Preventing mental, emotional, and behavioral disorders among young people: Progress and possibilities.* Washington, DC: The National Academies Press.
O'Connor, T.G., Deater-Deckard, K., Fulker, D., Rutter, M., & Plomin, R. (1998). Genotype–environment correlations in late childhood and early adolescence: Antisocial behavioral problems and coercive parenting. *Developmental Psychology, 34*(5), 970.
Oliver, R.M., & Reschly, D.J. (2010). Special education teacher preparation in classroom Management: Implications for students with emotional and behavioral disorders. *Behavioral Disorders, 35*(3), 188–199.
Ollendick, T.H., Weist, M.D., Borden, M.C., & Greene, R.W. (1992). Sociometric status and academic, behavioral, and psychological adjustment: A five-year longitudinal study. *Journal of Consulting and Clinical Psychology, 60*(1), 80–87.
Partin, T.C.M., Robertson, R.E., Maggin, D.M., Oliver, R.M., & Wehby, J.H. (2009). Using teacher praise and opportunities to respond to promote appropriate student behavior. *Preventing School Failure: Alternative Education for Children and Youth, 54*(3), 172–178.
Pope, A.W., Bierman, K.L., & Mumma, G.H. (1991). Aggression, hyperactivity, and inattention-immaturity: Behavior dimensions associated with peer rejection in elementary school boys. *Developmental Psychology, 27,* 663–671.
Posner, M.I., & Rothbart, M.K. (2000). Developing mechanisms of self-regulation. *Development and Psychopathology, 12,* 427–441.
Reid, R., Gonzalez, J.E., Nordness, P.D., Trout, A., & Epstein, M.H. (2004). A meta-analysis of the academic status of students with emotional/behavioral disturbance. *Journal of Special Education, 38,* 130–143.
Rosenberg, M.S., Sindelar, P.T., & Hardman, M.L. (2004). Preparing highly qualified teachers for students with emotional or behavioral disorders: The impact of NCLB and IDEA. *Behavioral Disorders, 29*(3), 266–278.
Ruhl, K.L., & Berlinghoff, D.H. (1992). Research on improving behaviorally disordered students' academic performance: A review of the literature. *Behavioral Disorders, 17*(3), 178–190.
Sacks, G., & Kern, L. (2008). A comparison of quality of life variables for students with emotional and behavioral disorders and students without disabilities. *Journal of Behavioral Education, 17,* 111–127.
Sameroff, A.J., & Chandler, M.J. (1975). Reproductive risk and the continuum of caretaking casualty. In F.D. Horowitz, E.M. Hetherington, S. Scarr-Salapatek, & G.M. Siegel (Eds.), *Review of child development research* (pp. 187–244). Chicago: University of Chicago Press.

Scales, P.C., Benson, P.L., Leffert, N., & Blyth, D.A. (2000). Contribution of developmental assets to the prediction of thriving among adolescents. *Applied Developmental Science, 4*(1), 27.

Shores, R.E., Gunter, P.L., & Jack, S.L. (1993). Classroom management strategies: Are they setting events for coercion? *Behavioral Disorders, 18,* 92–102.

Skiba, R.J., Peterson, R.L., & Williams, T. (1997). Office referrals and suspension: Disciplinary intervention in middle schools. *Education & Treatment of Children, 20*(3), 295–315.

State, T.M., Kern, L., Starosta, K.M., & Divatia Mukherjee, A. (2011). Elementary pre-service teacher preparation in the area of social, emotional, and behavioral problems. *School Mental Health, 3,* 13–23.

Sugai, G., & Horner, R.H. (2009). Responsiveness-to-intervention and school-wide positive behavior supports: Integration of multi-tiered system approaches. *Exceptionality, 17*(4), 223–237.

Sutherland, K.S., & Wehby, J. (2001). The effect of self-evaluation on teaching behavior in classrooms for students with emotional and behavioral disorders. *Journal of Special Education, 35*(3), 161–172.

U.S. Department of Education, Office of Special Education and Rehabilitative Services, Office of Special Education Programs. (2009). *28th annual report to Congress on the implementation of the Individuals with Disabilities Education Act, 2006* (Vol. 1). Washington, DC: Author.

Van Acker, R. (2004). Current status of public education and likely future directions in teacher preparation for students with emotional and behavioral disorders. In L.M. Bullock & R.A. Gable (Eds.), *Quality personnel preparation in emotional/behavioral disorders: Current perspectives and future directions* (pp. 79–93). Denton, TX: University of North Texas Press.

Vander Stoep, A., Weiss, N.S., Kuo, E.S., Cheney, D., & Cohen, P. (2003). What proportion of failure to complete secondary school in the U.S. population is attributable to adolescent psychiatric disorder? *Journal of Behavioral Health Services and Research, 30,* 119–124.

Wagner, M. (1993). The secondary school programs of students with disabilities. A report from the National Longitudinal Transition Study of Special Education Students.

Wagner, M., & Davis, M. (2006). How are we preparing students with emotional disturbances for the transition to young adulthood? Findings from the National Longitudinal Transition Study-2. *Journal of Emotional and Behavioral Disorders, 14*(2), 86–98.

Wagner, M.M., & Blackorby, J. (1996). Transition from high school to work or college: How special education students fare. *The Future of Children, 6,* 103–120.

Walker, J., Geddes, A., Lever, N., Andrews, C., & Weist, M.D. (2010). Reconsidering the term "emotional disturbance": A report from Maryland. *Advances in School Mental Health Promotion, 3*(2), 46–52.

Wehby, J.H., Symons, F., & Shores, R.E. (1995). A descriptive analysis of aggressive behavior in classrooms for students with emotional and behavioral disorders. *Behavioral Disorders, 20*(2), 87–105.

Wehby, J.H., Tally, B.B., & Falk, K.B. (2004). Identifying the relation between the function of problem behavior and teacher instructional behavior. *Assessment for Effective Instruction, 30,* 41–51.

Weist, M.D., Lever, N., Bradshaw, C., & Owens, J. (2014). *Handbook of school mental health: Research, training, practice, and policy* (2nd ed.). New York, NY: Springer.

Youngstrom, E., Weist, M.D., & Albus, K.E. (2003). Exploring violence exposure, stress, protective factors and behavioral problems among inner-city youth. *American Journal of Community Psychology, 32*(1–2), 115–129.

2

Schoolwide Positive Behavior Support

SWPBS is a systems approach for structuring school environments so that all students receive sufficient behavioral and academic support to achieve success in school. The approach focuses on establishing, teaching, and reinforcing consensually agreed upon behavioral expectations and applying clearly outlined consequences, both for adhering to and for violating the behavioral expectations (Kern, Hilt-Panahon, & Sokol, 2009). SWPBS is grounded in a behavioral perspective, a philosophical orientation recommended by the Surgeon General for working with at-risk and delinquent children and youth in school settings (U.S. Office of the Surgeon General, National Center for Injury Prevention and Control, National Institute of Mental Health, & Center for Mental Health Services, 2001). The behavioral perspective posits that human behavior is learned, predictable (given sufficient knowledge of the environmental conditions surrounding it), and modifiable (Baer, Wolf, & Risley, 1968). Because behavior is learned, SWPBS uses educational methods and approaches aimed at teaching appropriate behaviors and preventing and reducing problem behaviors. As a result, the school environment is enhanced to support behavior change (Sugai, O'Keeffe, & Fallon, 2013).

SWPBS focuses on all students in the school environment, even those students presenting the most severe and challenging behaviors. Teachers in schools that use SWPBS, especially those who work with students having behavior problems, are likely to have certain advantages over teachers who work in more traditional schools. Accumulating empirical evidence suggests that schools using SWPBS show improvements in school climate (Bradshaw,

Koth, Thornton, & Leaf, 2009), greater rule-following behavior (Kellam, Rebok, Ialongo, & Mayer, 1994), lower rates of teacher-reported bullying (Waasdorp, Bradshaw, & Leaf, 2012), fewer ODRs (Barrett, Bradshaw, & Lewis-Palmer, 2008), fewer suspensions (Bradshaw, Mitchell, & Leaf, 2010), and perhaps even fewer referrals of students in the category of serious emotional and behavioral disorders.

In this chapter, we describe the features of SWPBS and how the SWPBS approach distinguishes itself from traditional school discipline. We also describe its three-tiered model of prevention and intervention, with particular emphasis on Tiers 1 and 2 and with only a brief description of Tier 3. We cover Tier 3 in greater detail in Chapters 7 and 8. By placing the description of SWPBS early on in this book, we underscore its importance as a foundational component for guiding school personnel in supporting the needs of all students but especially for children and youth experiencing problems in schools. In addition, we provide a process for getting started and introducing the SWPBS approach in a school setting; although there likely are many processes for doing so, we believe the one we outline here is efficient.

FEATURES OF SCHOOLWIDE POSITIVE BEHAVIOR SUPPORT

SWPBS has a number of unique features that help differentiate it from traditional approaches to school discipline. In some instances, the differences between SWPBS and more traditional school approaches are simply a matter of emphasis; for example, adults focusing on students' appropriate behaviors rather than their misbehaviors. Other aspects are substantially different and require the development of new procedures altogether; for example, the alignment of various teams throughout the school and the proactive teaching of positive social behavior. A discussion of a number of these distinguishing features follows below.

A Different Perspective

The use of a SWPBS approach calls for a change in the way schools have operated in the past (and the way many still operate today). Traditional forms of school discipline primarily involve prescriptive and reactive responses to rule infractions (see Table 2.1). *Prescriptive* means the consequences for students are predetermined. A school authority needs only to look up the disciplinary violation in the Code of Conduct and find its accompanying consequence. *Reactive* means the consequence follows a rule violation. Administrators and teachers wait for a rule infraction and then deliver the associated punishment. For example, when a middle school student violates a school rule such as chewing gum in class, the teacher responds by writing an ODR and sending the offending student to the administrative office for a brief meeting with a school authority, usually the assistant principal. The assistant principal confers with the student about the rule infraction and checks the Student Code of Conduct to find the predetermined or prescribed consequence

Table 2.1. A comparison of traditional codes of conduct and schoolwide positive behavior support

Traditional	Schoolwide positive behavior support
Large number of rules	Five or fewer expectations
Rules largely unknown until violated	Rules directly taught and made clear
Prescriptive	Contextual and individualized
Stated as prohibitions (telling students what not to do)	Stated positively (telling students how to succeed)
Focuses adult attention on misbehavior	Focuses adult attention on appropriate behavior
Reacts to the occurrence of misbehavior	Prevents misbehavior from occurring
Predominately punitive	Predominately reinforcing

for chewing gum in class. A consequence is then issued (usually an after-school detention) with the hope that students make the connection between chewing gum and spending time after school and learn the additional lesson that chewing gum in school is prohibited and violates school rules. The consequence in this case is reactive, meaning it happens after the student was caught "misbehaving." It is also punitive, meaning it is designed to cause discomfort and distress so as to encourage the student to avoid the behavior (chewing gum) and its accompanying punishment in the future. Chewing gum in class a second time will likely result in a more severe punishment—perhaps an additional or longer detention after school. Here the notion of discipline resembles a pharmacological intervention in that it uses a stronger dosage of the consequence, in this case punishment, to treat more virulent and recurrent forms of misbehavior. Scenarios such as this one occur many times daily in American schools. Again, the aim is to teach students the lesson that chewing gum is prohibited in school and students should follow the rules at all times. The SWPBS approach to discipline stands in stark contrast. Within the SWPBS approach, teachers are encouraged to look for and reinforce compliant behavior rather than look for and punish negative behavior.

A Proactive Approach

Unlike traditional school discipline characterized by the application of reactive and negative consequences for rule-violating behaviors, SWPBS relies on an approach that is proactive and instructional for teaching appropriate behavior in schools. In the SWPBS approach, every student is taught the rules and expectations in advance of performing the expected behavior. A proactive response is based on the notion that children desire to do well in school and simply need to learn or be reminded of the behaviors that lead to school success. Outlining expectations clearly and reminding students often about the proper ways to behave in school help educate them about socially appropriate ways of interacting with others and decrease episodes of low-level misbehaviors, especially those misbehaviors resulting from mistakes or lack of knowledge. Examples of low-level misbehaviors are play fighting, teasing, flicking hats, loud talking, disrespectful speech, excessive talking, side talking in class, and other relatively minor or irritating behaviors that interfere with instruction and decorum within the school. Low-level misbehaviors sometimes lead to more serious misbehaviors. Play fighting, for example, may lead to real fights. By reducing levels of low-level misbehaviors, school staff are actively working to prevent episodes of higher intensity, more serious behaviors from occurring throughout the school (Skiba & Peterson, 2000).

An Instructional Approach

SWPBS is also instructional in nature. If, as the behavioral perspective postulates, behavior is learned, then it can be taught. Within the SWPBS framework, behavior is taught in the same way academics are taught, by using a direct instruction approach. In a direct instruction approach, students are explicitly taught the behavioral expectations so they know exactly what is expected of them. In addition to the expectations, the specific behaviors required to meet those expectations are taught, rehearsed, and repeatedly reviewed so that every student has the opportunity to succeed.

Teaching behavior, like teaching academics, requires forethought and planning. Taylor-Greene et al. (1997) listed some of the elements for teaching students the proper ways to behave in school:

- Introduce and define the specific behavior
- Provide a reasonable rationale for the behavior
- Describe the physical setting where instruction will be provided
- List examples of the behavior (what to do) as well as non examples (what not to do)
- Provide opportunities for students to practice the behavior
- Provide feedback on the performance of the behavior
- Publicly recognize students who demonstrate expected behaviors (p. 103)

From an instructional perspective, misbehaviors are treated as "social errors" and gently corrected, just as a math teacher might gently correct a calculation error in math class. Returning to the example of the gum-chewing student, rather than send the student to the office for a mild punishment, a teacher's response might be to instead issue a statement such as "Remember the expectations; part of being responsible in school means following the rules about chewing gum in class. Please discard your gum and continue to follow along with the lesson." The appropriate behavior is directly taught, and the reminder is instructive in that it reviews the school rule on gum chewing and gives the offending student the opportunity to practice the rule. As important, little time is taken away from valuable classroom instruction, unlike the typical ODR procedure in which the teacher must take the time to write a referral and the student must leave class, walk to the office, meet with a school authority, and await the consequence, a process that can take 20 minutes or more. Under optimal conditions, the teacher's reminder to the offending student is delivered privately so as to avoid bringing further attention to or embarrassment for the student.

A Systems Approach

SWPBS emphasizes the development and alignment of systems to support evidence-based practices throughout the entire school. A systems approach implies a structure that clearly identifies the interconnections between people within the school (e.g., teacher grade-level teams, special education teachers, counselors, school psychologists, administrators, federally funded remedial programs, transportation personnel, cafeteria workers, consultants), allowing work to be coordinated and resources distributed to efficiently meet organizational goals (Latham, 1988). Within the SWPBS approach, school teams are primarily responsible for developing most of the SWPBS activities, such as establishing schoolwide expectations, providing focused and ongoing professional development, adopting new policies, incorporating schoolwide data collection activities, and implementing new disciplinary procedures. Many of these activities have an impact on a wide audience, including parents associated with the school environment, and reinforce the need for integrating school teams within the organizational structure of the school. Aligning various participant groups effectively reduces inefficiencies and eliminates frustrating barriers. Personnel are well trained and know exactly how to respond across different situations, making routines predictable and secure. Resources are sufficient for promoting success, and when teachers are successful, job satisfaction increases and teaching becomes increasingly rewarding. (For more information about how to create SWPBS infrastructure, see http://www.PBIS.org.)

A Collaborative Process

The SWPBS process, as described in the previous subsection, is predicated on a collaborative, team approach for solving problems and making improvements in the school environment. A school team composed of volunteers and key stakeholders in the school enterprise, such as building principals, teachers, union representatives, parents, related services personnel, and community members, meets to establish and promote a vision for the school, examines schoolwide and individual student data, develops procedures for accomplishing important outcomes, creates celebration activities, and builds morale (Horner, Sugai, Todd, & Lewis-Palmer, 2005). When teachers and administrators commit to the SWPBS approach, they sacrifice some autonomy they have traditionally held in the school setting in exchange for greater cooperation with their fellow colleagues. Effective teams meet regularly, communicate effectively, and have the authority to disperse resources.

A First Step in Schoolwide Social Skills Instruction

The SWPBS emphasis on teaching appropriate school and classroom behaviors for enhancing success in school directly links SWPBS with a schoolwide social skills curriculum. In some schools, the introduction of SWPBS becomes the first step to developing a comprehensive social skills curriculum for all students in a school's population. Behaviors comprising responsibility, respect, politeness, and following adult directions are explicitly defined, directly taught, modeled, rehearsed, and reinforced within the various school settings in which they are expected to occur, increasing the probability that the behaviors will occur with greater frequency in the future.

Data-Driven Decisions

Decision making within the SWPBS approach is driven by the use of data. Schools collect voluminous information on students and their performances, both socially and academically, that often goes unused. A distinguishing feature of the SWPBS process is the use of multiple sources of information for making improvements in the school (Horner, Sugai, & Todd, 2001). Data are collected to track the progress of groups and individuals throughout the year and determine the degree to which schoolwide and individual interventions have been effective in achieving predetermined goals. Adjustments are regularly made when data reveal the need for greater improvement.

A Resource for Consistent Decision Making

When the school team has defined and clearly explicated the rules and expectations that guide and govern the school and has communicated them effectively to the faculty, staff, and students, there is a greater chance that staff and students will know and understand the rules and expectations and, as important, adhere to them. Students and adults alike can more readily recognize acceptable and unacceptable conduct, and faculty and staff can become consistent with one another in their responses to student behavior. As a result, when intervening with student behavior, opportunities for confusion and conflict among adults are minimized.

A TIERED PREVENTION MODEL

Improving the social and academic outcomes for every student in a school setting requires implementation of a "broad range of systemic and individualized strategies" (Turnbull et al., 2002, p. 377). SWPBS organizes and deploys these strategies through a three-tiered model of prevention and intervention similar to the one employed by the U.S. Public Health Service. The three tiers of prevention and intervention—primary, secondary, and tertiary—refer to the intensity of the services available at each level. This gradation of interventions allows for a system of increasingly intensive responses that match the increasing severity of behavior problems (Walker et al., 1996).

No single tier is effective for resolving all problem behaviors, because some students require more intensive assistance to achieve school success. At the same time, if interventions are highly effective at the primary or universal tier, fewer students will require more intensive and time-consuming interventions at subsequent tiers (Walker & Shinn, 2010). On the other hand, if schools find that too many students are in need of the intensive services offered at Tiers 2 and 3, more attention and work may be warranted at the universal level (Sprick & Borgmeier, 2010).

Universal or Tier 1 interventions target all students in the school and outline the rules and expectations every student needs to meet in order to be successful in school. Tier 2 interventions focus on a smaller group of students (5%–15%) who for various reasons require additional support to reach success. Tier 3 interventions target a much smaller group of students, perhaps 1%–5% of the school population, who need even more intensive supports to thrive in school despite previous access to Tier 1 and Tier 2 interventions. Note that base rates of problems vary across communities, and in some schools or districts, the percentage of students benefitting from programs at each tier will vary. For example, in a middle school in an inner-city neighborhood with high levels of poverty and violence, 20% or more of students may benefit from Tier 3 interventions. Increasingly, SWPBS programs are connecting to expanded school mental health services, wherein community mental health providers join with schools to deepen and expand effective services, especially at Tiers 2 and 3 (Barrett, Eber, & Weist, 2013).

Candidates for Tier 2 and Tier 3 services are identified on the basis of data collected on aspects of school performance deemed socially and academically important. Data may include the number of ODRs, suspensions from school, failing grades, and unexcused absences that indicate students are experiencing difficulties in school. A school team identifies the sources of data for making these decisions. Because students are specifically targeted with the use of meaningful data, the three-tiered system is parsimonious in its distribution of more intensive, complex, and time-consuming intervention services, granting them only to students who clearly need them. Each of the tiers is described in more detail in the following subsections.

Tier 1

Tier 1 interventions answer the question, "What do I need to know and do to succeed in school?" Tier 1 interventions are designed to first identify and then teach the basic standards of conduct to all students across all settings in the school. The goal is to promote prosocial behavior and prevent occurrences of misbehavior by ensuring that every student, at the very start of the school year, clearly knows and understands the rules and expectations needed to maximize success in school. Reviewing and teaching the behavioral standards in advance of an expected behavioral response promote compliance (increase the likelihood that students will perform the expected behavior) and decrease opportunities for social errors to occur. This proactive approach (i.e., the establishment, review, and direct teaching of the behavior expectations prior to the expected performance of the behavior) is a hallmark of SWPBS and one of the key features that distinguish SWPBS from traditional forms of school discipline.

A clear set of schoolwide behavioral standards provides school officials a framework for making consistent and predictable responses to student conduct in the school. When school personnel know what behaviors are acceptable as well as unacceptable for students, they know which behaviors to reinforce and which behaviors to discourage. For example, if school staff establish the standard that appropriate hall behavior is defined as "walking on the right-hand side of the hallway with hands to oneself," every staff person in the school who encounters play fighting in the hallways will know how to intervene and remind the offending students of the expectation that hands should be kept to oneself. As important, every staff person can recognize and call attention to students who are walking in the halls appropriately—on the right side of the hallway with their hands to themselves—thereby reinforcing the desired hallway behaviors. Tier 1 interventions are termed "universal interventions" because they are taught to every student in the school.

Tier 2

Tier 2 interventions are designed for students who require more assistance for achieving success in school than that provided at Tier 1. Students are screened and identified as candidates for Tier 2 interventions on the basis of data that are deemed appropriate by a school team and collected over time. For example, the number of ODRs or days of suspension from school are two data sources that might be used for making this determination. Interventions are more intensive at Tier 2, designed to match the intensity of the behavior problem, and are usually more time-consuming to implement. The ultimate goal, of course, is improvement in the student's behavior so that he or she no longer needs Tier 2 support, but for some students, maintenance of behavioral reductions with ongoing Tier 2 support becomes the long-term goal. Tier 2 interventions that have been described in the literature include Check In Check Out (CICO), social skills training, First Step to Success, and mentoring (Hawken, Alphonson, MacLeod, & Shumann, 2009; see descriptions of these interventions in later subsections of this chapter).

Tier 3

Tier 3 interventions are the most intensive interventions, designed for those relatively few students in the school population, approximately 1%–5%, who require the most intensive, individualized supports for achieving school success (as mentioned earlier, this percentage may be higher in some schools). Interventions at this level are highly individualized, complex, and more time-consuming than Tier 1 and Tier 2 interventions and may involve multiple participants, including personnel from community agencies, such as mental health, juvenile justice, and parent advocacy, as well as the parents themselves. Interventions at Tier 3 are almost always grounded in FBAs, a process that gathers data to learn more about the conditions under which challenging behavior occurs (see Chapter 8). Data are typically derived from reviews of students' records, classroom and school observations, and interviews of parents as well as school personnel who have had direct contact with the students, and sometimes from interviews of the students themselves, including focused psychosocial assessment (Kern, Dunlap, Clarke, & Childs, 1994).

Most often, the use of FBAs requires additional resources, especially in terms of personnel. Members of a behavior support team, composed of school and community personnel, at least one of whom has expertise in the techniques of SWPBS, distribute the duties associated with conducting FBAs and meet together to develop an individualized behavior support plan. Examples of Tier 3 interventions include person-centered planning, direct instruction in alternative adaptive skills, monitoring and measurement of students' progress toward individualized goals, frequent reminders and performance feedback, tangible rewards for acceptable performances, and services from collaborating community agencies designed to support and enhance students' school performances (see Chapter 9 for additional detail on developing an individualized support plan).

SCHOOLWIDE POSITIVE BEHAVIOR SUPPORT IMPLEMENTATION: A PRACTICAL PROCESS FOR SCHOOL IMPROVEMENT

The SWPBS framework offers broad guidance to school officials and a process for designing and implementing school change. SWPBS is a process, not a specific curriculum or program. The process is amenable to modification in order to meet the unique needs of a particular school district or school. Local teams are encouraged to modify the process, and, because school teams drive the process, the final form of SWPBS is likely to look different across districts and schools. Nonetheless, the process has a number of common features that we describe in the following subsections.

Getting Started

Schoolwide reform usually begins with the notion that things are not working as well as they should. Too many ODRs, too many suspensions, and too many students and parents expressing concerns about student safety (Public Agenda, 2004) are but a few of the many indicators that might cause school officials to begin looking for ways to improve the functioning of a school setting. Recently, when confronted with escalating behavior problems, many schools have relied upon "get tough" stances like zero-tolerance policies. However, there is little empirical evidence to show that such policies have been effective and mounting evidence to show that they may actually work at cross-purposes for creating safe learning environments, inadvertently resulting in lower academic achievement, poorer school climates (American Psychological Association, 2008), and more suspensions, expulsions, and referrals to juvenile justice (Council of State Governments Justice Center & Public Policy Research Institute at Texas A&M University, 2011).

SWPBS offers an alternative to the "get tough" approaches for addressing problem behaviors and begins with the straightforward question, "Is there a need for change?" (Lewis, Barrett, Sugai, & Horner, 2010). The first step to answering this pivotal question is self-assessment and documentation of the problem behaviors within the school.

Assessment of the School Environment An assessment of the school environment includes a review of information from multiple data sources. Numbers of in- and out-of-school suspensions, discipline referrals for rule infractions, after-school detentions, and perhaps parent complaints are examples of the types of data that might be used to assess and document a need for change. Although most schools already possess these data, such data are not frequently compiled, graphed, analyzed, and used for making decisions. As a result, few adults within the school setting have a clear understanding of the extent of problem behaviors throughout the school, much less where and when the behavior problems occur. Summarized and graphically displayed extant school discipline data provide school officials with an unmistakable view of the magnitude of the problem behaviors throughout the school, where they occur, when they occur, and with whom they occur. Electronic systems are commercially available that are designed to track and display SWPBS data (see http://www.pbis.org).

In addition, tapping into teachers' perceptions is often helpful for determining that a change is needed. Teachers and staff are a rich source of information about working conditions within the school, especially about the barriers that interfere with accomplishment of their job duties. A quick way to tap into teachers' perceptions is the Three-Question Survey, a three-question assessment of teachers' satisfaction with working conditions and school climate (see Figure 2.1).

Assessment of the School's Capacity to Implement Schoolwide Positive Behavior Support In addition to an assessment of current behavior problems within the school, the school (or district) should assess its capacity to implement the SWPBS model (Lewis et al., 2010). Of chief concern is whether someone with the proper level of behavioral expertise is available to help guide the SWPBS initiative and provide training and ongoing professional support for sustaining the initiative once it is launched. Ideally, the local school or district cultivates the necessary expertise internally, ensuring readily available assistance whenever it is needed. However, should local expertise be lacking, many states across the nation have supported the adoption of SWPBS by retaining consultants who can assist schools and districts in building local expertise.

Three-Question Survey
1. What do you like best about your job at school?
2. What do you like least about your job at school?
3. What would you like to change about your job at school?

Figure 2.1. Three-Question Survey.

Staff commitment to implementing an SWPBS initiative is an additional source of information and may prove critical for successful implementation. Acquiring this information may entail nothing more complicated than a vote among teachers and staff as to whether they would like to move forward with implementation of a SWPBS initiative in the months ahead (Lane, Kalberg, & Menzies, 2009). A number of assessment instruments are available for the school (district) self-assessments, such as School-wide Assessment Surveys and the Effective Behavior Support Survey. These and other instruments can be found at http://www.pbis.org/school.

A Vision of a Well-Functioning School Once a district or school determines that a change is in order, the driving question becomes, "Change to what?" In other words, what would a more productive and beneficial school environment look like? What is the desired outcome? Answering these questions necessarily requires a projection into the future—a vision of a more desirable school setting.

A vision is a picture or an image of a desired future state; in this case, it is an image of how the school community (teachers, staff, parents, and students) would like to see the school operate in the future. A vision takes the description of the need for change and transforms it into a description of a more effective and efficient school environment, one that is at once pleasant for students and faculty to work within as well as for parents and community members to visit. For example, if the general behavior among students is raucously inappropriate and chaotic, a vision for the future is a school that is orderly and respectful. Rather than displaying impolite, uncivil, and aggressive behavior, students are calm, polite, trusting of school staff, and respectful of themselves, peers, school officials, and school property.

The creation of the vision is dependent on people familiar with the current functioning of the school and who understand clearly any strengths the school has to offer as well as any barriers or roadblocks that threaten success. Organizational theorists have developed a number of practical strategies for engaging others in the process of creating a vision of the future. Figure 2.2 shares an example of an activity that faculty can use to reach consensus on a description and future vision of a well-functioning school program (G.P. White, personal communication, April 1, 2002). Once a vision has been created, the next step is to design goals and procedures for turning the vision of the future school into a reality.

School Teams School teams are the loci of decision making within the SWPBS approach. For some schools, team-centered discussions and decision making on school issues, especially schoolwide issues, represent a radical departure from the status quo in which top-down decision making traditionally prevails. By no means does the SWPBS approach preclude administrators from making decisions about their schools. It does suggest, however, that administrators make decisions using information and data supplied by the members of the SWPBS teams (Liaupsin, Jolivette, & Scott, 2004). Within the SWPBS approach, there are at least three teams: a school or Tier 1 team, a Tier 2 team, and a Tier 3 team (or multiple Tier 3 teams). Some schools empanel other teams as well (e.g., teams or committees for designing and implementing schoolwide activities such as awards, assemblies, and other schoolwide events and celebrations).

Ideally, teams are composed of key individuals and leaders within the school setting. The schoolwide team, for example, might include the building principal, teacher leaders, association representatives, special education teachers, parents, counselors, related services personnel, and community members (Muscott, Mann, & LeBrun, 2008). Important duties of the school team involve establishing a vision that guides future school improvement efforts and communicating the vision to others. As important, the school team creates action plans for achieving the school's vision and goals and works to remove any perceived or real barriers to success.

Tier 2 and Tier 3 teams include personnel possessing academic and behavioral programming expertise, such as school psychologists, counselors, and behavior consultants, as well as general and special education teachers. For Tier 3, the student's parents should also be team members. Tier 2 and Tier 3 team members are knowledgeable about students' school performances and the availability of resources within the school, and they have expertise in the methods of positive behavior support. Like schoolwide team meetings, Tier 2 and Tier 3 team meetings are driven by the use of data displays that track students' past successes and difficulties in the school setting. Tier 2 and 3 teams should share at least one representative with the schoolwide team. For many schools, having three separate teams to manage SWPBS can be quite challenging and also creates additional work for the teams to communicate and coordinate with one another. Alternatively, one larger, more inclusive team can meet the needs of a school, provided that

RUBRIC FOR VISIONING ACTIVITY

ELEMENTS OF A WELL-FUNCTIONING SCHOOL

Always see	Never see
Always hear	Never hear
Always feel	Never feel

INSTRUCTIONS

Ask the audience to break into several small groups. Within each work group, choose a chairperson, a scribe, a timekeeper, and a spokesperson (5 minutes). The chairperson's role is to help the group reach consensus. The scribe's role is to record the thoughts and ideas of the group. The timekeeper's role is to track the amount of time for each task. The spokesperson's role is to present the group's findings.

1. Brainstorm a list of features or characteristics under each of the three headings within the two columns. For example, what things would you always see and never see in a well functioning school program? List as many features as you can within 13 minutes.
2. Through a discussion led by the chairperson, reach consensus on which feature under each heading is most important to your team. Place a star by the most important characteristic. (4 minutes)
3. Share your findings with one other group. Everyone except the spokesperson should proceed to another table to hear another team's findings. Spokespeople should remain at their tables to present to the group visiting from another table. Note the similarities and differences. (7 minutes)
4. As a final activity, each spokesperson should prepare a short presentation of the group's findings for the entire audience (15 minutes).

Figure 2.2. Rubric for Visioning Activity.

it has the right people on it, that it is well led, that data are used in decision making, and that follow-up actions to completed decisions are strong. In this scenario, the team can include subteams at Tiers 2 and 3, with each team having relevant conversations, conducting planning, and engaging in follow-up actions for the work at their respective tier. Ideally, school teams are augmented by community providers, such as mental health personnel, to promote depth and quality of programs at each tier (Barrett et al., 2013). An example school team might include a school psychologist, school counselor, general education teacher, community social worker, school principal, school assistant principal, school nurse, parent, school resource officer, and student (especially if older).

Selection of team members should be strategic, with consideration given to the unique expertise each person brings to the table. School teams that include a building administrator tend to be poised for success because school principals wield authority to garner and distribute resources (Kartub, Taylor-Greene, March, & Horner, 2000). Ideally, parents are active members on these teams. Including parents on the team helps ensure a family voice is heard and helps cultivate parents' feelings of empowerment and commitment to the school. Students, especially at the middle or high school levels, too can play an important role on SWPBS teams by offering their perspectives of what works well within the school setting. Once appointed, team members should be committed to 1) adhering to a schedule of future meetings, 2) coming prepared to the meetings, 3) analyzing school data, 4) working together to set and achieve mutually agreed upon goals, 5) following up on decisions to support effective practices at each tier, and 6) communicating the outcomes of the team meetings effectively and regularly with others in the school environment.

An important but often overlooked and underemphasized duty of team leaders is to keep team meetings interesting and productive. Many educators have come to perceive school committee meetings as time-consuming competition for other "more important" matters confronting them. Poorly managed or mismanaged meetings quickly arouse feelings of dissatisfaction and often lead to absenteeism. Table 2.2 shows a number of strategies for keeping meetings productive and engaging.

Ground Rules Ground rules help organize team meetings. Ground rules are the mutually agreed upon expectations about how team meetings should unfold and include rules governing the agenda, members' interactions with one another, and decision making. Developed by the team, ground rules are the expectations that govern the behavior of team members before, during, and after the team meetings. Speak one at a time, remain focused on issues and solutions, use polite and respectful language, keep statements brief, come prepared to the meetings, listen, refrain from interrupting others, and manage conflict civilly are a few examples of ground rules team members might wish to develop to regulate the behavior of one another

Table 2.2. Strategies for conducting engaging and productive team meetings

1. Choose members strategically.
   - Identify each member's potential contribution; attributes to look for in team members are leadership qualities, social and legal status (e.g., teacher leaders, association representation) among members of the larger school population, and abilities in verbal and written communication.
   - Ensure expertise in positive behavior support.
2. Pay attention to meeting logistics.
   - Schedule meetings with sufficient prior notification.
   - Choose a comfortable meeting room with adequate privacy.
   - Build in breaks for longer meetings.
   - Discuss in advance role expectations and the decision-making process.
   - Develop and distribute meeting notes or summaries to constituents throughout the building.
3. Prepare an agenda and adhere to it.
   - Make the agenda available for input prior to the meeting.
   - Develop procedures for others to add to the agenda.
   - Include sections for "Unfinished Business" (issues left unfinished or unattended to from the last meeting) and "New Business" (items newly introduced to the agenda for discussion and decision).
   - Include a section for "Announcements" (time-saving printed messages that substitute for verbal announcements).
   - Consider including a time for "check ins" (announcements of any personal business that may interfere with one's attendance at the team meeting; e.g., "I need to excuse myself from the meeting in 20 minutes to make a phone call").
   - Consider including a time for "check outs" (evaluative statements at the close of the meeting; e.g., "I thought the meeting was productive and I want to thank the group for working well together" or "Although I am uncomfortable with the agreements reached by the group during the meeting, I will support them because they represent the consensus of the team").
   - Review the agenda before starting the meeting, giving team members the opportunity to add to the agenda any recent or urgent issues that need to be addressed.
   - List and attend to the most urgent and important agenda items first.
   - Use the agenda to organize the meeting and focus discussions.
4. Develop ground rules and review at the beginning of the meeting.
5. Conduct efficient and effective meetings.
   - Begin and end meetings on time.
   - Stay focused and remain faithful to the agenda.
6. Allow the agenda to govern the length of the meeting (e.g., if there are fewer agenda items, shorten the meeting length; if there are many agenda items, carry some over to the next meeting). Identify a mode of communication (written notes in teachers' mailboxes, e-mail, bulletin board postings, newsletters).
   - Determine a process for communication (who, when, how).

during the course of the team meetings. A ground rule governing decision making is important (see the subsection on Decision Making later in this section), as is a ground rule about publicly supporting the team decisions once they have been made. When individual team members fail to support the decisions of the team, it undermines the team's efforts and may confuse and polarize the faculty. Because ground rules articulate the specific ways team members conduct themselves during and after team meetings, it is best for the members of the school team to discuss and come to agreement on ground rules during the first few scheduled meetings of the committee.

The Meeting Agenda The meeting agenda supplies the framework that organizes team meetings. It ensures equitable participation among members of the team and serves as a vehicle for bringing issues from school personnel to the team for discussion. In theory, the meeting agenda is accessible to every member of the school so that all voices have the opportunity to be heard and everyone has input in the future operation of the school. Because it is simply not feasible for everyone in the school to attend team meetings, school teams often structure input from others into the agenda through any variety of ways. For example, some schools use electronic formats that allow school staff to add to the meeting agenda remotely. Other schools funnel faculty and staff input to the meeting agenda through appointed members of the school team. For example, when a teacher who is not a member of the school team wishes to place an item for discussion on the meeting agenda, the teacher contacts a member of the school team so that he or she can add the item.

Many formats exist for developing meeting agendas. Figure 2.3 displays one example. The items for discussion are listed in terms of their importance, and a rank order is made by the members of the team at the beginning of every meeting. Some meeting agendas include estimations of the length of time that is needed for discussion and debate to take place; these estimated times are listed next to the respective agenda item. Some meeting agendas include a few moments for members to "check in" or alert the whole team to any situations that might affect their individual participation, such as leaving the meeting early. Regardless of its format, the meeting agenda serves as the gateway for individuals throughout the school to bring important issues to the school team for discussion and serves as a tool for organizing efficient meetings.

Decision Making Decision making is an important function of team meetings. Lengthy discussions and debates about the future direction of the school are culminated in decisions made by the team. In order to avoid decision making that is marred by acrimony and bitterness, the process needs to be managed properly to ensure it is harmonious and civil. Managing decision making is best accomplished by talking with the team in advance of making any important decisions and coming to agreement about the process that will be used. Therefore, it is important for the group to establish ground rules and clear expectations for making decisions.

Establishing ground rules for decision making is helpful because they help describe how the school team resolves issues under discussion and minimize the opportunities for conflict during the meetings. Decisions affecting proposed program changes are usually reached in one of three ways: 1) consensus (wherein members agree by majority vote), 2) consultation (a decision by the administrator or team leader after soliciting opinions and advice from team members), or 3) command (a decision by the administrator, team leaders, or circumstances alone). Command decisions are frequently dictated by the circumstances surrounding the issue (e.g., procedures adopted automatically because of new legally binding regulations such as IDEA 2004). Sometimes administrators make command decisions on the basis of their knowledge and past experiences with certain issues. Consensus and consultative decision making require cooperation among team members, and the best way to ensure cooperation is to have clear expectations in place.

MEETING AGENDA

Group: SWPBS School Team ______ **Facilitator:** ______

Date: ______ **Time:** ______ **Location:** ______

AGENDA/ITEM	NAME	TIME	TYPE	EXPECTED OUTCOME
1. Agenda review		2 min.	d	
2. Additional agenda items		3 min.	d	
3. Check in		2 min.	d	
4. Review consolidated ground rules		10 min.	d/D	Review ground rules document for team leaders
5. Old business		15 min.	d	Discuss proposal for effective meeting training and make recommendations for change
6. New business		10 min.	d/D	
7. Future agenda items		5 min.	d	
8. Check out		5 min.	d	
9. Announcements				

Attachments: Proposed Consolidated Ground Rules
Proposed Effective Training Handout

Next Meeting:
Date/Time: ______
Location: ______
Recorder: ______

Agenda Item Type
D = Decision
d = Discussion/input
I = Informational

Facilitator:

Figure 2.3. Example of a meeting agenda. (From Helphand. M. [n.d.]. *Example of the meeting agenda.* Unpublished form; reprinted by permission.)

TIER 1 INTERVENTION

As mentioned earlier, Tier 1 interventions are designed to identify the basic standards of conduct for all students across all settings in the school. The goal is to clearly describe prosocial behavior so that every student knows and understands the rules and expectations needed to be successful in school. The following sections describe a process for developing a Tier 1 or universal intervention.

Defining School Rules and Expectations

It is usually school faculty and staff who define the schoolwide rules and expectations, although some schools include students as well as parents in the process, ensuring that cultural differences are honored and accommodated. School team members might begin the development of rules and expectations by asking themselves some guiding questions such as "What do we want our school to look like?" "How do we want students to treat one another?" "How do we want students to behave in the classroom?" and "What behaviors are desired from students when they walk in the hallways?"

Within the SWPBS framework, school personnel are encouraged to specify the appropriate social behaviors students need to perform to achieve success, and to do this across every physical location in the school—both instructional settings (classroom and labs) and noninstructional settings (hallways, cafeteria, gymnasium, commons areas, bus loading zones, and school buses). Once the specific behaviors for achieving school success have been enumerated, the school team is encouraged to develop a small set, usually five or fewer, of behavioral expectations sufficiently broad to encompass a number of more discrete behaviors (Sugai & Horner, 2002).

In the first documented schoolwide intervention, Taylor-Greene et al. (1997) developed five broad expectations they called the "High Five." The High Five expectations have since served as a model for many schools around the country. For example, Centennial School of Lehigh University developed a similar set of expectations called the "Take Five" (see Table 2.3). Like the High Five expectations, the Take Five were defined and taught across the various physical locations in the school (e.g., classrooms, hallways, gym, common

Table 2.3. Example of schoolwide expectations

Take Five expectations
Be there, be ready
Be respectful
Be responsible
Personal space
Follow directions

From Centennial School of Lehigh University. (n.d.). *Take five expectations.* Bethlehem, PA: Author; reprinted by permission.

areas, and the bus) and described in accordance with the behavioral demands of each setting. "Be respectful" in the common areas and hallways, for example, was defined as "stay to the right, respect others' space, and use an inside voice and appropriate language." In the media center, "be respectful" was defined as "enter with a quiet voice, wait your turn, speak to others with respectful voices, and say please and thank you." It is important to note that all the behavioral expectations are stated positively, telling students the appropriate ways to conduct themselves in order to succeed in school instead of telling them what not to do so that they may avoid punishment. School rules and expectations are more easily remembered when they are brief and positively describe the expected behaviors.

Different expectations for different settings highlight the important relationship between behavior and the physical setting. People behave differently in different physical settings. For example, in the school library, students typically sit at tables or study carrels for long periods of time and have little or no interaction with their peers. In the gymnasium, students run, jump, shout, and interact frequently with one another, expending vast amounts of energy. Although the student behavior differs greatly between the two settings, the behavior must be appropriate for each respective setting. If students were to behave in the library like they do in the gymnasium, their behavior would be quickly judged inappropriate. This example illustrates the functional relationship between a student's behavior and the physical environment and the importance of defining behavioral expectations with the physical setting in mind.

To facilitate the development and organization of rules and expectations across the physical settings in the school, some school teams use a rule matrix (Table 2.4). The rule matrix organizes behavioral expectations across the various physical settings of the school by listing three to five major rules down the left-hand side of the chart, with the different physical locations listed across the top of the chart (Sugai & Dickey, 2006). As the school team fills in the boxes with positive behavioral expectations, the similarities and differences among the expectations within each setting are displayed. When choosing which expectations are appropriate for a particular setting, the school team begins with those that are similar across various settings, emphasizing similar wording whenever possible, as doing so contributes to the establishment of a common language, which is hypothesized to be a major contributor to the development of school culture.

Teaching School Rules and Expectations

Rules and expectations are meaningless unless they are known and understood by everyone in the school setting. They need to be distributed widely and frequently reviewed. A common error among school teams is to seldom refer to the rules and expectations after they have been explicated and agreed upon. Posting school rules, although important, is insufficient

Table 2.4. Example of a schoolwide rule matrix

Expectations	Classroom	Hallway	Cafeteria	Recess	Bus/bus area	Library	Gymnasium
Be there, be ready	Enter class on time Have materials ready	Wait for bell Walk on the right-hand side	Wait for bell Line up for lunch Have money ready	Wait for bell Line up at door	Wait for bell Be prompt and on time Enter bus one at a time	Report on time Enter quietly Check in at front desk Have materials ready	Have appropriate materials Wear appropriate attire Focus eyes on speaker
Be responsible	Work quietly Participate in class Keep area and notebook organized Hand in homework	Go directly to assigned area Carry hall pass Walk using soft voice Focus on self	Wait quietly in line Sit at assigned table Clean up area after eating	Follow rules of game Display good sportsmanship	Stay seated Fasten seat belt Keep equipment safe	Handle books with care Follow procedures for checking out and returning books	Participate in activities Cooperate with teammates Accept outcomes of games or activities
Be respectful	Raise hand to speak Remain quiet when others speak Use polite language Ask for help or assistance when frustrated	Speak politely and maintain appropriate voice volume Wait patiently Carefully handle school property	Speak politely using soft voice volume Remain at table until finished eating	Take turns on equipment Resolve conflicts using polite words	Speak politely and maintain appropriate voice volume Use anger management strategy when upset	Speak politely and maintain appropriate voice volume	Speak politely and maintain appropriate voice volume Resolve conflicts using polite words
Keep hands and feet to self/ personal space	Maintain appropriate social distance Use materials appropriately	Maintain appropriate social distance Keep hands and feet to self	Keep hands and feet to self	Gentle touching only Respect others' space	Keep hands and feet to self Keep body parts inside the windows	Be gentle with equipment Maintain social distance Stay safe	Handle equipment appropriately Maintain social distance Stay safe
Follow directions	Follow directions the first time Ask questions if unsure or confused	Follow directions the first time Ask questions if unsure or confused	Follow directions the first time Ask questions if unsure or confused	Follow directions the first time Ask questions if unsure or confused	Follow directions the first time Ask questions if unsure or confused	Follow directions the first time Ask questions if unsure or confused	Follow directions the first time Ask questions if unsure or confused

Source: Sugai and Dickey (2006, http://www.pbis.org/common/pbisresources/presentations/gsgettingstarted0107.ppt).

as a sole strategy for motivating and guiding school staff and students to change their behaviors in accordance with expectations. The teaching of the schoolwide expectations needs to be ongoing throughout the school day and throughout the school year and not an episodic or one-time event. The rules and expectations must be taught repeatedly so that everyone in the school setting, students and adults alike, know precisely how to proceed for achieving school success.

Creative activities for teaching the schoolwide expectations are abundant and limited only by a lack of imagination. To get an early start on teaching the rules and expectations, some schools spend the entire first full day of school reviewing and rehearsing the expectations across the various school settings. In some schools, students carry a "passport" (see Figure 2.4) to the different physical locations such as the gym, lunchroom, hallways, laboratories, and playground (Sugai & Dickey, 2006). Teachers or students in each of the settings describe the rules and expectations and the rationales for abiding by them in each setting. Sometimes skits are performed for the students, showing them what to do to succeed as well as what not to do (examples and

Passport

Name: ______________________

Date: ______________________

Classroom			
Library	Common areas	Principal's office	Gym
Bus area	Cafeteria	Award ceremony	Playground

Figure 2.4. Example of a student passport.

nonexamples). As students move from one setting to another, school staff sign or stamp the passports, documenting students' attendance and exposure to the presentations of rules and expectations.

In other schools, teachers briefly review the small set of three to five school rules and expectations before every class period and transition, clearly describing how each rule applies to the specific setting (and specific activities) the student is about to participate in and precisely how adherence to the rules and expectations leads to success. The teacher explains (using the Centennial School Take Five expectations) what it means to "be there, be ready," to "be responsible," and to "be respectful" prior to class and describes the specific behaviors needed to meet the expectations. For example, "be there, be ready" means to quietly enter class on time and have materials ready on the desk. "Be responsible" means to work quietly, hand in homework, and participate in class. Reviewing these expectations prior to an activity precisely describes the specific behaviors students need to perform to experience success in that particular class or activity and helps prevent the commission of errors.

Other opportunities for directly teaching school rules and expectations occur throughout the day. Attentive teachers look for teachable moments, or situations involving students where inferences from student behaviors can be drawn to illustrate examples of school rules and expectations. An example of teaching and reinforcing rule-following behavior is simply calling on a student who is raising his or her hand to get the teacher's attention (a teachable moment). The teacher responds, "Tristan, thank you for following the expectation of following directions by quietly raising your hand to get my attention." In another example of using a teachable moment, the teacher reinforces the expectation of being respectful by responding to a student's behavior, saying, "Alexa, I like how you spoke so nice and politely to Jeremiah during the break; you were very respectful to him."

In addition to interactions with specific students, school rules and expectations can also be taught and reinforced by embedding them in general and routine conversations with the pupils. For example, when students are following the expectations appropriately, the teacher might say, "I like how everyone is being there and being ready by having your desks cleared and quietly awaiting my instruction." Or "Thank you for being responsible learners by working quietly at your seats."

References to the rules and expectations can also be incorporated when privately correcting students' misbehaviors. For example, "Remember, John, being there and being ready means having your desktop cleared except for your textbook." As soon as John clears his desk, the teacher states, "Thank you for following that direction."

Teachers who repeat the phraseology of the school rules and expectations in general conversations with students not only teach and reinforce the rules and expectations, but also achieve other important objectives.

Repeated recitations of the rules and expectations help establish a common language among faculty as well as students and signal adherence to a common set of social standards. Moreover, making public the rules and expectations essentially gives students permission to do the right thing. What does that mean? When adults use praise liberally and publicly, they demonstrate to students that it is acceptable within the school culture to use polite words and to praise others (Skinner & Belmont, 1993). Students believe they have support and encouragement for being polite and courteous, a far cry from some school cultures, where praise of students by peers and staff may lead to ridicule and harassment.

Recognition and Acknowledgment for Adherence to Rules and Expectations

Teachers and students who demonstrate adherence to the newly created rules and expectations should be recognized and acknowledged for a job well done, not unlike employees in American industries and enterprises. Recognition and acknowledgments take many forms, ranging from social praise to tangible awards. For example, administrators should recognize and acknowledge teachers who incorporate school rules and expectations into their daily vocabulary and conversations with students and check in frequently with faculty to remind them of the important role of repetition when establishing a common language and building the school culture.

Students too should receive frequent recognition and acknowledgment from school faculty (teachers, paraprofessionals, related staff, and administrators) and others (volunteers) for abiding by the schoolwide rules and expectations. Verbal praise is a powerful form of recognition for many students, especially when contextually appropriate for students' ages and, whenever possible, their interests. A simple "thank you" in response to a desired behavior can result in future compliance. Some schools use tangibles, such as tickets or small slips of paper, as recognition for a job well done. The use of such extrinsic incentives serves to recognize appropriate behavior and makes visible to all students the behaviors that are valued. The tickets or slips represent tokens that can be exchanged at a later time for more desirable items, such as school store points or other tangible rewards. Distributed by faculty throughout the day, the tickets or slips not only acknowledge students' compliance with a particular school rule or expectation but also serve as a prompt about the importance of the schoolwide program to other students in the area.

An award ceremony is another tangible form of recognition and acknowledgment often used to emphasize the importance of appropriate social behavior throughout the school. The award ceremony is a time for recognizing students for demonstrating appropriate behavior over a specified period of time (usually weekly or monthly). Awards are designed and distributed by faculty in celebration of students' achievements in specific areas such as "Most Respectful Student," "Most Responsible Student," "Outstanding Sportsmanship Award," "Homework Award," and "Attendance Award." Award ceremonies are usually brief assemblies of the student body (some are conducted by way of the intercom) that recognize students for "doing the right thing." Faculty usually select the award recipients, although some schools include peers in the nomination and selection process. Awards consist of paper certificates with the name of the award, the date, and the name of the student prominently displayed. Copies of the awards are displayed in the school for all to see.

TIER 2 INTERVENTIONS

Check In Check Out

CICO (Campbell & Anderson, 2008), also known as the Behavior Education Program (Crone, Hawken, & Horner, 2010), is the most frequently reported program used at Tier 2 (Mitchell, Stormont, & Gage, 2011). Implementation involves identifying a staff member to check in with the student before school each day. The staff member provides the student with a daily CICO card that lists behavioral goals (usually SWPBS expectations), a rating scale (usually points earned) for scoring how the student performs each behavior or expectation, and a schedule for checking in with staff throughout the day (e.g., the end of each period, half-hour intervals). The staff discusses ways the student can meet the goals and how to be successful that day. Using the check in schedule, the student carries the card and presents it to each school staff member for evaluation at the predetermined times. At the end of the day, the student again meets with the designated staff member for check out. The staff reviews the daily CICO card, totals the number of points earned, and provides feedback to the student. The student is provided a summary of that day's performance, which he or she takes home in the form of a report for his or her parent or guardian to sign and then returns to school for the next day's check in. Detailed steps for implementation are described in the book *Responding to Problem Behavior in Schools: The Behavior Education Program* by Crone et al. (2010).

Social Skills Training

At Tier 2, social skills programs are usually implemented in small groups made up of students with similar skill deficits. Social skills instruction (see Chapter 6) focuses on a particular skill (e.g., making friends, maintaining hygiene, initiating interactions with peers). Groups usually convene for relatively short periods of time (e.g., a few months) to learn and practice the skills using instruction, role play, and other procedures. As we describe in Chapter 6, it is essential that the instruction include both procedures for generalizing the skill to typical settings where social problems occur and for measuring acquisition of the skill in those settings.

First Step to Success

First Step to Success is a structured, commercially available program that uses a behavior coach to work with Tier 2 students in grades kindergarten through third and their peers, teacher, and parents for roughly 50–60 hours over a 3-month period. The program consists of three interrelated modules. The first module, screening, involves teacher nomination and ranks order of students in the classroom with behavioral challenges followed by a rating of the severity of behavior problems. The second module, classroom intervention, includes identifying specific performance criteria (i.e., behavior the student needs to exhibit) and providing the student with regular feedback about whether the performance criteria have been met (e.g., displaying green card if met, red card if not met) at predetermined intervals. Data are recorded on a card that is taken home each evening. The parent or guardian provides encouragement and/or rewards for meeting criteria and signs the card, which the student returns to school. This phase is implemented for a minimum of 30 days or until criteria have been achieved. In the third module, parent education, a coach meets with the family for 6 weeks (45–60 minutes weekly) and teaches the parents strategies and activities they can use with their child that will increase success at school. For more information, see What Works Clearinghouse, http://ies.ed.gov/ncee/wwc/interventionreport.aspx?sid=179.

Mentoring

Mentoring is another common Tier 2 intervention that shares characteristics of CICO. Mentoring involves identifying an adult mentor who creates a relationship with a Tier 2 student, providing encouragement, support, and problem solving. Mentors meet regularly with students (e.g., weekly) across a substantial period of time (e.g., up to 2 years) so that they may build and maintain a relationship (DuBois & Neville, 1997). Some mentoring programs, such as Check & Connect (Anderson, Christenson, Sinclair, & Lehr, 2004), offer a structured framework to track behavior and academic performance. Although research on the long-term effects of school-based mentoring is limited, some studies suggest positive results, including improvements in emotional and psychological functioning, reductions in problem behavior, increases in social competence, improvement in academic performance, reductions in dropout, and increases in post-school employment (e.g., DuBois, Holloway, Valentine, & Cooper, 2002; Silverthorn, Dubois, & Crombie, 2005).

SUMMARY

SWPBS is an easy-to-use and efficient approach for restructuring school environments. Empirical research shows that sustained and reliable implementation of the SWPBS approach leads to reductions in problem behaviors and increases in prosocial behavior among students in the school environment. Schools that have successfully implemented and sustained the SWPBS approach have reported reductions in student misbehaviors ranging from 30% to 80% and sometimes even more, as measured by decreases in ODRs and suspensions. The SWPBS approach's relationship to academic improvements is less clear. Although it has been hypothesized that SWPBS should result in enhanced academic outcomes for students, this relationship has not been fully demonstrated empirically.

The success of the SWPBS approach in schools has an additional positive outcome. It clearly points out that in schools experiencing high frequencies of student misconduct, much of the student misbehavior is not the sole responsibility of the students. Instead, through its success, the SWPBS approach has shown that high levels of student misbehavior can be attributed to a failure of systems within schools—a failure to teach appropriate behavior. This important lesson reaffirms past research findings pointing to the critical role of environment in shaping behavior and provides a starting point for the information contained in this book.

Self-Reflection

1. How would you characterize the discipline in your school or the school you have visited on a continuum of predominantly reactive to mostly positive? How balanced are these two approaches?
2. How collaboratively do staff members address problem behavior in the school where you work or have visited? Can you think of ways that increased collaboration among staff could benefit you as a teacher? What are ways it could benefit students?
3. To what extent are data used to make decisions about how to intervene with problem behavior in the school where you work or have visited? In what ways would the collection and use of data improve behavior management?
4. Does the school where you work or have visited emphasize and reward appropriate behavior? What are some specific ways the school could increase its emphasis on appropriate behavior?
5. What Tier 2 interventions are in place in the school where you work or have visited (regardless of whether a tiered system is in place)? How could these Tier 2 interventions be expanded to thoroughly address student needs?

REFERENCES

American Psychological Association. (2008). Are zero tolerance policies effective in schools? *American Psychologist, 63,* 852–862.

Anderson, A.R., Christenson, S.L., Sinclair, M.F., & Lehr, C.A. (2004). Check and connect: The importance of relationships for promoting engagement with school. *Journal of School Psychology, 42,* 95–113.

Baer, D.M., Wolf, M.M., & Risley, T.R. (1968). Some current dimensions of applied behavior analysis. *Journal of Applied Behavior Analysis, 1,* 91–97.

Barrett, S., Bradshaw, C., & Lewis-Palmer, T. (2008). Maryland state-wide PBIS initiative: Systems, evaluation, and next steps. *Journal of Positive Behavior Interventions, 10,* 105–114.

Barrett, S., Eber, L., & Weist, M.D. (2013). *Advancing education effectiveness: An interconnected systems framework for positive behavioral interventions and supports (PBIS) and school mental health.* Center for Positive Behavioral Interventions and Supports (funded by the Office of Special Education Programs, U.S. Department of Education). Eugene: University of Oregon Press.

Bradshaw, C.P., Koth, C.W., Thornton, L.A., & Leaf, P.J. (2009). Altering school climate through school-wide positive behavioral interventions and supports: Findings from a group randomized effectiveness trial. *Prevention Science, 10,* 100–115.

Bradshaw, C.P., Mitchell, M., & Leaf, P.J. (2010). Examining the effects of school-wide positive behavioral interventions and support on student outcomes: Results from a randomized controlled effectiveness trial in elementary schools. *Journal of Positive Behavior Interventions, 12,* 133–148.

Campbell, A., & Anderson, C. (2008). Enhancing effects of targeted interventions with function-based support. *Behavioral Disorders, 33*(4), 233–245.

Council of State Governments Justice Center, & Public Policy Research Institute at Texas A&M University. (2011). *Breaking schools' rules: A statewide study on how school discipline relates to students' success and juvenile justice involvement.* New York, NY: Council of State Governments Justice Center.

Crone, D.A., Hawken, L.S., & Horner, R.H. (2010). *Responding to problem behavior in schools: The Behavior Education Program.* New York, NY: Guilford Press.

DuBois, D.L., Holloway, B.E., Valentine, J.C., & Cooper, H. (2002). Effectiveness of mentoring programs for youth: A meta-analytic review. *American Journal of Community Psychology, 30,* 157–197.

DuBois, D.L., & Neville, H.A. (1997). Youth mentoring: Investigation of relationship characteristics and perceived benefits. *Journal of Community Psychology, 25,* 227–234.

Hawken, L.S., Alphonson, S.L., MacLeod, K.S., & Shumann, J. (2009). Secondary tier interventions and supports. In W. Sailor, G. Dunlap, G. Sugai, & R. Horner (Eds.), *Handbook of positive behavior support* (pp. 395–420). New York, NY: Springer.

Horner, R.H., Sugai, G., & Todd, A.W. (2001). "Data" need not be a four letter word: Using data to improve school-wide discipline. *Beyond Behavior, 11*(1), 20–22.

Horner, R.H., Sugai, G., Todd, A.W., & Lewis-Palmer, T. (2005). School-wide positive behavior support. In L.M. Bambara & L. Kern (Eds.), *Individualized supports for students with problem behaviors* (pp. 359–390). New York, NY: Guilford Press.

Individuals with Disabilities Education Improvement Act (IDEA) of 2004, PL 108–446, 20 U.S.C. §§ 1400 *et seq.*

Kartub, D.T., Taylor-Greene, S., March, R.E., & Horner, R.H. (2000). Reducing hallway noise: A systems approach. *Journal of Positive Behavior Interventions, 2,* 170–182.

Kellam, S.G., Rebok, G.W., Ialongo, N., & Mayer, L.S. (1994). The course and malleability of aggressive behavior from early first grade into middle school: Results of a developmental epidemiological based preventive trial. *Journal of Child Psychology and Psychiatry, 35*(2), 259–281.

Kern, L., Dunlap, G., Clarke, S., & Childs, K.E. (1994). Student-assisted functional assessment interview. *Diagnostique, 19,* 29–39.

Kern, L., Hilt-Panahon, A., & Sokol, N.G. (2009). Further examining the triangle tip: Improving support for students with emotional and behavioral needs. *Psychology in the Schools, 46*(1), 18–32.

Lane, K.L., Kalberg, J.R., & Menzies, H.M. (2009). *Developing schoolwide programs to prevent and manage problem behaviors: A step-by-step approach.* New York, NY: Guilford Press.

Latham, G. (1988). The birth and death cycles of educational innovations. *Principal, 68*(1), 41–43.

Lewis, T.J., Barrett, S., Sugai, G., & Horner, R.H. (2010). *Blueprint for school-wide positive behavior support training and professional development.* Eugene, OR: National Assistance Center on Positive Behavior Interventions and Support. Retrieved from www.pbis.org/Common/Cms/files/pbisresources/PBIS_PD_Blueprint_v3.pdf

Liaupsin, C.J., Jolivette, K., & Scott, T.M. (2004). Schoolwide systems of behavior support: Maximizing student success in schools. In R.B. Rutherford, M.M. Quinn, & S.R. Mathur (Eds.), *Handbook of research in emotional and behavioral disorders* (pp. 487–501). New York, NY: Guilford Press.

Mitchell, B.S., Stormont, M., & Gage, N.A. (2011). Tier two interventions implemented within the context of a tiered prevention framework. *Behavioral Disorders, 36*(4), 241–261.

Muscott, H.S., Mann, E.L., & LeBrun, M.R. (2008). Positive behavioral interventions and supports in New Hampshire: Effects of large-scale implementation of schoolwide positive behavior support on student discipline and academic achievement. *Journal of Positive Behavior Interventions, 10,* 190–205.

Public Agenda. (2004). *Teaching interrupted.* Retrieved from www.publicagenda.org/media/teaching-interrupted

School Climate Committee. (1997). *The High Five program.* Fern Ridge, OR: Author.

Silverthorn, N., Dubois, D.L., & Crombie, G. (2005). Self-perceptions of ability and achievement across the high school transition: Investigation of a state-trait model. *The Journal of Experimental Education, 73,* 191–218.

Skiba, R.J., & Peterson, R.L. (2000). School discipline at a crossroads: From zero tolerance to early response. *Exceptional Children, 66,* 335–346.

Skinner, E., & Belmont, M. (1993). Motivation in the classroom: Reciprocal effects of teacher behavior and student engagement across the school year. *Journal of Educational Psychology, 85,* 571–581. doi:10.1037//0022-0663.85.4.571

Sprick, R., & Borgmeier, C. (2010). Behavior prevention and management in three tiers in secondary schools. In H.M. Walker & M.R. Shinn (Eds.), *Interventions for achievement and behavior problems in a three-tier model including RTI.* Bethesda, MD: National Association of School Psychologists.

Sugai, G., & Dickey, C. (2006). *Schoolwide positive behavior support: Getting started.* Retrieved October 2, 2007 from http://www.pbis.org/common/pbisresources/presentations/gsgettingstarted0107.ppt.

Sugai, G., & Horner, R.H. (2002). The evolution of disciplinary practices: School-wide positive behavior supports. *Child and Family Behavior Therapy, 24,* 23–50.

Sugai, G., O'Keeffe, B.V., & Fallon, L.M. (2013). A contextual consideration of culture and school-wide positive behavior support. *Journal of Positive Interventions, 14*(3), 197–208.

Taylor-Greene, S., Brown, D., Nelson, L., Longton, J., Gassman, T., Cohen, J., . . . Hall, S. (1997). School-wide behavioral support: Starting the year off right. *Journal of Behavioral Education, 7*(1), 99–112.

Turnbull, A., Edmonson, H., Griggs, P., Wickham, D., Sailor, W., Freeman, R., & Warren, J. (2002). A blueprint for school-wide positive behavior support: Implementation of three components. *Exceptional Children, 68,* 377–402.

U.S. Office of the Surgeon General, National Center for Injury Prevention and Control, National Institute of Mental Health, & Center for Mental Health Services. (2001). Prevention and intervention. In *Youth violence: A report of the Surgeon General.* Rockville, MD: Author. Retrieved from http://www.ncbi.nlm.nih.gov/books/NBK44295/

Waasdorp, T.E., Bradshaw, C.P., & Leaf, P.J. (2012). The impact of school-wide positive behavioral interventions and supports on bullying and peer rejection. *Archives of Pediatric and Adolescent Medicine, 166*(2), 149–156.

Walker, H.M., Horner, R.H., Sugai, G., Bullis, M., Sprague, J.R., Bricker, D., & Kaufman, M.J. (1996). Integrated approaches to preventing antisocial behavior patterns among school-age children and youth. *Journal of Emotional and Behavioral Disorders, 4,* 194–209.

Walker, H.M., & Shinn, M.R. (2010). Systemic, evidence-based approaches for promoting positive student outcomes within a multitier framework: Moving from efficacy to effectiveness. In H.M. Walker & M.R. Shinn (Eds.), *Interventions for achievement and behavior problems in a three-tier model including RTI, 1* (1–26). Bethesda, MD: National Association of School Psychologists.

3

Assessing the Classroom Environment

Classrooms that promote academic achievement and foster appropriate social behavior do not just happen; they are the result of careful planning. Because the environment greatly influences child behavior, the classroom structure and the types of activities conducted within it are important elements in a child's school life. Regardless of the classroom type (i.e., ranging from inclusive classrooms in general education environments to self-contained classrooms within alternative school settings), basic elements of classroom structure, teacher–student interactions, and instructional procedures remain the same. To ensure optimally functioning classroom environments, teachers must periodically review their physical settings and instructional practices to ensure they are aligned with the goals and anticipated outcomes they have for their students. In this chapter, we describe a number of informal assessments that will help teachers evaluate their classroom structures along a number of different dimensions.

INFORMAL SELF-ASSESSMENTS

Over the years, a variety of assessments have been developed that aid in understanding important components of an effective classroom. Stewart, Evans, and Kaczynski (1997), for example, identified four major factors for teachers to consider when assessing classroom structures: 1) physical environment, 2) time/instructional management, 3) behavior management, and 4) teacher effectiveness. Neel, Cessna, Borock, and Bechard (2003) identified six quality indicators of special education classrooms for students with emotional and behavior disorders, including 1) school environmental and resource management, 2) behavior support, 3) affective education, 4) individual processing, 5) academics, and 6) career/life skills/transitions. In 2006, Boreson expanded these components by describing the following eight factors of an effective program for students with socioemotional behavioral problems: 1) academics, 2) affective education (e.g., feelings, personal awareness, conflict negotiation, self-management skills), 3) behavior management, 4) collaboration and communication, 5) evaluation and assessment, 6) life skills/transition, 7) staff–student interactions and student engagement, and 8) miscellaneous (e.g., policies/procedures, mission statement, related services). These factors provide guidance for teachers by describing important features to incorporate into their classroom designs and provide a starting point for teachers who wish to strengthen their classroom structure in order to improve student behavioral and academic functioning.

Self-assessment is one method that we highly recommend for promoting the use of effective practices by teachers (Kilbourn, 1991; Stronge, 1997) because it can be completed on an ongoing basis with no additional resources. Early studies by Johnston and Afflerbach (1983) and Hoover and Carroll (1987) demonstrated that self-evaluation of teaching behaviors can lead to increased use of desired and effective teaching behaviors.

We present two informal teacher self-assessments that draw upon the past work of our colleagues as well as our own experiences over the years. Like past self-assessments, the ones presented here allow teachers to examine classroom environments along dimensions aligned with the body of literature on best practices. Through this self-assessment process, teachers identify features that are working well for them as well as areas in need of refinement and improvement. We call our self-assessments the Teacher Self-Assessment of Classroom Management Practices and the Self-Assessment of Effective Teaching Strategies.

THE TEACHER SELF-ASSESSMENT OF CLASSROOM MANAGEMENT PRACTICES

The Teacher Self-Assessment of Classroom Management Practices (shown in Figure 3.1) addresses six key features of the physical classroom as well as practices in the area of behavioral support. It can be used in general and special education classrooms and provides teachers an opportunity to examine their own teaching practices in light of the teaching practices that have been shown to increase student performance in the classroom. Using this checklist, teachers are able to assess their use of each strategy and identify areas of strength as well as areas that may need to be strengthened to ensure optimal teacher effectiveness.

A brief description of the six features follows, along with specific elements and definitions that comprise the key features. This information is meant to assist teachers in determining the degree to which the feature is

TEACHER SELF-ASSESSMENT OF CLASSROOM MANAGEMENT PRACTICES

+ = Feature in place − = Feature partially in place × = Feature not in place

Directions: Read each item relating to classroom management practices and assess whether the feature is currently in place, partially in place, or not in place within your classroom, using the code shown above. Use the final section of the assessment to identify those features that need strengthening.

PHYSICAL ORGANIZATION OF CLASSROOM SPACE

1. ____ Desks and tables are arranged to optimize instructional activities.
2. ____ Work areas are established for different types of skills development.
3. ____ There is adequate separation of space between work areas.
4. ____ All areas of the classroom are visible and easily accessible to staff.
5. ____ Instructional materials are easily accessible to staff and students.
6. ____ The setting is safe (potentially unsafe materials are stored out of reach), and there are procedures for addressing dangerous behaviors.
7. ____ The classroom is neat, visually pleasing, and inviting to students.
8. ____ There is adequate space for students to store their belongings.

Comments: ____

____

____

CLASSROOM EXPECTATIONS

1. ____ There are three to five clear, positively stated, and operationally defined classroom expectations.
2. ____ Classroom expectations are displayed in a prominent place in the classroom.
3. ____ Classroom expectations are explicitly taught, using examples and nonexamples.
4. ____ Students are acknowledged positively for following the classroom expectations.
5. ____ Private corrective feedback is provided to students when expectations are not followed.

Comments: ____

____

____

CLASSROOM ROUTINES AND PROCEDURES

1. ____ Efficient classroom routines are in place and are directly taught to students (i.e., entry into class, review of daily schedule, homework collection, transition between activities, dismissal).
2. ____ Classroom management procedures are developed and directly taught to students (i.e., teachers routinely teach and reinforce expected behaviors and use a predictable sequence of behavioral prompts for addressing low-level misbehaviors and for maintaining decorum).
3. ____ An attention signal is developed to gain students' attention.
4. ____ Procedures are in place for enhancing the efficiency of transitions.

Comments: ____

____

____

Figure 3.1. Teacher Self-Assessment of Classroom Management Practices.

(continued)

Figure 3.1. *(continued)*

TEACHER–STUDENT INTERACTIONS AND EMOTIONAL CLIMATE

1. ____ The emotional climate of the classroom fosters a sense of belonging and connection to school.
2. ____ There are positive staff–student relationships.
3. ____ Staff model appropriate social skills and behavior, including patience, persistence, and problem-solving.

Comments: ______________________________

____

____

PROCEDURES FOR TEACHING AND REINFORCING APPROPRIATE BEHAVIOR

1. ____ Explicit instruction is used to teach appropriate social behavior, including self-management and self-control skills.
2. ____ A high rate of specific, contingent praise is used to reinforce appropriate behavior.
3. ____ A 4-to-1 ratio of teacher attention is given to positive versus negative events.
4. ____ Positive reinforcement procedures to strengthen appropriate behavior are varied and designed to meet students' needs.
5. ____ Individualized strategies are developed to teach and strengthen appropriate behavior.

Comments: ______________________________

____

____

PROCEDURES FOR MANAGING BEHAVIOR PROBLEMS

1. ____ There is an adequate level of supervision and monitoring of student behavior.
2. ____ Procedures are in place to respond to low-level problem behavior (e.g., talking out, off-task behaviors).
3. ____ Positive behavior support plans, based on functional behavior assessment, are in place for students whose behavior impedes their own learning or the learning of others.
4. ____ Procedures are in place for the prevention of serious problem behavior (e.g., physical aggression, behavior that causes safety concerns), including de-escalation and crisis management procedures.

Comments: ______________________________

____

____

GOAL SETTING

1. List one or two areas that you would like to target for improvement.

2. Identify activities to strengthen these areas.

3. Identify the types of assistance or resources that are needed to accomplish these goals.

in place, partially in place, or not in place in their classrooms. The six key features are as follows:

1. Physical organization of classroom space
2. Classroom expectations
3. Classroom routines and procedures
4. Teacher–student interactions and emotional climate
5. Procedures for teaching and reinforcing appropriate behavior
6. Procedures for managing behavior problems

Physical Organization of Classroom Space

Structuring the physical environment is an important first step in creating a well-managed classroom. Classrooms contain many items and pieces of furniture: desks, tables, filing cabinets, whiteboards, televisions, computers, and bookshelves. More and more, modern classrooms contain an abundance of interactive technology, such as SMART Boards, laptop computers, iPads, and iPods, to supplement and enhance the delivery of lesson content, and some classrooms today may even have green screens as backdrops for the production of in-class movies. Following are features to consider when arranging the physical environment, along with descriptions to help determine whether the feature is in place.

1. Desks and tables are arranged to optimize instructional activities.

   Feature in Place: Arrangement of furniture facilitates achievement of lesson objectives. Furniture is treated as objects that can be manipulated to accommodate various lesson formats and foster achievement of behavioral expectations. Tables, for example, are available for small-group lessons and placed strategically so the teacher can continue to visually monitor the remainder of the class during small-group instruction. In lieu of table groups, student desks are moved to form configurations conducive to either large- and small-group activities, again allowing the teacher visual contact with the other students in the room.

   Feature Not in Place: Arrangement of furniture causes difficulties in monitoring and supervision. Lessons repeatedly fail to reach successful conclusions due to misbehavior among students who are in too close proximity to one another or are unobserved by the teacher.

2. Work areas are established for different types of skills development.

   Feature in Place: Different areas of the room are routinely designated for different skill activities such as academics, social skills, leisure skills, and job-related skills. For instance, reading and math instruction take place with student desks aligned facing a whiteboard or SMART Board, but students choose individual spaces in the classroom for independent reading. An open space in the rear of the room is dedicated for social skills instruction, role-plays, or other activities. Student seating during various lessons and activities is predictable and promotes harmonious transitions throughout the day.

Feature Not in Place: Spaces are not designated for skill development activities. Students frequently compete verbally and physically for desks or spaces during transitions to skill development activities.

3. There is adequate separation of space between work areas.

   Feature in Place: Different skill development groups are separated by physical space or the configuration of furniture (e.g., two groups facing away from one another), allowing for completion of each lesson's agenda without disturbance or interruption from other groups.

   Feature Not in Place: Different skill development groups are disturbed and interrupted frequently by verbal comments and physical touching from one group or activity to the other.

4. All areas of the classroom are visible and easily accessible to staff.

   Feature in Place: Desks and tables are configured in such a manner as to permit supervision (visual contact) of every student at all times. Teachers and staff can easily move about the room to reach students and use proximity control when needed.

   Feature Not in Place: Some desks, tables, and cubbies are shielded from staff vision, making supervision of certain students impossible. Configuration of furniture prohibits staff movement to certain parts of the instructional space, leaving students inaccessible to staff.

5. Instructional materials are easily accessible to staff and students.

   Feature in Place: Instructional materials and supplies for each skill development group are readily accessible to students and staff, allowing for prompt initiations, uninterrupted implementation of lesson objectives, and efficient transitions.

   Feature Not in Place: Instructional materials and supplies are inaccessible, causing lessons to begin late or resulting in interruptions to lessons while staff and students search to locate missing items.

6. The setting is safe (potentially unsafe materials are stored out of reach), and there are procedures for addressing dangerous behaviors.

   Feature in Place: Floors and carpets are in good repair; disinfectants are labeled properly and stored; potentially dangerous items such as scissors, knives, and paints are stored and secured; emergency exit maps are posted; electrical cords are in good repair and removed from aisles;

furniture is in good repair; ceiling lights are working properly; equipment is secured and in good working order; and personal items such as keys and purses are securely stored. A written plan for managing emergencies and episodes of dangerous behaviors is in place and communicated to aides, support personnel (e.g., school psychologists, social workers, nurse, cafeteria workers, bus drivers), and building administrators.

Feature Not in Place: Omission of any of the items mentioned in "Feature in Place."

7. The classroom is neat, visually pleasing, and inviting to students.

   Feature in Place: Classroom appears tidy, papers and books are neatly stored, and wall displays are colorful and visually pleasing. Displays of student products are rotated often.

   Feature Not in Place: Classroom is cluttered and unkempt; papers, books, and materials spill off of shelves and out of closets to litter the floor. Wall displays are messy, outdated, and unappealing to the eye.

8. There is adequate space for students to store their belongings.

   Feature in Place: Students' personal items such as backpacks, coats, hats, lunches, projects, and homework are neatly stored under desks or in cubbies and closets.

   Feature Not in Place: Storage space for students' personal items is insufficient.

Classroom Expectations

Research clearly shows that developing, teaching, and reinforcing adherence to classroom expectations are chief characteristics of an effective classroom and contribute to improvements in student behavior and academic achievement (Johnson, Stoner, & Green, 1996; Shores et al., 1993). A good beginning point for developing classroom rules is answering the simple question, "How would I like the students to behave in my class?" Following is a description of classroom expectations on the self-assessment to determine whether expectations are in place in a way that optimally benefits students.

1. There are three to five clear, positively stated, and operationally defined classroom expectations.

   Feature in Place: Expectations are few in number and sufficiently broad to encompass every behavior that could occur within the classroom. Expectations are briefly stated, using fewer than five words, and describe behaviors students should perform; for example, "be respectful." Expectations are operationally defined using examples and nonexamples.

Feature Not in Place: The number of expectations exceeds five. Expectations are lengthy, worded negatively, and describe behaviors teachers wish to eliminate (e.g., "There shall be *no* cursing in this room.").

2. Classroom expectations are displayed in a prominent place in the classroom.

   Feature in Place: Expectations are posted on one of the classroom walls and, if used, on individual students' point sheets.

   Feature Not in Place: Expectations are not visible anywhere within the classroom or instructional areas.

3. Classroom expectations are explicitly taught, using examples and non-examples.

   Feature in Place: Time is spent every day reviewing the classroom expectations. Classroom expectations are embedded verbally throughout the day. Teachers describe and model behaviors that constitute fulfillment of the classroom expectations as well as behaviors that constitute violations of the expectations. Natural contexts are used to illustrate appropriate achievement of the classroom expectations.

   Feature Not in Place: Classroom expectations are seldom if ever mentioned or are referred to only when students fail to meet them. Teachers expect students to comply with expectations but take little or no time to teach students the discrete behaviors required for meeting them.

4. Students are acknowledged positively for following the classroom expectations.

   Feature in Place: Teachers use verbal comments (e.g., "thank you," "good job," "way to go") and motoric feedback (e.g., thumbs up, winking, head nod) to signal students who are meeting classroom expectations.

   Feature Not in Place: Students who behave appropriately and strive to meet expectations are generally ignored while students who violate expectations receive constant teacher feedback and attention, usually through reprimands, warnings, and exclusions.

5. Private corrective feedback is provided to students when expectations are not followed.

   Feature in Place: Teachers walk to the student's desk or area and deliver corrective feedback quietly and privately, using a calm but firm voice to state, for example, "Being respectful means listening and remaining quiet when the teacher is speaking." Teachers tell students what they should be doing, not what they should stop doing.

   Feature Not in Place: Misbehavior is addressed publicly; for example, by halting instruction and calling across the room to an offending student.

Classroom Routines and Procedures

Similar to classroom expectations, routines and procedures promote order and efficiency within a classroom. Structure and routine lead to predictability. When students can predict events throughout their school day, they are more likely to be engaged in learning and less likely to display problem behaviors (Kern & Clemens, 2007). Teachers should structure every period of the day, even those "unstructured" times that appear in the school schedule, such as recess, lunch, and break. The following are descriptions of features of routines and procedures, as denoted on the self-assessment.

1. Efficient classroom routines are in place and directly taught to students (i.e., entry into class, review of daily schedule, homework collection, transition between activities, dismissal).

   Feature in Place: Students self-regulate and appear to know, understand, and behave in accordance with previously taught routines for entering and exiting the room, beginning the school day, storing personal belongings, ordering lunches, turning in homework, sharpening pencils, gaining the teacher's attention, and distributing and retrieving materials. Activities generally progress without disruptive incidents.

   Feature Not in Place: Transitions are accompanied by turmoil; students wander the room at inappropriate times; the classroom lacks decorum and appears disorderly and chaotic.

2. Classroom management procedures are developed and directly taught to students (i.e., teachers routinely teach and reinforce expected behaviors and use a predictable sequence of behavioral prompts for addressing low-level misbehaviors and for maintaining decorum).

   Feature in Place: Teachers routinely teach and reinforce desired appropriate behavior and reliably use a predetermined sequence of verbal prompts and warnings when confronted with misbehavior. The strategies and techniques for maintaining desired behavior eventually become predictable to students, signaling to them whether teachers perceive their behaviors to be appropriate.

   Feature Not in Place: Teachers seldom teach and reinforce desired behavior, and responses to student misbehavior are random and unpredictable.

3. An attention signal is developed for gaining students' attention.

   Feature in Place: Teachers reliably use a verbal or motoric signal to gain students' attention and provide a transition into the next activity. For example, before each activity, the teacher says, "May I have your attention please?" or "Eyes up front!" Alternatively, teachers use a motoric signal such as silently raising a hand in the air or clapping a rhythm to signal students to stop talking and focus their eyes on the teacher.

Feature Not in Place: Teachers do not have a signal for gaining student attention, and students, unaware a new teacher-directed activity is ready to begin, often continue to converse with one another or fail to transition to the new activity.

4. Procedures are in place for enhancing the efficiency of transitions.

   Feature in Place: Students know and follow routines that govern movement between activities and instructional periods. Transitions between one activity and another are quick and efficient, with little "down" time.

   Feature Not in Place: Transition procedures are not in place, and transitions are chaotic and haphazard or disorderly.

Teacher–Student Interactions and Emotional Climate

Positive and supportive teacher–student relationships are important for all students but are critical for students experiencing academic and behavioral difficulties. A clear and unmistakable connection exists between positive teacher–student relationships and more favorable student responses in school, including reductions in behavior problems and increases in academic achievement (Marzano, Marzano, & Pickering, 2003). Wentzel (2006) noted that when students perceive their involvement and relationships with teachers as emotionally supportive and nurturing, they more readily engage in social and academic activities (see Chapters 6 and 11 for more information on enhancing positive relationships). As one writer mused, when students respect and like their teachers, they are likely to go to great lengths to please them, even so far as doing algebra!

Strategies for communicating emotional support and a sense of caring for students include greeting students joyfully by name at the start of each day; learning about students' interests, strengths, and needs; initiating personal conversations; and praising students for their efforts as well as their accomplishments. Listening to students is extremely important as well. According to William Glasser, student attempts to have someone listen to them are the source of 95% of discipline problems in schools (Brandt, 1988). The following are features of teacher–student interactions and emotional climate along with definitions to facilitate self-assessment.

1. The emotional climate of the classroom fosters a sense of belonging and connection to school.

   Feature in Place: Students are eager to be part of the school and classroom environments. Attendance rates are high. Students' work-products are prominently displayed, their interests are reflected in instructional materials, and they behave in ways to preserve their access to the school culture. School is perceived as a safe place where needs can be met and futures enhanced. New students are welcomed and assisted in adjusting to the routines. Students have friends at the school.

Feature Not in Place: Rates of absenteeism and truancy are high. Students misbehave in order to acquire suspensions from school. Students do not respect school, as evidenced by property destruction (e.g., graffiti, vandalism).

2. There are positive staff–student relationships.

   Feature in Place: Staff greet students by name and are knowledgeable about student interests at home and in the community. Positive comments to students exceed negative comments by a ratio of 4-to-1. Staff initiate and engage students in conversation. Teachers listen to students and honor their reasonable requests.

   Feature Not in Place: Teachers seldom initiate conversations with students outside of directives associated with the curriculum. Dialogue is characterized by the issuance of prohibitions, reprimands, and warnings. Students seldom initiate conversation with staff. Students seek staff attention in inappropriate ways.

3. Staff model appropriate social skills and behavior, including patience, persistence, and problem-solving.

   Feature in Place: Staff demonstrate appropriate social behavior, even during times of stress, by using calm voices, listening, honoring polite requests, focusing upon and reinforcing appropriate behaviors, ignoring honest mistakes, using polite words, dressing appropriately for school, remaining civil during crises, and celebrating classroom successes.

   Feature Not in Place: Staff engage in inappropriate social interactions with students. Staff appear irritated or frustrated with students and address student misbehavior through intimidation or threats. Staff make disrespectful comments, engage in name calling, or use sarcasm with students.

Procedures for Teaching and Reinforcing Appropriate Behavior

It is important that teachers develop procedures for explicitly teaching appropriate social behaviors and self-management skills. Features that need to be addressed in the design of the classroom include explicit instruction for teaching prosocial behavior; procedures for teaching alternative, appropriate behavior; and positive reinforcement for strengthening appropriate social skills (also see Chapter 11). These features are defined below to assist teachers using the self-assessment.

1. Explicit instruction is used to teach appropriate social behavior, including self-management and self-control skills.

   Feature in Place: Teachers demonstrate, reinforce, and provide ample opportunities for the practice of important prosocial behaviors. Teachers assume students have not mastered social skills and use naturally occurring contexts as platforms for social skills instruction, emphasizing the acquisition of self-management and self-control skills. Misbehaviors are viewed as "social errors" and correctible with direct feedback that tells students how and when to use more socially appropriate responses in given situations. Teachers problem-solve ways to help students gain self-control in difficult situations. Teachers provide specific strategies for helping students recognize and handle frustration.

Feature Not in Place: Potential teaching episodes in naturally occurring contexts go unrealized. Students are expected to know how to behave in social situations and receive feedback only when social errors are committed, usually in the form of corrections or warnings coupled with mild threats to take something away if the behavior persists. Teachers assume misbehavior is purposeful and calculated to disrupt. Punishment, rather than teaching, is the preferred method of intervention.

2. A high rate of specific, contingent praise is used to reinforce appropriate behavior.

   Feature in Place: Teachers recognize prosocial behavior throughout the day by using statements that link verbal praise with the behavior for which the praise is given, telling students the precise behavior deemed appropriate. For example, when a student raises his or her hand to signal teacher attention, the teacher states, "I like how you quietly raised your hand to get my attention," thus verbally reinforcing the appropriate social behavior of quiet hand-raising.

   Feature Not in Place: Teachers fail to recognize desired behaviors, and when they do, the praise is general and nondescript; for example, "good job." Prosocial behavior receives little teacher attention. Most teacher attention is directed at students who misbehave, taking the form of prohibitions, reprimands, and warnings.

3. A 4-to-1 ratio of teacher attention given to positive versus negative events.

   Feature in Place: Teachers look for and focus on positive events and interactions that occur in the classroom. Teachers acknowledge students and draw attention to their appropriate behaviors using verbal or motoric signals. The goal is to reinforce students based on the principle that reinforcing prosocial events increases the likelihood the events will occur again and with greater frequency in the future. Low-level misbehavior is either ignored (if it is relatively minor and not harmful or disruptive to others) or treated as a behavioral error and gently corrected by telling or showing students the preferred replacement behavior. For example, saying, "A better way (rather than calling out "teacher") to get my attention is to quietly raise your hand." The overall ratio of positive to negative teacher statements is 4-to-1.

Feature Not in Place: Teachers focus predominately on negative events, even low-level misbehaviors, occurring in the room in an attempt to eliminate them. For example, a student who curses receives immediate attention from the teacher (in the form of a reprimand), whereas a student who uses polite language is ignored. Positive statements for appropriate behavior are rarely issued.

4. Positive reinforcement procedures for strengthening appropriate behavior are varied and designed to meet students' needs.

   Feature in Place: Teachers use a variety of methods to recognize and reinforce desired behaviors; for example, verbal praise, social reinforcement, tangible reinforcement, access to preferred activities, token economies, level systems, individual and group contingencies.

   Feature Not in Place: Reinforcement is not in place and not used consistently. Those reinforcement measures in place are largely inaccessible to students due to their lack of skill, despite genuine effort on the part of students to acquire them. Student behavior is not improving; the novelty and power of the selected reinforcers has diminished.

5. Individualized strategies are developed to teach and strengthen appropriate behavior.

   Feature in Place: Time is set aside for formal individualized instruction in social skills, including anger management skills, that targets the unique needs of individual students. New skills are directly taught, rehearsed, and reinforced. Teachers use goal setting, behavioral contracts, data graphs, point cards, and self-monitoring strategies to encourage use of newly acquired skills across settings.

   Feature Not in Place: Although group social skills lessons may be provided using a packaged curriculum, individualized strategies that target the unique needs of the students in the class are not provided.

Procedures for Managing Behavior Problems

The use of positive behavior support strategies dramatically reduces the incidence of problem behaviors in the classroom. Specifically, classroom procedures need to be in place to supervise and monitor students in order to identify sources of tension or frustration, respond preventively to low-level behaviors, address more serious behaviors, and implement individualized behavior support plans, when needed.

All students experience frustration, interpersonal conflicts, and other challenging situations that trigger outbursts of disruptive behavior at some time or another. Students differ vastly in their responses to frustrating situations. Students diagnosed with educational disabilities are likely to experience frustrations more frequently and with more intensity than others.

In designing the classroom structure, teachers should thoughtfully develop management procedures that address potential behavioral concerns in the following areas.

1. There is an adequate level of supervision and monitoring of student behavior.

   Feature in Place: Students are under adult supervision at all times. When working with small groups, teachers have visual contact with students who are working independently. Alternatively, supervision has been delegated to another adult in the room. Procedures are in place for ensuring supervision of students during recess, breaks, lunch, assemblies, bus drop-off and pickup, and field trips. Those charged with supervision are apprised of medical conditions (e.g., heart problems, allergies, medication) and potentially dangerous behaviors (e.g., elopement, aggression) the students might have.

   Feature Not in Place: Students are unsupervised or easily escape adult supervision. Critical medical and behavioral information is unknown to those who are delegated responsibility for supervision.

2. Procedures are in place to respond to low-level problem behavior (e.g., talking out, off-task behaviors).

   Feature in Place: Teachers develop and employ a sequence of steps for managing low-level misbehavior; for example, 1) reviewing expectations for success, 2) issuing explicit directives to the student about what he or she should be doing, 3) using quiet and private prompts, 4) maintaining proximity, 5) offering redirection, and 6) issuing warnings about what will occur if problem behavior continues (e.g., "You need to be sitting in your seat to earn your points."). The procedures should be predictable, fair, instructive, and provide ample opportunities for students to correct their behavior and rejoin the lesson.

   Feature Not in Place: Teachers respond to undesirable low-level behavior with warnings, reprimands, coercion, and exclusions. Students cannot predict teachers' responses and perceive them as variable, leading to feelings of being treated unfairly. Teacher responses escalate behavior problems.

3. Positive behavior support plans, based on FBA, are in place for students whose behavior impedes their own learning or the learning of others. (See Chapter 9 for further information on behavior support plans.)

   Feature in Place: Individualized plans, based on FBAs, are in place for students who are not responsive to school and classroom supports. Individualized strategies are implemented as designed and result in reductions in behavior problems. Plans are communicated to significant members of the school community who will be asked to play a role in supporting the target students.

Feature Not in Place: Modifications and adaptations based on FBAs are missing. Alternatively, positive behavior support plans with modifications and adaptations are in place but are poorly communicated to significant adults in the school community and therefore implemented poorly. Modifications and adaptations lead to a lowering of academic and behavioral standards, stigmatizing students and calling undesirable attention to them.

4. Procedures are in place for the prevention of serious problem behavior (e.g., physical aggression, behavior that causes safety concerns), including de-escalation and crisis management procedures.

   Feature in Place: Written procedures are in place for preventing behavioral crises (see procedures for classroom management) and describe how teachers and staff should respond to behavioral crises. The procedures employ safe, hands-off de-escalation strategies. Each student's individual crisis plan is communicated to key school personnel (e.g., counselors, social workers, school administrators) as well as parents. School personnel implementing the plan have received training in safety procedures and have rehearsed the plan.

   Feature Not in Place: Prevention and de-escalation strategies are not in place. Procedures are not articulated, and there is no coordinated response by school officials. Crisis procedures may escalate student behavior problems and do not ensure student and staff safety.

After completing the Teacher Self-Assessment of Classroom Management Practices, teachers should be able to list areas they would like to target for improvement and identify changes to strengthen these areas. Finally, by comparing the features of their classrooms to those listed in the assessment, teachers can begin identifying the types of assistance and additional resources they need to improve their classrooms.

TEACHER VERBAL BEHAVIOR

The data collection tool Teacher Verbal Behavior Assessment, shown in Figure 3.2, allows teachers to assess the use of positive statements in the classroom. Teacher language plays a key role in the development of a positive classroom environment. Words do more than deliver content. Denton (2007) suggested that language may be the teacher's most powerful tool for influencing students' self-identity and sense of well-being in the classroom. How educators speak with children can influence development of their self-control, sense of belonging, and confidence in their academic and social abilities. Simply saying to a student with school adjustment problems at the beginning of the day, "I notice you've been working so hard to do well in school. Let me know how I can help you succeed," goes a long way to building rapport and commitment to the process of schooling.

TEACHER VERBAL BEHAVIOR ASSESSMENT

Teacher name:	Observer:
Date of observation:	Class/activity:

Teacher Verbal Behavior: Record the teacher's statements under each heading.

+ = positive statement made to the class as a whole
+S = positive statement made to an individual student
N = neutral statement (e.g., open your books to p. 65, move your desks into a circle)
– = negative statement (e.g., reprimand, correction)

+	+S	N	–

Figure 3.2. Teacher Verbal Behavior Assessment.

Walker, Colvin, and Ramsey (1995) reminded teachers that what they say or do may be the most powerful strategy they possess for remedying disruptive behavior. Indeed, what teachers say and how they say it (tone and volume of voice, expression) can either escalate or de-escalate behavioral outbursts. In contrast to what many people commonly believe, negative comments can actually serve to increase misbehavior. Maintaining a high ratio of positive to negative statements (i.e., a minimum of four positive to every negative) is one way to ensure students experience support and affirmation from their teachers.

The data collection tool Teacher Verbal Behavior Assessment can help teachers determine the nature of their interactions with students by recording the numbers of positive, neutral, and negative statements (e.g., reprimands) made during an instructional period. Positive statements are affirmations and other kind remarks (e.g., "You're working hard today." "I appreciate the way you are helping Jenna." "Thank you for being polite."). Negative statements are reprimands, warnings, criticisms, and put-downs (e.g., "You are not following the rules." "You can't do any better?" "Didn't your mother teach you better?"). Teachers' classroom language is complemented by neutral statements or simple directives and commands such as "Please open your books to page 10."

We recommend teachers use predominately positive statements in their work with students. The use of positive language adds greatly to the social climate of the classroom and helps make the classroom a place where students want to be. The use of positive statements is a skill that teachers can work to develop, but, like the acquisition of any skill, it takes practice. Rephrasing a statement such as "Stop, don't run" to "Please walk" is simply a matter of mindfulness, rehearsal, and repeated practice.

Because feedback from others often accelerates skill acquisition, we recommend that teachers have a colleague (a fellow teacher or teacher assistant) use the Teacher Verbal Behavior Assessment to collect data on the type of statements used in the classroom. This is done by simply tallying the number of each type of statement in the appropriate column on the checklist. Typically, the data are recorded during one instructional lesson or even part of a lesson—for instance, the first 20 minutes or so.

The checklist can also be modified to record which students in the room are provided the most teacher feedback and whether that feedback is positive, negative, or neutral in nature. Determining which students receive the most teacher directives and the type of language—positive, neutral, or negative—can be important. For example, a teacher may be using a 4-to-1 ratio of positive to negative statements in the classroom but inadvertently directing all of the negative comments to one particular student.

SELF-ASSESSMENT OF EFFECTIVE TEACHING STRATEGIES

Many factors contribute to students' academic success—individual characteristics as well as family and neighborhood experiences. Although these nonschool factors influence student achievement, most of them are largely outside the control of school personnel. Research strongly suggests that among school-related factors, what teachers do in the classroom matters most (Bain, Lintz, & Word, 1989; Wright, Horn, & Sanders, 1997).

Effective teachers know their students, their learning styles, and their accompanying strengths and weaknesses. Effective teachers are masters of the subject matter, and as important, they focus tenaciously on students' learning. Teachers, whether working in general or special education, must constantly monitor and adjust their teaching techniques. What they do not have to do is reinvent the wheel. Good teachers can draw upon an accumulation of evidence-based practices that extend across many years and have been shown to improve student learning (Bateman, 2004). These findings are applicable today. Good teaching, characterized by careful planning and instruction, keeps students actively engaged in learning and is a powerful behavior management strategy as well. Because effective classroom managers maximize the time that students spend actively engaged in academic tasks, they also maximize their students' opportunities to learn academic content and consequently, improve their achievement (Brophy, 1983; Deno, 1998; Sutherland & Wehby, 2001). In a study examining effective practices in programs serving students with emotional and behavioral disorders, researchers pointed out that strong academic instruction and intervention may be the "first line of defense" in working with students with challenging behaviors (Farley, Torres, Wailehua, & Cook, 2012).

The Self-Assessment of Effective Teaching Strategies is an informal assessment tool for examining six key components of effective classroom instruction (see Figure 3.3). The checklist allows teachers to thoughtfully evaluate each of the six areas, using a rating scale ranging from Not Implemented to Fully Implemented, to identify areas of strength as well as areas in need of improvement. Effective teaching strategies are defined in the following to help teachers determine the extent to which they are in place in their classroom.

1. I set high expectations for student achievement.

   Fully Implemented: Academic standards parallel district and state standards for grade-level achievement and include modifications and adaptations to accommodate students' present levels of academic functioning and provide alternative pathways (specially designed instruction in the case of special education students) to meeting the district and state standards. Similarly, standards of behavior parallel district standards for proper school conduct, again with additional group and individualized strategies in place for helping students learn how to achieve those standards. Although the academic and behavioral standards for students with EBD remain the same as for students in the general school population, the strategies for achieving those standards are modified from those commonly used with the general population.

SELF-ASSESSMENT OF EFFECTIVE TEACHING STRATEGIES

Read each item and consider the degree to which you implement it in your classroom. Circle the number that corresponds to your overall implementation of that item using the following code:

1 = Not implemented 2 = Inconsistently implemented 3 = Fully implemented

1. I set high expectations for student achievement.

   1 2 3

2. I use creative and stimulating curriculum materials to involve students and motivate learning.

   1 2 3

3. I utilize diverse teaching methods within each lesson (e.g., lecture, group work, seatwork) to maintain high rates of on-task behavior.

   1 2 3

4. I differentiate instruction based on my students' skill levels to ensure high rates of student success.

   1 2 3

5. I am aware of and include students' interests when preparing my lessons.

   1 2 3

6. I structure lessons to actively engage all my students in learning.

   1 2 3

7. I use strategies for smooth, efficient transitions between activities.

   1 2 3

8. I use a brisk pace of instruction to maintain student attention.

   1 2 3

9. My lessons include explicit instruction, frequent checks for understanding, and opportunities for guided practice.

   1 2 3

10. I routinely monitor my students' progress and reteach skills to ensure that students reach mastery.

   1 2 3

Interpreting Results: Add the circled numbers and calculate the total points. Total: ______

25–30 points: Strong use of effective teaching practices
20–25 points: Moving toward effective teaching practices
19 or fewer points: More emphasis on effective teaching practices needed

List one to three teaching strategies that you would like to strengthen. Make a plan for addressing these features.

Figure 3.3. Self-Assessment of Effective Teaching Strategies.

Not Implemented: Expectations for student achievement do not match district and state standards for grade-level achievement. Modifications and adaptations are not in place, are not evidence-based, or do not match student needs.

2. I use creative and stimulating curriculum materials creatively to involve students and motivate learning.

   Fully Implemented: Student interest is piqued by the format and presentation of the curriculum materials chosen for lessons. Materials are selected that challenge students academically yet contain skills within their ability levels and academic reach. Supplementary materials, including the integration of technology and media formats, build upon and enhance core instruction.

   Not Implemented: Curriculum materials are uninteresting and redundant (e.g., students are frequently provided worksheets). Tasks do not challenge students.

3. I utilize diverse teaching methods within each lesson (e.g., lecture, group work, seatwork) to maintain high rates of on-task behavior.

   Fully Implemented: Formats vary within each lesson, and students anticipate or "look forward" to a preferred lesson format. Students are alerted to the lesson format via outlines and reviews of the lesson provided in advance of the presentation.

   Not Implemented: There is little variety in lessons, which are primarily characterized by teacher lecture or independent seatwork.

4. I differentiate instruction based on my students' skill levels to ensure high rates of student success.

   Fully Implemented: Modifications and adaptations are made to the content to ensure it is accessible and matches the different skill levels of the students. Students achieve a high rate of success, with very few errors.

   Not Implemented: The same curriculum is used with all students.

5. I am aware of and include students' interests when preparing my lessons.

   Fully Implemented: Students' interests are assessed through conversations, informal surveys, and parent contacts and are incorporated in lesson preparation whenever feasible.

   Not Implemented: Lessons are planned and taught without regard to student interests.

6. I structure lessons to actively engage all my students in learning.

   Fully Implemented: I use a number of different strategies, such as response cards, choral responding, voting, whiteboards, and thumbs up, that offer all students the opportunity to respond to the curriculum.

Not Implemented: Lessons are predominantly characterized by teacher lecture with students called upon to answer questions individually, providing the opportunity for only one student in the class to respond to each question.

7. I use strategies for smooth, efficient transitions between activities.

   Fully Implemented: Procedures for transitions throughout the day are developed and taught, including transitions to less structured activities such as recess (for younger students), break (for older students), lunch, assemblies, study hall, departure, and bus drop-off and pickup.

   Not Implemented: No procedures are in place for transitions. Transitions take away from instructional time and are often chaotic.

8. I use a brisk pace of instruction to maintain student attention.

   Fully Implemented: Lessons move along briskly, keeping students focused on tasks and engaged.

   Not Implemented: Lessons progress slowly, and student interest is lost. Lessons are not well planned or organized, slowing the pace.

9. My lessons include explicit instruction, frequent checks for understanding, and opportunities for guided practice.

   Fully Implemented: Lessons rely on "errorless learning" so that students are highly successful. Checks for student understanding occur frequently throughout the lesson, using a variety of techniques, such as "thumbs up" for correct answers, writing answers on small whiteboards, and evaluating written products. Opportunities for guided practice occur prior to evaluating student understanding through independent work.

   Not Implemented: Lessons proceed without attention to student learning and acquisition of material.

10. I routinely monitor my students' progress and reteach skills to ensure that students reach mastery.

    Fully Implemented: Student progress is assessed at various time intervals (e.g., review of previous lesson at beginning of next day's class, end of lesson, and end of unit) using a variety of formal and informal methods (e.g., teacher questioning, review of independent seatwork, curriculum-based monitoring, end of chapter assessment). Skills that students have not fully acquired are retaught.

    Not Implemented: Student progress is haphazardly (e.g., teacher only notices significant deficits) or infrequently (e.g., end of unit) monitored, and lessons and units proceed regardless of student acquisition of material.

ASKING STUDENTS ABOUT THE CLASSROOM ENVIRONMENT

Students' perceptions of the classroom setting can be an important source of information as teachers develop and refine classroom practices (see Chapter 11). After all, students are the ones who benefit directly from a well-designed and engaging classroom environment. Researchers studying student perceptions about classroom environments found that student satisfaction with their classrooms leads to improved student learning (Diamantes, 2002; Johnson, 2006; Woolfolk & Weinstein, 2006).

Student surveys are a quick and easy way to gather student impressions about the classroom environment. Good student surveys focus on what matters; that is, what teachers actually do in the classroom and the quality of the learning environment they create (Bill and Melinda Gates Foundation, 2012). When using informal student surveys, questions should be worded clearly and designed to gain candid information from participants. Students will answer questions more honestly when they know their answers will be confidential. Usually, these student surveys can be completed anonymously without students putting their name on them.

Two examples of informal student surveys are provided in Figures 3.4 and 3.5. The first student survey, the Five-Question Student Survey, is a short, open-ended instrument that asks students to identify what they like and do not like about their classroom and to suggest what they would like to change (see Figure 3.4). It can serve as the basis for teachers to reflect on student perceptions about the design of the classroom and quality of the classroom culture and may be used as the focus for discussion in future class meetings.

Similar in some ways to the Five-Question Student Survey, the second informal student survey, the Student Survey of Classroom Environment, is a 10-question survey that can be used to gain student perceptions about the design and workings of the classroom (see Figure 3.5).

The information obtained from student surveys should be used constructively and talked about in terms of its helpfulness and usefulness to the future functioning of the classroom and the quality of relationships within it. Sometimes the information students provide points to unnecessary barriers to success that the teacher can easily remove, once those barriers have been identified. Although inviting evaluation from one's students may engender feelings of vulnerability, including opinions by students can enhance their involvement in the school and allow them to feel a greater sense of belonging within the classroom (see discussion of ways to promote student empowerment in Chapter 11).

USING PEER OBSERVATIONS FOR ENHANCING CLASSROOM PRACTICES

Peer observation, that is, teachers observing teachers, is another means of assessing teaching practices. This kind of observation can be used to provide feedback on classroom design or to share instructional techniques

THE FIVE-QUESTION STUDENT SURVEY

Students: Please complete this short survey, giving your honest thoughts about our classroom. No names, please: this is confidential.

1. One thing I like about my classroom is

   ____

   ____

2. One thing I don't like about my classroom is

   ____

   ____

3. One thing I would like to change in my classroom is

   ____

   ____

4. One thing that I would like my teacher to *keep doing* is

   ____

   ____

5. One thing that I would like my teacher to *stop doing* is

   ____

   ____

Figure 3.4. The Five-Question Student Survey.

STUDENT SURVEY OF CLASSROOM ENVIRONMENT

Directions: Please read each item and circle the response that shows how you feel, using the following code:

☺ = Yes, I agree! ㋡ = I sometimes agree. ☹ = I do *not* agree.

1. I feel comfortable and safe in my classroom.

   ☺ ㋡ ☹

2. My teacher welcomes me to class and talks with me about my interests.

   ☺ ㋡ ☹

3. I have friends in my classroom.

   ☺ ㋡ ☹

4. I know the rules and routines in my classroom.

   ☺ ㋡ ☹

5. My teacher notices me when I follow the rules and praises me.

   ☺ ㋡ ☹

6. My teacher quietly corrects my behavior when I do not follow the rules.

   ☺ ㋡ ☹

7. I know how to get help from my teacher if my work is too hard.

   ☺ ㋡ ☹

8. My teacher helps me when I am unsure about how to complete my work.

   ☺ ㋡ ☹

9. The one thing I like *best* about my classroom is

   ____.

10. The one thing I would like to *change* about my classroom is

    ____.

Figure 3.5. Student Survey of Classroom Environment.

and can serve as an informal tool for professional development. Blackwell and McLean (1996) outlined a number of potential benefits from peer observations; for example, positive feedback from colleagues can provide reassurance and affirmation, dispel anxiety and increase confidence in one's abilities (especially for new and inexperienced teachers who may feel uncertain about their teaching abilities), and lead to the acquisition of new skills and techniques.

The process of peer observation is straightforward and involves four steps: 1) meet with a colleague and ask him or her to attend a teaching session, 2) identify the main targets for observation and feedback, 3) have the colleague observe and takes notes on the implementation of a lesson, and 4) meet afterward to share data and discuss the results of the observation. The observer can provide feedback, if asked, on what aspects of the lesson went well and suggest changes that might improve the teaching session (e.g., clarity of expectations, types of statements made during the lesson, responsiveness to students' needs, pacing of the lesson, and percentages of student engaged time). For those who observe, watching others almost always evokes reflection on one's own teaching.

Two informal observation forms are presented that can be used to collect data during peer observation sessions. These protocols provide the observer with a focus for the observation and a means to collect objective data that can be shared later with the teacher. The first form, Instructional Practices Observation Form (Figure 3.6), focuses the observer's attention on the planning and organization of the lesson. The observer indicates which instructional features were or were not observed during the lesson. In the comments section, the observer can note details to share with the teacher in the follow-up discussion.

The second observation form, Classroom Management Observation Form (Figure 3.7), allows the observer to quickly assess the overall organization and design of the classroom, including features that support effective behavior management. The protocol allows the observer to check whether a program design feature is present and to briefly describe what he or she sees during each observation. As noted previously, the information is then shared with the classroom teacher during a follow-up meeting with the peer observer.

The follow-up meeting should be a conversation between colleagues, not the delivery of a judgment. The classroom teacher should be allowed time to review the observation data before scheduling the meeting. The follow-up discussion should include both positive feedback, which builds confidence and provides reassurance, and sharing of data that may signal areas in need of improvement. The data should drive the discussion, which may include the following:

- What went well in the session?
- What could be improved or developed?
- What steps will be taken to address any areas of concern?

INSTRUCTIONAL PRACTICES OBSERVATION FORM

Name: ____________________ Date: ____________

Directions: Using this checklist, record your observations using the following code:

+ = Observed — = Not observed NA = Not applicable

PLANNING AND ORGANIZATION

Materials are prepared, organized, and available.	+	–	NA
Lesson plan reflects students' strengths and needs.	+	–	NA
High quality materials/media are used.	+	–	NA
Materials are varied and interesting to students.	+	–	NA

INSTRUCTION

Lesson begins promptly.	+	–	NA
Student attention is gained prior to lesson.	+	–	NA
Prior knowledge/previously learned skills are linked to the current lesson.	+	–	NA
Students actively participate in the learning activities.	+	–	NA
Modeling and demonstration are used to teach concepts.	+	–	NA
Examples and guided practice are provided.	+	–	NA
Adaptations are made to lesson to accommodate needs of individual students.	+	–	NA
Student understanding is checked during the lesson.	+	–	NA
Activities keep students focused and engaged.	+	–	NA
Errors are corrected or clarified with patience and encouragement.	+	–	NA
Students achieve a high success rate.	+	–	NA
Lesson ends on time with appropriate closure activities.	+	–	NA

CLIMATE AND RAPPORT

Teacher–student interactions are positive.	+	–	NA
Teacher is enthusiastic and shows interest in lesson.	+	–	NA
Instruction reflects students' interests and experiences.	+	–	NA
Teacher treats students equitably and respectfully.	+	–	NA

Comments:

Figure 3.6. Instructional Practices Observation Form.

CLASSROOM MANAGEMENT OBSERVATION FORM

Name: ______________________________ Date: ____________________
Observer: ____________________________ Subject: __________________

1. Classroom is neatly organized and uncluttered.

   Yes ☐ No ☐

   What did I see?

2. Behavioral expectations are displayed and addressed during the lesson.

   Yes ☐ No ☐

   What did I see?

3. Classroom routines and procedures are evident.

   Yes ☐ No ☐

   What did I see?

4. Overall level of student engagement

   High ☐ Medium ☐ Low ☐

   What did I see?

5. Appropriate behavior is reinforced with positive statements.

   Yes ☐ No ☐

   What did I see?

6. Off-task behavior is addressed through private prompts and/or redirection.

   Yes ☐ No ☐

   What did I see?

7. Teacher circulates around the classroom and monitors multiple activities.

   Yes ☐ No ☐

   What did I see?

8. Lessons begin and end promptly, with minimal transition time between activities.

   Yes ☐ No ☐

   What did I see?

9. Lessons are well planned, and students are actively engaged.

   Yes ☐ No ☐

   What did I see?

10. Problem-solving strategies are implemented to address behavioral concerns.

    Yes ☐ No ☐

    What did I see?

Figure 3.7. Classroom Management Observation Form.

SUMMARY

Creating a well-designed classroom that incorporates high-quality instruction and sound behavior management practices is a challenging process that requires thoughtful attention and ongoing scrutiny. The use of informal tools such as those offered in this chapter allows teachers to assess their environment and identify areas of strength and areas needing improvement. These informal tools are easy to use and require very little (if any) cost. As we suggested, a combination of self-assessment and colleague observation is ideal. Teachers need to continuously evaluate their own practices. In addition, observation by others ensures that important elements are not missed. We recommend ongoing classroom evaluation until classrooms are orderly, efficient, and productive. Thereafter, only periodic monitoring is needed.

Self-Reflection

1. Using the Teacher Self-Assessment of Classroom Management Practices tool, identify the areas where you need improvement. List your first, second, and third priorities in implementing change.
2. Using the Teacher Verbal Behavior Assessment tool, identify the areas where you need improvement. List your first, second, and third priorities in implementing change.
3. Using the Self-Assessment of Effective Teaching Strategies tool, identify the areas where you need improvement. List your first, second, and third priorities in implementing change.
4. Using The Five-Question Student Survey, identify the areas where you need improvement. List your first, second, and third priorities in implementing change.
5. Using the Student Survey of Classroom Environment tool, identify the areas where you need improvement. List your first, second, and third priorities in implementing change.
6. Using the Instructional Practices Observation Form, identify the areas where you need improvement. List your first, second, and third priorities in implementing change.
7. Using the Classroom Management Observation Form, identify the areas where you need improvement. List your first, second, and third priorities in implementing change.

REFERENCES

Bain, H., Lintz, N., & Word, E. (1989). *A study of fifty effective teachers whose class average gain scores ranked in the top 15% of each of four school types in Project Star.* Paper presented at American Educational Research Association annual meeting, San Francisco, CA.

Bateman, B. (2004). *Elements of successful teaching: A best practices handbook for beginning teachers.* Verona, WI: Attainment.

Bill and Melinda Gates Foundation. (2012). *Asking students about teaching: Student perception surveys and their implementation.* Retrieved from http://www.metproject.org/downloads/Asking_Students_Summary_Doc.pdf

Blackwell, R., & McLean, M. (1996). Peer observation of teaching and staff development. *Higher Education Quarterly, 50*(2), 156–171.

Boreson, L. (2006). *Effective programs for students with emotional behavioral disabilities (EBD).* Ashland, WI: Wisconsin Department of Public Instruction.

Brandt, R. (1988). On students' needs and team learning: A conversation with William Glasser. *Educational Leadership, 45,* 38–45.

Brophy, J. (1983). Classroom organization and management. *Elementary School Journal, 83,* 264–285.

Deno, S.L. (1998). Academic progress as incompatible behavior: Curriculum-based measurement (CBM) as an intervention. *Beyond Behavior, 9,* 12–17.

Denton, P. (2007). *The power of our words: Teacher language that helps children learn.* Turners Falls, MA: Northeast Foundation for Children.

Diamantes, T. (2002). Improving instruction in multicultural classes by using classroom-learning environments. *Journal of Instructional Psychology, 29,* 277–282.

Farley, C., Torres, C., Wailehua, C.T., & Cook, L. (2012). Evidence-based practices for students with emotional and behavioral disorders: Improving academic achievement. *Beyond Behavior, 21,* 37–43.

Hoover, N.L., & Carroll, R.G. (1987). Self-assessment of classroom instruction: An effective approach to inservice education. *Teaching and Teacher Education, 3,* 179–191.

Johnson, L. (2006). Elementary school students' learning preferences and the classroom learning environment: Implications for education practice and policy. *Journal of Negro Education, 75,* 506–518.

Johnson, T.C., Stoner, G., & Green, S.K. (1996). Demonstrating the experimenting society model with classwide behavior management interventions. *School Psychology Review, 25,* 199–214.

Johnston, P.H., & Afflerbach, P.A. (1983). Measuring teacher and student change in remedial reading clinic. In J.A. Niles & L.A. Harris (Eds.), *Searches for meaning in reading/language processing and instruction* (pp. 304–312). Rochester, NY: National Reading Conference.

Kern, L., & Clemens, N.H. (2007). Antecedent strategies that promote appropriate classroom behavior. *Psychology in the Schools, 44,* 65–75.

Kilbourn, B. (1991). Self-monitoring in teaching. *American Educational Research Journal, 28,* 721–736.

Marzano, R., Marzano, J., & Pickering, D. (2003). *Classroom management that works.* Alexandria, VA: Association for Supervision and Curriculum Development.

Neel, R.S., Cessna, K.K., Borock, J., & Bechard, S. (2003, Spring). Quality program indicators for children with emotional and behavior disorders. *Beyond Behavior,* 3–9.

Shores, R.E., Jack, S.L., Gunter, P.L., Ellis, D.N., DeBriere, T.J., & Wehby, J.H. (1993). Classroom interactions of children with behavioral disorders. *Journal of Special Education, 1,* 27–39.

Stewart, S.C., Evans, W.H., & Kaczynski, D.J. (1997). Setting the stage for success: Assessing the instructional environment. *Preventing School Failure, 41,* 53–56.

Stronge, J.H. (Ed.). (1997). *Evaluating teaching: A guide to current thinking and best practice.* Thousand Oaks, CA: Sage.

Sutherland, K.S., & Wehby, J.H. (2001). Exploring the relation between increased opportunities to respond to academic requests and the academic and behavioral outcomes of students with emotional/behavioral disorders. *Remedial and Special Education, 22,* 113–121.

Walker, H., Colvin, G., & Ramsey, E. (1995). *Antisocial behavior in school: Strategies and best practices.* Pacific Grove, CA: Brooks/Cole.

Wentzel, K. (2006). A social motivation perspective for classroom management. In C. Evertson & C. Weinstein (Eds.), *Handbook of classroom management: Research, practice, and contemporary issues.* Mahwah, NJ: Lawrence Erlbaum.

Woolfolk, A., & Weinstein, C. (2006). Students' and teachers' beliefs and perspectives about classroom management. In C. Evertson & C. Weinstein (Eds.), *Handbook of classroom management: Research, practice, and contemporary issues* (pp.181–223). Mahwah, NJ: Lawrence Erlbaum.

Wright, S.P., Horn, S.P., & Sanders, W.L. (1997). Teacher and classroom context effects on student achievement: Implications for teacher evaluation. *Journal of Personnel Evaluation in Education, 11,* 57–67.

4

Managing Classroom Behavior

There are a number of "basics" that should be in place in every classroom. When these basics are in place, most problem behavior can be avoided or eliminated. Well-designed classrooms present the context for developing academic competence, teaching prosocial skills, expressing creativity, building trust, and cultivating friendships. For children with long-standing emotional and behavioral problems, an organized and structured classroom becomes a place for them to experience success, maybe for the first time in their young lives.

In Chapter 3, we described a number of assessments that help teachers to self-evaluate the environment in their own classroom and identify features that are already in place and those that can be improved upon. The assessments focused on two broad areas: classroom management and instructional practices. This chapter and the next chapter (Chapter 5) are aligned with the assessments (particularly the Teacher Self-Assessment of Classroom Management Practices) and offer specific strategies to enhance classroom features that teachers identified as needing improvement through the self-assessment. This chapter focuses on classroom management and Chapter 5 addresses instructional practices. Throughout this chapter, we focus on the practices and modifications that a teacher, Mr. Daniels, put in place in his fifth-grade classroom to improve the climate and the behavior of his students, after using self-assessment to evaluate his teaching practices.

IMPROVING THE ARRANGEMENT OF CLASSROOM SPACE

The arrangement of furniture and other classroom items should be strategic. That is, organization should match the types of routines and activities that will take place. In other words, form (structure and design) should follow function (groups and activities). The design of the classroom should reflect the different teaching and learning arrangements that will be used, such as whole-class instruction, small-group instruction, and individual seatwork.

One way to approach the task of organizing a classroom is to think about the types of instructional activities planned throughout the day as well as the expectations for students during those activities. Thought should be given to the number of students in each group and each subgroup for every period of the day, the nature of the instructional groupings (large group, small group, and individual), the materials required (e.g., paper and pencils, books, laptops, iPads), and any expected movement of students that will occur during the activities (e.g., moving from their desk to the SMART Board in front of the room). Another important consideration is the behavior and dynamics of students in the classroom.

A starting point is to make sure desks, tables, labs, and work areas are arranged so that they are conducive to the expectations of the activity. If problem behaviors are observed during a particular activity (e.g., small-group instruction), modifications can be made. For instance, Mr. Daniels' self-assessment reflected numerous classroom management features that either were not in place or were only partially in place in his fifth-grade classroom. He noted that few problems occurred during whole-group and individual activities, but the noise level increased substantially, as did problem behaviors (e.g., yelling out, side-talking, touching of other's property), during small-group activities.

Mr. Daniels began by closely examining the classroom space. He noted that there were two particular groups of students who tended to be most disruptive. Mr. Daniels subsequently made two changes. The first was to decrease the size of small groups from five students to three students. This required rearranging the desks so that three, rather than five, students were clustered together. In addition, he changed the composition of the groups so that each of the students who tended to be disruptive was grouped with two students who were routinely engaged and productive, had the academic skills to lead small-group activities, and were mature in peer contexts. This rearrangement substantially decreased problem behaviors during small-group activities, causing Mr. Daniels to judge the self-assessment of his classroom and subsequent restructuring of the physical classroom environment a success.

Optimally arranged classrooms make it easy for students to complete relevant activities in the space provided. For example, lab activities in which limited supplies and equipment are available (e.g., microscopes) need to be carefully organized so that students smoothly rotate through in pairs (e.g., examining and coding cells) while the rest of the class completes a preplanned and related independent assignment. Teachers should also ensure that there is adequate space for each activity. When space is insufficient or crowded, it may be necessary to modify or eliminate an activity or to rearrange the classroom.

When designing classroom space, ease of movement also should be considered. When a student is asked to go to the board, for example, what route will he or she follow? If board work is a regular activity, then the classroom needs to be arranged for easy access between the board and each student's seat. Similarly, teachers must ask what is the best (or least disruptive) route to the pencil sharpener (yes, even the placement of the pencil sharpener will greatly influence the traffic patterns in a classroom!), the wastebasket, and the teacher's desk. Strategic placement of these items minimizes disruptions and makes the most of classroom time. For younger children, arrangement considerations include sufficient space near the door to line up when it is time to leave the room, on the floor for circle time, and in the play area.

In addition to easy student movement, a well-arranged classroom allows the teacher to easily move about. There is research to support that teacher proximity to students can result in reductions in problem behavior (Gunter & Shores, 1995; Wubbels & Brekelmans, 2005). Classroom space should allow teachers to regularly and easily move about the classroom, monitoring student behavior and academic performance.

Another consideration when arranging space pertains to classroom materials. When materials needed for a lesson are organized and readily available, instructional time is maximized, and downtime, which is associated with increased occurrences of problem behavior, is minimized (Hayling, Cook, Gresham, State, & Kern, 2008). For instance, Mr. Daniels was provided one cabinet for storage, which was located in the back corner of the classroom. Although storing the supplies in the cabinet kept the classroom tidy, it led to disruption when many students needed materials at the same time. Also, opening and closing the cabinet added unnecessary noise and distraction. Seeking a solution to the problem, Mr. Daniels reorganized the classroom by removing the cabinet (which added classroom space) and installing portable shelving placed in three separate areas in the classroom. Supplies for different activities and subject areas were placed in the three distinct locations in the room so that they were accessible and convenient to students. Materials Mr. Daniels needed for teaching and demonstration were moved to shelving in the front of the classroom near the SMART Board, where he usually stood to provide group instruction. Student supplies were stationed at each side of the classroom, where they were easily accessible. In addition, a row of hooks was placed in the back of the classroom for students to store their backpacks and jackets.

A classroom environment that is safe, well organized, and visually pleasing creates an inviting atmosphere for everyone. A neat and orderly classroom with materials properly stored enhances and promotes organization and minimizes distractions. Colorful room decorations not only reflect the personalities of the teacher and students, but also create energy and excitement about learning. Walls and bulletin boards may be used to display student work, post classroom expectations and schedules, and highlight newly acquired skills. This extra effort is important because researchers have found that teacher and student satisfaction with the classroom environment enhances learning (Fullerton, 2010; Johnson, 2006) and has a positive effect on behavior (Evans, Evans, Gable, & Schmid, 1991).

CLASSROOM EXPECTATIONS

Classroom expectations follow the same logic as schoolwide expectations (described in Chapter 2): making the behavioral standards expected in the classroom setting clear to students and offering a framework for responding consistently to student conduct. As with schoolwide expectations, the emphasis should be on praising students for following the expectations.

When schoolwide expectations are in place, consideration should be given to modeling classwide expectations after the schoolwide expectations. Doing so contributes to the consistency of expectations across the school environment (clarifying what is appropriate and what is not) and helps build a common language for teachers to use when reinforcing and correcting behaviors. If schoolwide expectations are not in place, it is even more important to establish classwide expectations so that students are directly instructed in the expectations and fully understand the consequences for following and not following the expectations.

Classwide expectations differ from schoolwide expectations in that classwide expectations are directly applicable to the classroom needs and climate. That is, they are aligned with the activities that take place in the classroom and reflect a teacher's instructional style and preference. For example, in a chemistry class, it might be important to establish a rule that pertains to the use of equipment and materials (e.g., "Respect classroom property."). In a kindergarten classroom, expectations will be simple to facilitate understanding and may pertain to interacting with others (e.g., "Be kind."), listening (e.g., "Use ears and eyes."), taking turns (e.g., "Show respect."), and so forth. Classroom expectations differ among teachers. Some teachers expect students to be quiet throughout class, while others prefer students to confer with one another. Different expectations among classrooms is a given in schools. What is important is that they are applied consistently within classrooms.

Sugai and Horner (2002) offered a few guidelines for enhancing the effectiveness of classroom expectations. First, the number of expectations should not exceed five, because having just a few expectations helps ensure students easily remember them. For young children, three expectations are appropriate. Next, the expectations should be worded simply and stated positively so that students understand what to do to meet expectations, rather than what to stop doing. For example, when addressing movement around the classroom, a positively worded rule would be "Ask permission before leaving your seat" as opposed to a rule that states "Do not get out of your seat." A third suggestion entails providing students a role in formulating the expectations. Student input into the development of class expectations creates a sense of fairness and increases feelings of commitment to the mutually agreed-upon expectations.

After formulating the expectations, it is essential that students receive instruction on the expectations and how to behave in accordance with them. As a result of instruction, students should understand how each rule applies. This involves providing examples and nonexamples of the classroom expectations (e.g., "*Be polite* means listening when the teacher or your classmates are talking. *Be polite* does not mean wandering around the classroom or playing with toys in your desk when the teacher or your classmates are talking."). Expectations should be referred to frequently, especially when they are first taught. In particularly challenging classrooms, it may be helpful to refer to the expectations prior to each activity, including typically less structured activities such as lunch or recess. When reviewed frequently, the expectations not only help to develop appropriate classroom behaviors, but also serve as a basic framework for social skills instruction. Finally, the expectations need to be prominently displayed in the classroom. For older students, we recommend also placing copies of the expectations in their folders or binders. This will assist them in learning and internalizing the expectations. Figure 4.1 provides examples of expectations from Mr. Daniels' fifth-grade classroom, Mr. Keith's kindergarten classroom, and Ms. Lopez's chemistry class.

When schoolwide expectations are in place, they can often be easily extended to the classroom. For example, rubrics can be developed to illustrate

Mr. Daniels' Daily Directions

Be in your seat when the bell rings.
Be respectful to your teacher and classmates.
Be responsible for your personal items.
Complete your work on time.
Do your best.

Mr. Keith's Kindergarten Expectations

1. Be kind.
2. Listen.
3. Keep hands and feet to self.

Ms. Lopez's Chemistry Class Expectations

1. Be in your seat, ready for class when the bell rings.
2. Bring materials to class.
3. Be respectful when others are talking and working.
4. Use equipment appropriately.
5. Complete assignments on time.

Figure 4.1. Examples of classroom expectations.

how the schoolwide expectations apply to various activities in the classroom. Figure 4.2 provides a rubric showing how to apply the expectations across common activities in the school as well as in the classroom.

For expectations to be effective, they need to be accompanied by consequences. All too often, teachers design an explicit set of expectations but fail to follow through, both when expectations are adhered to and when they are violated. This lack of following through generally renders the list of expectations completely ineffective. It is most important for teachers to determine how they will recognize students for following the expectations. Emphasizing adherence to expectations helps instruct students about what they should be doing and also encourages good behavior, because teacher acknowledgment is valuable to most students. Positive feedback for adhering to the expectations can range from specific verbal praise (e.g., stating, "Jenna is following the rule *Be polite* by being in her seat and listening to my instructions.") to a more complex system of rewards for more challenging classrooms. Complex systems may involve an incentive program wherein students earn rewards throughout the day. For example, a chart can be developed listing each student's name. Students receive stars or checks during predesignated intervals throughout the day for adhering to the classwide expectations. These intervals should be short (even as brief as 10–15 minutes) for classes with students who have great difficulty following the expectations. Longer intervals can be used for classes with fewer problem behaviors. For example, Mr. Daniels' students had a moderate amount of problem behaviors at the start of the school year, so he decided to use a chart to monitor adherence to the expectations at 30-minute intervals. He set a timer for 30 minutes as a reminder. Whenever the timer sounded, he placed a check mark by the name of each student who had followed all of the expectations during that interval. At the end of each school day, students who earned more than 80% of the possible checks (i.e., 10 of 12 possible checks) received 10 minutes of free time. Within a few months, he was able to fade the intervals to hourly checks, and by the end of the school year, he no longer needed to use the system.

Along with rewards for following the expectations, consequences for not following the expectations also need to be developed and made explicit to students. Consequences must be consistently delivered in order to discourage inappropriate classroom behavior. Minor behavior problems or rule violations can sometimes be ignored, resulting in only a failure to receive checkmarks or points. This helps to avoid drawing notice to students who are misbehaving and may find attention rewarding (even if it is negative attention). Other examples of consequences for minor infractions include providing a quiet prompt or redirection (e.g., "Please go to your seat." or "It is time to complete your lab work."), providing specific corrective feedback (e.g., "Using your cell phone during class is not permitted; please put it away."), or reteaching (e.g., "The expectation is that you respect others. Telling Sarah that you do not like her picture is not respectful to her. Please give me an example of something respectful you could say to her.").

Rubric of Expectations Across Areas

	Be safe	Be cooperative	Be respectful	Be prepared
All settings	• Walk • Keep hands and feet to self • Watch out for others • Open doors slowly	• Follow adult directions • Wait to be dismissed • Help out peers	• Follow adult directions • Clean up after yourself • Treat others the way you would want to be treated • Use calm voice	• Dress appropriately • Be prepared to leave on time
Classroom	• Keep hands and feet to self • Remain in assigned seat or location	• Cooperate with others • Speak kindly about self and others	• Follow directions the first time • Use quiet raised hand • Use appropriate language and tone	• Get materials out; be prepared to work as soon as you enter the classroom
Transitions	• Walk	• Wait for directions before leaving	• Walk quietly so other students can continue learning	• Walk quietly
Hallway	• Watch where you are walking • Keep your hands and feet to yourself	• Follow expectations without adult reminders	• Use polite language • Follow adult directions	• Enter classrooms quietly
Cafeteria	• Walk • Keep hands and feet to self • Watch out for others • Open doors slowly • Keep food on your tray	• Follow adult directions • Sit at assigned table • Wait to be dismissed	• Follow adult directions • Wait in line in order • Eat only your own food • Clean up after yourself • Allow everyone to sit • Use polite words	• Bring lunch money with you • Be prepared to leave on time

Figure 4.2. Example of schoolwide expectations applied across various school settings.

Responses to more serious problem behaviors may include a phone call home, loss of minutes from recess, detention, or an after-school family conference. It should be noted that any corrective feedback that is provided to students should be delivered privately to both prevent attention for misbehavior and to avoid humiliating or stigmatizing the student.

ESTABLISHING ROUTINES AND CLASSROOM PROCEDURES

As we recommended in Chapter 3, structure can be included throughout every activity in the school day, even during times that are seemingly "unstructured." Increasing the structure in a classroom involves establishing predictable routines and procedures. This requires first identifying activities and transitions throughout the school day. For example, common segments of the day or activities may include 1) the beginning of the day or the beginning of class, 2) instructional activities, 3) ending class, 4) lunchtime, 5) recess, 6) requesting use of the restroom, and 7) fire drill.

After important activities have been identified, they can be broken into substeps (i.e., each necessary step required to complete the activity in an efficient, orderly, and timely manner is delineated). For example, Mr. Daniels identified the following steps for a smooth class entry at the start of the day: 1) place personal items away (i.e., lunch in bin, coats on rack, book bag and personal items in cubby), 2) take seat, 3) check board for story starter, 4) begin journal writing. Instructional activities may involve procedures such as how students should move about class during instruction; what students should do if they have a question or need to get the teacher's attention (and what to do if the teacher is busy); and how to obtain materials such as pencils, books, or paper.

Finally, transitions (e.g., from subject to subject, between activities within a content area subject, from the classroom to the lunchroom) tend to be associated with higher rates of problem behavior and, when longer than necessary, can interfere with instructional time. Thus, it is helpful to develop steps and procedures for such transitions. This process may include strategically placing items so that access to them is easy and convenient. For instance, students can keep materials in their desk (e.g., paper, journals, extra pencils) and have them readily available when the teacher makes a transition during the lesson from a listening activity to a writing activity (within-activity transitions). Alternately, materials can be placed on students' desks or science kits can be compiled and placed in each student's lab area prior to class. Another strategy to reduce transition time when alternative materials are needed is to designate students in each section of a classroom to hand out materials or books to the other students in their section.

After routines and procedures are delineated, they should be taught to students in much the same way as expectations are taught. That is, the teacher can model completion of the routine, illustrating both examples and nonexamples, and students can practice the routines. It is sometimes helpful to write out and post routines, particularly if they are complicated or not regularly followed. The teacher can then remind students who are not following instructions by simply referring to the posted routine.

In classrooms where students have difficulty adhering to a particular classroom routine, teachers can link adherence to contingencies. For example, Mr. Daniels' students had particular difficulty settling down at the start of the school day, sometimes taking as long as 10 minutes to get to their seats and start journal writing. Therefore, he decided to set a goal of completing the morning routine in 3 minutes. He informed the class that he would mark a tally each day of the week they met the goal and if they earned at least four tallies by the end of the week, they would receive 5 minutes of additional recess time. In the long run, this incentive actually saved a great deal of instructional time, and Mr. Daniels was easily able to fade it out entirely within a few months by changing the extra recess time to biweekly, followed by monthly, and then eliminating it altogether.

As with expectations, in addition to rewarding students for following routines, procedures also need to be in place when a student is consistently unable to follow the routine. It is first useful to determine if the student would benefit from additional supports. For example, occasionally students, such as some with ADHD, have difficulty keeping track of time. In this situation, an individual timer or digital vibrating watch might be helpful. The student can be taught to frequently check the time or respond to vibrations and determine whether steps in a routine have been completed. Similarly, a student who has difficulty completing the routine without socializing excessively can be given a desk close to the class entry and storage areas, allowing minimal interaction with peers. In some cases, when a student does not have deficits that might affect organization or time management but is simply clowning around or attempting to avoid work, it might be necessary to add a consequence, such as owed time during recess or detention.

ENHANCING TEACHER–STUDENT INTERACTIONS AND CLASSROOM CLIMATE

Creating a positive, supportive, and nurturing classroom climate may be the most important tactic a teacher can employ, with both short- and long-term benefits. As we noted in Chapter 3, research indicates that students respond best to teachers who establish caring relationships with them (Woolfolk & Weinstein, 2006; see also Chapter 11). On several surveys, students have reported that when they perceive their teachers to be supportive, they are more likely to both follow the classroom expectations and be academically engaged (e.g., Plank, McDill, McParland, & Jordan, 2001; Thorson, 1996). Furthermore, positive relationships within the school and with adults who serve as mentors can increase student connections to school (as we describe in Chapter 11), which in turn is associated with reductions in delinquency, gang membership, substance abuse, and dropout (Catalano, Oesterle, Fleming,

& Hawkins, 2004; DuBois & Silverthorn, 2005). Finally, teachers who have good relationships with students report reductions in work stress (Roorda, Koomen, Split, & Oort, 2011).

An important way that teachers can create a positive classroom community is through interactions with their students. How educators speak with children can influence development of their self-control, sense of belonging, and confidence in their academic and social abilities. There are several simple strategies for developing student rapport that are meaningful to students and set a positive classroom tone. These include addressing students by name (at the middle school and high school levels, this begins with learning each student's name), greeting them at the door when they enter the classroom, and smiling often. Talking with students about their interests or concerns also demonstrates that teachers care about them beyond their performance in the classroom. Examples include asking a student what is troubling her or making it a point to acknowledge student success in sports, dance, chess, or other extracurricular activities.

Maintaining a high ratio of positive to negative statements is yet another important way to ensure students experience support and affirmation from their teachers. As described earlier, positive statements are affirmations and other kind remarks (e.g., "You did great on your last spelling test," "I like how you are responsible during class," "You have been putting a lot more effort into your handwriting."). Negative statements are reprimands, warnings, and criticisms (e.g., "You're late every day," "When will you hand in an assignment I can read?" "Did you forget your lunch again?") and should be avoided. Furthermore, teachers should be very careful to avoid overly critical comments of students that could be interpreted as putting them down or teasing them (e.g., "I am really not sure you can do this work," "You have more problems with peers than other students," "Your work is the sloppiest I have ever seen."). It is recommended that teachers maintain a minimum ratio of four positive statements to every negative statement. It is important that this applies to both individual students as well as the class as a whole, because research has shown that, although teachers' comments may be positive in general, teachers tend to issue far more negative comments (and fewer positive statements) to students with behavior problems (e.g., Wehby, Symons, Canale, & Go, 1998).

Beyond teacher language, there are a number of strategies that can help students feel connected to school. A simple strategy that helps students feel connected to school is to display their work, both inside and outside of the classroom. Another approach is expecting students to assume classroom responsibilities. Teachers can facilitate by assigning classroom jobs and requiring helpfulness. For elementary students, this could include serving as line leader, cleaning whiteboards, passing out materials, organizing the reading corner, caring for the classroom pet, and helping peers with their work. For older students, an in-school job program can engage struggling students by providing hands-on tasks within the school that allow them to work side by side with adults in nonacademic situations. Examples of jobs readily available in schools include clerical assistant (photocopying, filing, and answering phones), library assistant (shelving books, dusting shelves, cleaning tables), cafeteria assistant (setting up lunches, handing out milk, cleaning tables, collecting trays, recycling), and janitorial assistant (sweeping hallways, collecting trash, washing walls). In fact, schools can turn their in-school job program into a full-blown prevocational curriculum, requiring applications and interviews, time cards, daily evaluations of work performance, and letters of resignation when the students wish to leave their positions. Such activities not only teach valuable skills but also engender a general sense of ownership, belonging, and mutual support.

Finally, special consideration needs to be paid to highly mobile students. Changing schools is both disruptive and stressful for students and affects their sense of belonging. There are many ways to welcome new students and help them develop connections to their new school. First, students should be taught the school and classroom expectations. A peer buddy can facilitate this and support the new student in understanding and adapting to a new school culture. In addition, new students can be given the opportunity to introduce themselves, describe their interests, and map the travels that led them to their current school. New students should be provided with a range of opportunities to meet and interact with their peers. In the classroom, teachers can structure group projects or cooperative learning groups. Outside of the classroom, new students should be introduced to extracurricular activities. Furthermore, students who make frequent school transitions may benefit from an adult mentor with whom they can share concerns (see Chapter 11).

ENCOURAGING APPROPRIATE BEHAVIOR AND ADDRESSING INAPPROPRIATE BEHAVIOR

One of the distinguishing features of positive behavior support is the direct teaching and acknowledgment of appropriate social behaviors. Teachers are wise to give attention to the behaviors they value. Through encouragement and positive recognition, teachers strengthen newly learned social behaviors. Similarly, teachers need to discourage and redirect inappropriate behaviors in a gentle but firm and consistent manner. Procedures for acknowledging appropriate behaviors and discouraging problem behaviors are presented below.

Instruction and Reinforcement

We have emphasized the importance of providing explicit instruction to students about what is expected of them. We discussed this instruction in the context of teaching schoolwide expectations as well as classwide expectations. We reiterate the importance of teaching (including modeling, role playing, and using other strategies) the behavior that is expected of students across school contexts. This includes behavior encompassed in the expectations as well as other desirable school and classroom behaviors. In addition, we underscore the need to provide frequent positive feedback to students, in the form of specific verbal praise, when they engage in appropriate behavior.

Enhancing Systems Already in Place

Teachers are sometimes challenged by a particularly difficult mix of students in a classroom or by one or a few students with more intensive behavior problems than they are accustomed to facing. In these situations, when students are not responsive to the aforementioned classroom procedures, additional supports are needed. These supports can be applied with the entire class or with individual students. Our recommendations are to begin with supports that enhance the systems already in place. For instance, it might be that expectations have already been established for the classroom, but the associated level of reinforcement may not be sufficient for the classroom or specific students. That is, praise provided to students for adhering to the expectations may not be sufficiently powerful or preferred to compete with reinforcement that students receive from engaging in problem behavior.

To illustrate, Adrian greatly enjoys the peer attention he gets from yelling out funny comments during instructional time. This immediate and, from Adrian's perspective, high-quality peer attention competes poorly with the occasional group praise the class receives for following the classwide expectations. Thus, additional reinforcement is needed. This additional reinforcement can be linked to the presumed function of Adrian's problem behavior, peer attention. In this case, the function refers to Adrian's need for acquiring attention from his classmates; he is reinforced for his comical statements by the snickers of his peers and therefore his need for gaining status from his peers is fulfilled. As an example of reinforcement linked to the behavior's function, for every half hour that Adrian remains quiet unless called on, he may receive 1 minute of free time with a peer of his choice (recall that he highly values peer attention). As noted, reinforcement can be applied with the entire class, if needed.

The extra minute of free time with a favored peer is an example of an incentive (reinforcement) offered to induce appropriate behavior. Incentives play an important role in schools. Minutes of free time, praise, stars, gummy bears, merits, points, tokens, and stickers, as mentioned throughout this chapter, are a few examples of the different types of incentives used by teachers for motivating students to improve their performance in school. In today's world, incentives are ubiquitous. Parents exhort their children to do well in school in order to get a "good" job when they graduate. Younger children work diligently to acquire teacher praise and affirmation. Older students strive to achieve honor roll. Businesses offer salary increases for exceeding job expectations. For incentives to work, however, they must have some reinforcing value for the individual.

Incentives as part of behavioral interventions should be viewed as a means for rapidly shaping behavior in order to achieve the ultimate goal of self-management and independence. Although most students do well with the reinforcers commonly associated with school (e.g., teacher praise, stickers, good grades, honor roll), struggling students, like Adrian, cannot easily gain access to those reinforcements and may require more immediate reinforcement. Some students with more severe impairments may need reinforcers for their entire school experience. Table 4.1 offers a list of alternative types of reinforcement.

To diminish reliance on additional or alternative reinforcement, we recommend establishing a plan for fading it. Fading can be done by systematically reducing the quantity or frequency of reinforcement. For example, after appropriate behavior has occurred for 3 consecutive weeks, extra recess time can be reduced by 1 minute every 3 days. Similarly, a gummy bear provided for good behavior at each 30-minute interval can be faded to 45-minute intervals, followed by 60-minute intervals, and so forth. However, before

Table 4.1. Alternative options for reinforcement

Academic Activities
In-class reading break
Library privileges (pick a book to take home or read in library during free time in school)
Play school-based or academic computer games
Access to academic content on the Internet
Provide choices for learning activity from a list of preapproved activities
Select a friend as a "study buddy" on an in-class work assignment
Select friends to sit with to complete a cooperative learning activity
Read a story to younger children
Praise/Recognition
Public praise (schoolwide announcements for good behavior)
Private praise (during or after class by the teacher or other adult)
Nonverbal praise (sign from teacher indicating praise and approval)
Call or write note to student's parent or guardian to give positive feedback about the student
Post academic or other work items in the hallway (e.g., artwork)
Awards or other honors for good behavior
Privileges or Rewards
Earn points or tokens to be redeemed for prizes, privileges, or preferred activities
Listen to music or watch videos
Provide "tickets" that the student can use to enter into a classroom prize lottery
Lunch with teacher or other preferred adults
Work with parents or guardians to set up rewards at home for good school performance
Get extra gym or recess time
Select fun activity from list of approved activities in the classroom (e.g., computer games, board games, Internet use)
Participation
Be given responsibility for assigning other students in the class to helping roles, chores, or tasks
Deliver school announcements
Help the classroom teacher or specials teacher (e.g., art, music, gym) with chores in the class
Work at the school store
Mentor for peers or younger students

fading reinforcement, it is important that appropriate behavior is firmly established. That is, a repertoire of appropriate behavior should be exhibited across a sufficient period of time to instill confidence that the behavior is well established. The exact length of time will depend on characteristics of the specific student and the environment. For example, reinforcement may need to be maintained for a lengthy period with an older student who has engaged in problem behavior over a long period of time.

Likewise, fading should be delayed in classroom contexts that tend to encourage problem behavior. For instance, in spite of the aforementioned classwide procedures Mr. Daniels put in place, a few students continued to exhibit disruptive behavior. One student, Vincent, had struggled with behavior control since kindergarten. In addition to engaging in behavior problems over a lengthy period of time, he also was highly reinforced by the attention he received from several of his classroom peers (who also tended to engage in problem behavior). Therefore, Mr. Daniels decided to delay fading reinforcement until Vincent's problem behavior was reduced to low levels (no more than three occurrences per week) across 6 weeks.

Another strategy to enhance the classroom expectations is to establish group contingencies. In this case, contingencies or rewards for meeting preestablished behavioral expectations are provided to either the class as a whole or subgroups of students within the class. One structured way to implement group contingencies is the Good Behavior Game, an approach that has been demonstrated to be effective for all ages, from preschool to high school (Kleinman & Saigh, 2011; Rathvon, 2008). This approach involves identifying problematic time periods, determining particular behaviors that need to be improved, and allocating group or class merits for engaging in the expected behaviors. (See Chapter 6 for specific steps of the Good Behavior Game.)

A caveat when using this approach is that it must be implemented in a supportive way. That is, students must prompt and support one another to exhibit appropriate behavior. It is neither productive nor instructional if students begin to punish their peers for not following the expectations. In this case, a teacher may want to establish a response cost (removing a merit) if students are overheard being punitive.

As noted above, research has demonstrated that this strategy can effectively reduce problem behavior with older students. For example, Kleinman and Saigh (2011) implemented the Good Behavior Game in a diverse public high school in New York City. The intervention was implemented in a particularly disruptive ninth-grade history class. The procedures described previously were followed, including establishing and operationally defining classroom expectations. The class was then divided in half. When a student was seen not following the classroom expectations, the student was verbally identified, the infraction stated, and a checkmark placed on the board under his or her team. Daily and weekly rewards were provided for the team with the fewest number of checkmarks. Daily rewards included small pieces of candy, and weekly rewards included a cupcake or pizza party. The intervention resulted in large reductions in talking or verbal disruption, aggression or physical disruption, and leaving seats. Although the intervention was effective, one caution is that misbehavior was verbally noted, which could potentially garner either attention (a rewarding outcome) or embarrassment (a harmful outcome). An alternative approach is to reward the group of students who adhered to expectations at predetermined intervals.

Additional Strategies for Nonresponders

The strategies described in previous sections are designed to strengthen or enhance the procedures, expectations, and routines already in place. If one or a few students continue to engage in problem behavior in spite of these enhancements, additional strategies should be introduced. Typically, only one or two students will need these extra supports. This subsection describes individualized approaches.

One simple strategy with evidence to support its effectiveness is a behavioral contract (e.g., Wilkinson, 2010). To implement this intervention, the teacher first identifies and defines the observable behavior targeted for the contract. It is usually beneficial to involve the student in this step because soliciting student input increases motivation to change. Consistent with our recommendations throughout this book, the target behavior should be stated in a positive manner, describing a goal that is expected (e.g., raise hand in class, remain in seat in the cafeteria, complete assigned independent work). Next, the teacher and student determine the conditions under which the student will earn a reward for engaging in the targeted behavior. Generally, points, tokens, or stickers are used as rewards, which can later be exchanged for a specific, predetermined reward (see Table 4.1 for examples).

The effectiveness of the contract can be enhanced for some students (particularly those who have the target behavior well established in their repertoire) by including a penalty. For example, serious violations of the contract (e.g., calling out more than five times in a class, leaving one's seat in the cafeteria more than once, failing to complete at least half of the assignment) may cost the student a point, token, or sticker. In addition, bonuses can be included in the contract for particularly good behavior (e.g., completing all assignments) or consistently achieving the contract goal (e.g., consistently raising hand to be called on across three consecutive days). Finally, the behavior contract should be signed by both the teacher and the student to indicate their agreement to adhere to its terms. Other invested individuals may sign the contract as well, such as the student's parent or a school administrator. Figure 4.3 shows an example of a behavioral contract.

Behavioral contracts are versatile in that they have been demonstrated to be effective across a wide range of problem behaviors in addition to disruptive classroom behaviors. Studies have shown that behavioral contracts can decrease tardiness and truancy (DeMartini-Scully, Bray, & Kehle, 2000; Trice, 1990), improve personal hygiene (Allen & Kramer, 1990), and reduce

This contract will begin on ____________________ and will end or be modified on ____________ after a review meeting with the student, parent or guardian, and relevant school professionals.

My GOALS

1. I will complete my homework every night from 6 to 8 p.m.
2. I will bring my homework to my teachers on time.

What happens if I meet my goals for

1 full week?

I will earn $2.00.

3 weeks?

I will earn $6.00.

1 month?

I will earn $10.00.

CONSEQUENCES for not following the contract

My cell phone will be taken away until I finish 2 nights of homework in a row.

Additional terms:

If I cannot do my homework for some reason, I will discuss with Mom and Dad an alternative plan.

By signing this contract, I ______________________ (print name) agree that I understand the terms described above. This agreement will start today and will be renegotiated in ______ weeks, and changes will depend on how I am doing at that time.

Student Signature: ______________________________ Date: __________

Parent Signature: ______________________________ Date: __________

School Professional Signature: ____________________ Date: __________

Figure 4.3. Example of behavioral contract.

isolation and withdrawal (Jolivette & Wehby, 1999). In addition, they have been successful with students with diverse characteristics, including students without disabilities and those with ADHD, autism, and EBD.

In a study by Mzurek, Cohen, and Smith (2007), behavioral contracts were used with two students, one with ADHD and one with Asperger's syndrome. Contracts were developed indicating the expectations each student would adhere to that day. Examples of expectations included, "I will use polite and respectful language with my teachers and classmates" and "I will touch others without hurting them." The students earned stars or smiley faces every 60 minutes for adhering to the expectations, although initially up to two minor rule infractions each hour were permitted. Students could earn a 15-minute access to a preferred activity at the end of the day for earning a predetermined number of stars or smiley faces. The number required for earning the preferred activity was gradually increased. Within 10–12 weeks, the students were adhering to the expectations almost the entire day, with low levels of aggression, yelling, work refusal, and other behavior problems.

Goal setting is another relatively simple intervention that is particularly well suited to students nonresponsive to classwide interventions, because it can be easily individualized. The procedures involve having the student identify a future goal and then self-evaluating performance related to that goal. The goal can involve increasing a desirable behavior (e.g., homework completion, frequency of social initiations, positive interactions with peers) or decreasing an undesired behavior (e.g., tardiness to class, inappropriate social interactions). The teacher can assist the student in the goal selection process by ensuring that the goal identified by the student is realistic and achievable.

The first step in goal setting is to determine and operationally define the goal to be achieved (e.g., minutes on task, assignments completed, number of social initiations), a time frame, and a reward if the goal is achieved within the designated time period. Sometimes rewards can be naturally occurring, as in the case of a student passing a test or class; however, students who are nonresponsive to classwide expectations and procedures often benefit from additional rewards because they have tended to be unsuccessful in school.

If the goal cannot be easily achieved, intermediary goals can be established (Locke & Latham, 2006). For example, a student may earn a reward for staying in her seat for one 15-minute interval. After she has achieved this goal 3 days in a row, the reward requirements can be gradually increased (e.g., stay in seat for two 15-minute intervals, stay in seat for three 15-minute intervals). When behavior is being "shaped" in this way, it is important to be systematic. That is, the initial goal should not be set too high and should match the current rates of behavior. For example, if a student shouts out at least 12 times in a 60-minute period, a good starting point would be a goal of raising a hand before talking throughout at least one 10-minute interval. In addition, goals should be increased slowly and systematically. In the previous example, the goal might be increased by 5 minutes every 2–3 days, given that the student was successful on previous days. Finally, frequent feedback and discussion should occur regarding progress toward the goal (e.g., Krenn, Würth, & Hergovich, 2013). Figure 4.4 shows an example of a daily goal-monitoring sheet.

Self-management is another highly effective intervention with an abundance of research support (Briesch & Chafouleas, 2009). Self-management

Ella's Daily Goal Sheet

GOAL: I will sit at my desk for 3 minutes

Minute 1	Minute 2	Minute 3	Minute 4	Minute 5
–	+	–	+	+

Did I meet my goal? Yes X No ___

Figure 4.4. Example of student goal-setting format.

is a strategy wherein students are taught to manage their own behavior. This differs from strategies of external management in which an adult monitors students and informs them of the appropriateness of their behavior. Self-management helps students move toward independence by learning a set of skills; once they learn them, they no longer need support from their teachers (Halle, Bambara, & Reichle, 2005). There are two mechanisms that appear to account for its effectiveness. First, the process teaches students to become aware of, and thereby change, their behavior. In addition, reinforcement for engaging in appropriate behavior may enhance the effectiveness of the intervention (Chafouleas, Sanetti, Jaffery, & Fallon, 2012).

Self-management is a versatile intervention that can be implemented across a wide range of behaviors. It has also been used successfully with students with and without disabilities and using both an individual and class-wide format (Chafouleas et al., 2012; Lee, Simpson, & Shogren, 2007). In addition, self-management may enhance generalization to a greater extent than other interventions because of the focus on self-awareness (Briesch & Chafouleas, 2009; Mooney, Ryan, Uhing, Reid, & Epstein, 2005). Self-management procedures are, however, a bit more complicated to implement than the interventions described earlier in this chapter. Nonetheless, given that it is a highly effective and adaptable intervention, we strongly recommend taking the time to try it with students who have not been responsive to other intervention efforts.

The first step when implementing a self-management program is to identify and operationally define the targeted behavior. Next, a form should be created that the student can use to monitor the targeted behavior (see Figure 4.5 for an example). Behavior can be monitored using either yes/no responses or rating scales (e.g., 1 = none of the period, 2 = some of the period, 3 = all of the period). Certain behaviors are better monitored with yes/no responses (e.g., "I completed my homework." "I was in my seat when the bell rang."), while others may be more suited for scaling (e.g., "I worked well with my peers."). In addition, time intervals for monitoring the target behavior need to be determined. Interval length should be determined by the frequency of the target behavior. For high-frequency behaviors (e.g., frequent talk-outs, high rates of negative statements to peers), brief (e.g., 5 or 10 minutes) monitoring intervals should be used. Longer intervals can be used (e.g., a class period, a school day) for low-frequency behaviors such as handing in assignments.

The next step is to teach the student to identify the target behavior and use the monitoring form. This involves providing examples and nonexamples of the behavior and practicing coding on the form. Subsequently, the student should practice self-monitoring his or her behavior in the actual setting where it will be implemented. Initially, the teacher or staff member simultaneously monitors occurrences or absences of the target behavior to determine matches with the student. That is, the adult compares his or her coding with the student's and discusses discrepancies. When the student is reasonably

SELF-MANAGEMENT FORM

Student Name: ______________________ **Date:** ______________________

Teacher Name: ______________________

Class	Target behaviors	Yes	No
Homeroom	1. I interacted appropriately with others	Y	N
	2. I was focused on my work	Y	N
Language arts	1. I interacted appropriately with others	Y	N
	2. I was focused on my work	Y	N
Math	1. I interacted appropriately with others	Y	N
	2. I was focused on my work	Y	N
Gym	1. I interacted appropriately with others	Y	N
	2. I was focused on my work	Y	N
Social studies	1. I interacted appropriately with others	Y	N
	2. I was focused on my work	Y	N
Art	1. I interacted appropriately with others	Y	N
	2. I was focused on my work	Y	N
Other:	1. I interacted appropriately with others	Y	N
	2. I was focused on my work	Y	N

Total number of "Y" = __________ Goal for today = __________

Signed by

Student: ______________ Teacher: ______________ Parent: ______________

Notes

Figure 4.5. Self-Management Form.

accurate, he or she is ready to self-manage independently, although periodic matching is helpful with some students, particularly those with lower rates of accurate matching or students who tend to be dishonest about their self-rating.

Although self-management alone can reduce problem behavior, it is generally accompanied by reinforcement, particularly for students who have not been responsive to other supports. Rewards should be predetermined, along with the points required to earn a reward. For example, a student might earn a reward for earning at least 80% of her points for 5 days or making at least five social initiations across 3 consecutive days.

After implementing basic classwide strategies as well as a few individualized interventions, one student in Mr. Daniels' class, Aaron, continued to have difficulty staying engaged. Mr. Daniels was well aware that Aaron had a very short attention span and difficulty staying on task, particularly during independent seatwork. Therefore, Mr. Daniels developed an individualized self-management program that Aaron could use to self-monitor his behavior (see Figure 4.6). Mr. Daniels taught Aaron

Self-Management Form

Student Name: Aaron **Date:** ____________

Teacher Name: Mr. Daniels

Instructions: For each 5-minute interval you are on-task during independent work time, circle a "Y."

Interval	Target behaviors	Yes	No
1	I stayed on task	Y	N
2	I stayed on task	Y	N
3	I stayed on task	Y	N
4	I stayed on task	Y	N
5	I stayed on task	Y	N
6	I stayed on task	Y	N
7	I stayed on task	Y	N
8	I stayed on task	Y	N
9	I stayed on task	Y	N
10	I stayed on task	Y	N
	TOTAL NUMBER OF Ys		

Goal for today = 70% I earned iPad time today: Yes No

Signed by

Student: ____________ Teacher: ____________ Parent: ____________

Notes

Figure 4.6. Aaron's self-management form.

to recognize when he was on and off task through description, modeling, and role-play. To cue intervals, Mr. Daniels provided Aaron with a vibrating wristwatch. Because the signal was not audible, it did not disrupt Aaron's classmates, and the wristwatch was also discreet (other students wore wristwatches). Because Aaron was able to persist with work for about 7–8 minutes, Mr. Daniels had him begin self-monitoring at 5-minute intervals. Mr. Daniels built rewards into the system in the following manner. Aaron chose to earn time on the iPad. For each independent work session in which Aaron earned at least 70% "yes" responses, he earned 5 minutes to use the iPad at the end of the school day. Within 3 weeks, Aaron was regularly earning the iPad. At that time, Mr. Daniels began to gradually increase expectations to 80%, then 85%, then 90% on-task in order to earn iPad time. This was highly successful, so Mr. Daniels then increased the time intervals in 5-minute increments every 3 days. When Aaron reached 15-minute intervals, Mr. Daniels revised the monitoring form so that Aaron was self-monitoring throughout the day on a single form. Within 6 months, Mr. Daniels was able to eliminate the self-monitoring altogether, as Aaron had developed the self-control to stay engaged without the need to self-monitor.

PROCEDURES FOR MANAGING AND DECREASING MORE SERIOUS BEHAVIOR PROBLEMS

Many of the procedures described throughout this book, when implemented consistently over time, will help create safe, secure, productive, and welcoming learning environments that will serve to reduce the occurrence of escalated behavioral episodes in the classroom and school environments. The best way to manage crises is to prevent them from occurring in the first place. Nonetheless, as we have noted throughout the book, there are many "triggers" within school and classroom settings (e.g., work difficulty, peer provocations, perceptions of unfairness, deficient academic skills, harsh disciplinary interventions, boredom, uninteresting assignments) that may set the occasion for student behavior to escalate. One or any combination of these factors may trigger frustration, anxiety, and anger. Some students handle these emotions in appropriate ways; others do not. Rather than developing multiple individualized support plans, we recommend that teachers begin with a classwide management plan for escalating behavior.

Classwide Management Plan for Escalating Behavior

The purpose of a classwide management plan for escalating behavior is to provide students who have difficulty handling anger appropriately with an acceptable set of alternative behaviors they can use in the classroom. The plan for reducing negative behavior should include procedures for the students to use as well as procedures for classroom staff to follow.

Student Procedures Teaching students to manage their volatile behavior involves two steps: 1) assisting students in recognizing the conditions under which they experience sudden anger and frustration, and 2) developing and then teaching a series of simple alternative behaviors students can use in the classroom when they successfully recognize the early signs of anger and frustration. Assisting students in recognizing the conditions under which they experience sudden anger and frustration can begin with a private conversation between the teacher and student wherein the teacher prompts the student through a series of questions that help him or her identify the feelings and emotions leading to the serious problem behavior. This might include feeling hot and red in the face, anxious, tense, and shaky (e.g., feeling "butterflies in the stomach"). By helping students identify these feelings, teachers can then teach them to develop age-appropriate behaviors to signal frustration—for example, raise hand (all students), put head down on the desk (younger students), or put pencil down (older students)—and talk to them about ways to manage their emotions and reengage in the lesson when they are again feeling calm (also see Chapter 12 for specific descriptions of self-control and problem-solving strategies for students).

Teachers can facilitate the conversation by reviewing the expectations governing self-regulation in their classrooms. For example, the teacher might begin by stating, "Frustration, anxiety, and anger are naturally occurring feelings that are to be expected when you are learning new skills. It's okay to feel angry. We all get angry, but we need to learn to express our anger in appropriate ways."

When developing the alternative behaviors students can use in the classroom when experiencing feelings of anger, the teacher should consider a number of contextual features unique to the setting, such as students' ages, size of classroom, number of students, support personnel, and administrative support. Under ideal circumstances, students should engage in behaviors that are contextually appropriate for any classroom (e.g., raising their hands to seek teacher assistance or to take a break, or even removing themselves from the group and sitting in a designated break area at the back of the room). Less often, students may need to remove themselves from a distressing situation and proceed to a designated area outside the classroom (a caveat, however, is that breaks outside the classroom likely require administrative support and approval). At times, the plan may call upon the teacher to prompt the distressed and upset student to take a break. This step is especially important early in the learning process, when students cannot reliably identify the early signs of frustration and anger or are not yet fluent with the procedures. Here, the skill of observation is critical. Teachers need to become proficient at observing the telltale signs of frustration and anger that lead to serious problem behavior so they can intervene early and prompt students to use the predetermined strategy. When students use the strategy successfully, teachers should acknowledge them for making the effort to remain calm and for working through the frustrating episode appropriately.

Teacher Procedures As we have described, teachers can prevent problems from escalating by incorporating routines for addressing low-level behaviors. However, when behaviors continue to escalate, a hierarchy of procedures can be designed to gently prompt and encourage the student to comply with the classroom expectations. Use of structured procedures allows staff to respond in a calm, predictable manner and provides students opportunities for refocusing attention and gaining access to assistance to resolve the problem. An example of a structured sequence for managing students' low-level behaviors in efforts to prevent behavioral escalations might be as follows:

1. Teacher reviews the classroom expectations.
2. Teacher points out students who are behaving as expected.
3. Teacher uses proximity control (i.e., moves closer to the student with escalating behavior).
4. Teacher restates classroom expectation privately.
5. Teacher issues private warning to the student (e.g., "Please listen quietly or you will be asked to take a break.").
6. Teacher quietly directs student to use a pretaught anger management strategy (e.g., "Take a break.").
7. Teacher directs student to report to a designated staff member (e.g., counselor, social worker, principal) to resolve issues.

There are many variations in classroom procedures. Having a classwide management plan in place when behavior problems escalate is a benefit for the student, the teacher, and the rest of the class. With a plan in place, teachers and staff know exactly what to do when confronted with agitated students, and students know exactly what to do when agitated. Because the plan is in place in advance of any behavior problems and in fact anticipates them, it is proactive in nature and serves to defuse crises.

An additional advantage to having a classwide management plan for escalating behavior relates to the individualized support plan. Well-designed classwide plans can serve as the basis or starting point for developing a student's individualized behavior support plan and can be modified if indicated by the functional behavioral assessment (FBA). For example, if the function of a student's behavior is to escape academic instruction, directing students to the counselor's office may be contraindicated and therefore should be eliminated from the plan. On the other hand, that step of the plan could be retained but an additional component added wherein the student has to make up the work he or she missed because of being out of class—preferably during recess, lunch, or break (a natural consequence for missing the work in class).

SUMMARY

Students spend the majority of their school day in the classroom setting. Unfortunately, most teachers receive limited, if any, formal preservice coursework in the area of behavior management (State, Kern, Starosta, & Mukherjee, 2011). We described a number of classroom "basics" that every teacher should have in place. This will reduce the majority of behavior problems in a given classroom and also make it much simpler for teachers to put additional supports in place for the few students who are not responsive to classroom approaches. In the case of a student or a few students who continue to engage in behavior problems in spite of the classwide and individual interventions described in this chapter, we recommend convening a support team to consider initiating the FBA process described in Chapter 8.

SELF-REFLECTION

1. Identify ways your classroom arrangement works. Identify ways you can improve.
2. In terms of classroom expectations, identify the areas you do well. Identify the ways you would like to improve.
3. Identify how your classroom procedures and routines work. Identify ways you can better streamline processes and procedures.
4. Identify the ways you interact well with your students. Identify the ways you can improve.
5. Describe ways you encourage appropriate behavior. Identify additional ways you can encourage appropriate behavior.
6. Describe how you address problem behavior. Identify additional ways you can address problems.

REFERENCES

Allen, S.J., & Kramer, J.J. (1990). Modification of personal hygiene and grooming behaviors with contingency contracting: A brief review and case study. *Psycholology in the Schools, 27,* 224–251.

Briesch, A.M., & Chafouleas, S.M. (2009). Review and analysis of literature on self-management interventions to promote appropriate classroom behaviors (1988–2008). *School Psychology Quarterly, 24,* 106–118.

Catalano, R.F., Oesterle, S., Fleming, C.B., & Hawkins, J.D. (2004). The importance of bonding to school for healthy development: Findings from the Social Development Research Group. *Journal of School Health, 74*(7), 252–261.

Chafouleas, S.M., Sanetti, L.M.H., Jaffery, R., & Fallon, L.M. (2012). An evaluation of a class-wide intervention package involving self-management and group contingency on classroom behavior of middle school students. *Journal of Behavioral Education, 21,* 34–57.

DeMartini-Scully, D., Bray, M.A., & Kehle, T.J. (2000). A packaged intervention to reduce disruptive behaviors in general education students. *Psychology in the Schools, 37,* 149–156.

DuBois, D.L., & Silverthorn, N. (2005). Characteristics of natural mentoring relationships and adolescent adjustment: Evidence from a national study. *Journal of Primary Prevention, 26*(2), 69–92.

Evans, W., Evans, S., Gable, R., & Schmid, R. (1991). *Instructional management for detecting and correcting special problems.* Boston, MA: Allyn & Bacon.

Fullerton, E.K. (2010). Teacher and students' perceptions of a modified inclusion classroom environment. *Electronic Journal for Inclusive Education, 2,* 1–16.

Gunter, P.L., & Shores, R.E. (1995). On the MOVE: Using teacher/student proximity to improve students' behavior. *Teaching Exceptional Children, 28,* 12–14.

Halle, J., Bambara, L.M., & Reichle, J. (2005). Teaching alternative skills. In L.M. Bambara & L. Kern, (Eds.), *Individualized supports for students with problem behaviors.* New York, NY: Guilford Press.

Hayling, C.C., Cook, C., Gresham, F.R., State, T., & Kern, L. (2008). An analysis of the status and stability of the behaviors of students with emotional and behavioral difficulties: A classroom direct observation study. *Journal of Behavioral Education, 17,* 24–42.

Johnson, L. (2006). Elementary school students' learning preferences and the classroom learning environment: Implications for education practice and policy. *The Journal of Negro Education, 75,* 506–518.

Jolivette, K., & Wehby, J.H. (1999). My teacher said I did good work today! Using collaborative behavioral contracting. *Teaching Exceptional Children, 31,* 12–18.

Kleinman, K.E., & Saigh, P.A. (2011). The effects of the Good Behavior Game on the conduct of regular education New York City high school students. *Behavior Modification, 36,* 95–105. doi:10.1177/0145445511039221

Krenn, B., Würth, S., & Hergovich, A. (2013). The impact of feedback on goal setting and task performance: Testing the feedback intervention theory. *Swiss Journal of Psychology, 72*(2), 79.

Lee, S.H., Simpson, R.L., & Shogren, K.A. (2007). Effects and implications of self-management for students with autism: A meta-analysis. *Focus on Autism and Other Developmental Disabilities, 22,* 2–13.

Locke, E.A., & Latham, G.P (2006). New directions in goal-setting theory. *Association for Psychological Science, 15*(5), 265–268.

Mooney, P., Ryan, J.B., Uhing, B.M., Reid, R., & Epstein, M.H. (2005). A review of self-management interventions targeting academic outcomes for students with emotional and behavioral disorders. *Journal of Behavioral Education, 14,* 203–221.

Mzurek, D.W., Cohen, C., & Smith, T. (2007). Contingency contracting with students with autism spectrum disorders in a public school setting. *Journal of Development and Physical Disabilities, 19,* 103–114.

Plank, S.B., McDill, E.L., McParland, J.M., & Jordan, W.J. (2001). Situation and repertoire: Civility, incivility, cursing, and politeness in an urban high school. *Teachers College Record, 103,* 504–524.

Rathvon, N. (2008). *Effective school interventions: Evidence-based strategies for improving student outcomes.* New York, NY: Guilford Press.

Roorda, D.L., Kooman, H.M.Y., Split, J.L., & Oort, F.J. (2011). The influence of affective teacher–student relationships on students' school engagement and achievement: A meta-analytic approach. *Review of Educational Research, 81*(4), 493–529.

State, T.M., Kern, L., Starosta, K.M., & Mukherjee, A.D. (2011). Elementary pre-service teacher preparation in the area of social, emotional, and behavioral problems. *School Mental Health, 3,* 13–23.

Sugai, G., & Horner, R.H. (2002). Introduction to the special series on positive behavior interventions and supports in schools. *Journal of Emotional and Behavioral Disorders, 10,* 130–135.

Thorson, S. (1996). The missing link: Students discuss school discipline. *Focus on Exceptional Children, 29,* 1–12.

Trice, A.D. (1990). Adolescents' locus of control and compliance with contingency contracting and counseling interventions. *Psychological Reports, 67,* 233–264.

Wehby, J.H., Symons, F.J., Canale, J.A., & Go, F.J. (1998). Teaching practices in classrooms for students with emotional and behavioral disorders: Discrepancies between recommendations and observations. *Behavioral Disorders, 24,* 51–56.

Wilkinson, L.A. (2010). Using behavioral consultation to reduce challenging behavior in the classroom. *Preventing School Failure: Alternative Education for Children and Youth, 47,* 100–105.

Woolfolk, A., & Weinstein, C. (2006). Students' and teachers' beliefs and perspectives about classroom management. In C. Evertson & C. Weinstein (Eds.), *Handbook of classroom management: Research, practice, and contemporary issues.* Mahwah, NJ: Lawrence Erlbaum.

Wubbels, T., & Brekelmans, M. (2005). Two decades of research on teacher–student relationships in class. *International Journal of Educational Research, 43,* 6–24.

5

Effective Instructional Practices

In the previous chapters, we discussed strategies to address behavior problems. Many educators, however, neglect to see the relationship between academic expectations and student behavior. That is, they hold the belief that behavior problems need to be addressed separately from academic considerations. As we note throughout this book, student behavior bears a close relationship to contextual factors in the environment. Academic demands and instructional practices play a very important role in whether behavior problems occur. For example, in a recent study examining effective practices in programs serving students with emotional and behavioral disorders, researchers pointed out that strong academic instruction and intervention may be the "first line of defense" in working with students with challenging behaviors (Farley, Torres, Wailehua, & Cook, 2012).

A number of evidence-based approaches have been described in the literature that help to keep students engaged and motivated during academic instruction and also may enhance learning. In this chapter, we describe both broad and specific instructional practices that are applicable in either general or special education classrooms. The practices are linked to the Self-Assessment of Effective Teaching Strategies described in Chapter 3. If you are a current teacher, you can use the strategies in this chapter to strengthen areas that you identified as weak. If you are not yet a teacher, the strategies will help you to start your teaching career using best practices in instruction.

ESTABLISH ACADEMIC EXPECTATIONS

An important consideration when designing instruction is the academic expectations that are placed on students. As Lady Bird Johnson, the former First Lady of the United States, once said, "Children are likely to live up to what you believe of them." This is especially applicable to the American education system, where high expectations are universally viewed as important. For example, in a comprehensive review of 25 years of research on effective schools, Johnson, Livingston, Schwartz, and State (2000) found that high student expectations and the belief that all students can learn were consistent themes of importance among various stakeholder groups, including teachers, parents, and school administrators. Furthermore, this theme has remained central to effective schools and optimal student achievement across several decades of research (Johnson et al.). Unfortunately, underachieving schools can be found everywhere, and many teachers settle for mediocre student performance.

How can educators make high expectations come to life in the classroom? First, it is critical that teachers believe every student can succeed. The significance of this has been illustrated in numerous research studies showing that high teacher expectations can overcome student characteristics that function as barriers to achievement and also can have long-term effects on student achievement (Boer, Bosker, & Van der Werf, 2010; Hinnant, Brien, & Ghazarian, 2009). Of course, children and adolescents have different strengths and learn at different rates and in different ways. This means that, at times, students will need scaffolding and supports, such as breaking complex tasks into manageable parts and reteaching whenever necessary, which we discuss in the sections below. Nonetheless, having confidence that all students can learn is critical for optimal student achievement, and this message needs to be passed to students.

In addition, students need to understand the concept of high and low standards. This begins with helping them recognize basic academic expectations, as illustrated in the example in Table 5.1. However, encouraging students to achieve high standards requires more than simple discussion. Of primary importance is to make high standards explicit for each and every

Table 5.1. Example of high academic expectations

Expectations for assignments and classwork
• Be ready and prepared for class. • Hand in your assignments on time. • Try hard and do your best work. • Participate during class. • Listen to the teacher and your classmates. • Study for tests. • Reflect on your work and ask for help. • Try new things.

academic activity. Examples can be seen in the following statements: "The expectations for group today are to stay focused on the topic, make sure each group member participates, and generate a reasonable and thoughtful solution to the problem." "To do well on the test Friday, you will need to review the material every night this week." "Neat papers are expected. This means you erase stray markings and that I can easily read what you wrote." Second, teachers must constantly pay attention to student progress and provide encouragement, support, and modifications as needed. Third, students need to be acknowledged and praised when they meet high standards. For example, Mr. Bennett might point out that the students who were the most successful on their papers included details about the story characters, remembered punctuation rules, and submitted a neatly written paper. This acknowledgment should extend to students who put in a great deal of effort, even though they struggled with an assignment. Finally, students should be encouraged to push themselves to tackle difficult tasks and to set high personal standards. This might involve a discussion with a student about the exact steps he or she can take to improve performance in a particular area.

CRAFT A MOTIVATING CURRICULUM

There is a great deal of research to support the role that curriculum plays in student performance (Johnson et al., 2000). It is a common experience to find that studying a subject one enjoys can capture the attention, whereas the mind wanders during an uninteresting topic. Although the curriculum and academic standards are generally dictated at the district, state, or even federal level, teachers also have a large role in the content and delivery. That is, student learning can be viewed as a partnership between the teacher and curriculum (e.g., Russell, 1997). Specifically, the way that a teacher delivers and presents the curriculum plays a large role in student learning. Material that is delivered enthusiastically and creatively can motivate and impassion students. Mundane and unexciting delivery leaves students bored. In addition, delivering curriculum effectively entails understanding how each student approaches learning as well as making the modifications and enhancements necessary to fully motivate students.

There are numerous ways teachers can make the curriculum interesting and stimulating (see Table 5.2). To begin, teachers must fully understand the curriculum from start to finish, including scope, sequence, standards, goals, and objectives. With a thorough understanding of the curriculum, teachers can determine how additional competencies or programs can be added, as well as identify any gaps. This requires that a teacher become familiar with his or her students in order to identify additional competencies that need to be added to the curriculum. For instance, if a group of students is not fluent with the multiplication facts needed to solve more difficult mathematics problems, additional practice opportunities can be embedded in the curriculum. Similarly, a teacher may choose to include information about a local battle site

Table 5.2. Strategies for improving the curriculum

- Understand the curriculum from start to finish, including standards, goals, and objectives.
- Determine how to embed additional competencies or programs.
  - Identify gaps.
  - Include additional objectives.
  - Determine interdisciplinary overlap.
- Identify resources to enhance the curriculum.
  - District
  - School
  - Community
  - Internet
- Create relevant, topical, and engaging learning experiences.
  - Update
  - Enhance
  - Extend

that is not included in a unit on the history of the Civil War. Finally, potential overlap across disciplines can be identified, and teachers can plan diverse instruction embedded across the curriculum. For instance, students can identify shapes found in famous artwork to integrate art and geometry, or students can create public service announcements to integrate reading, writing, and oral communication. This type of curricular integration helps students make connections between learning and also provides additional opportunities for skill practice (see http://www.teachhub.com/integrate-science-across-curriculum for ideas about how to develop cross-curricular lessons).

Along with determining ways to add to and enhance the curriculum, the availability of additional resources should be identified. Often, resources are available at the school or district to supplement lessons and offer hands-on experiences. In addition, community resources, such as people or local facilities with expertise in a particular subject (e.g., science museum, art center), can be made available. Using these resources also helps students see the relevance and usefulness of their learning to the world outside of school. Finally, the Internet is replete with digital collections, interactive lessons, and other easily accessible materials to expand the curriculum.

The information and resources identified here can be used to create relevant, topical, and engaging learning experiences. This includes updating the curriculum where relevant. For example, recent world events or local issues may need to be incorporated into lessons. In addition, using a variety of resources can enhance lessons to increase student motivation and interest, as described later in this chapter. Finally, the curriculum can be extended to include related topics relevant to particular groups of students in the local community, or simply to capture student interests.

USE DIVERSE TEACHING METHODS

It can be difficult to keep students engaged in academic lessons day after day across the course of a school year. This is particularly so as students are increasingly exposed to captivating media outside of school that can render a simple lecture rather mundane. Thus, it is important that teachers regularly use diverse teaching methods, both to break the monotony of a single format of instruction and to capitalize on students' preferred modes of learning. Group size is one simple way of varying instruction. Although whole-group instruction or teacher lecture continues to be the predominant mode of instructional delivery (e.g., Hayling, Cook, Gresham, State, & Kern, 2008; Scott, Hirn, & Alter, 2014), small-group work holds many advantages for students, including offering greater opportunities to learn from one another, experiencing alternative ways of thinking, and enhancing their social skills. In addition, research has shown that small-group instruction may increase the engagement of students with attention difficulties (Imeraji et al., 2013). Furthermore, teachers can organize small groups so that multiple activities can occur simultaneously. Also, instructional activities can be tailored to meet the needs of specific groups of students. Table 5.3 provides examples of a variety of activities that can be used during small-group instruction.

DIFFERENTIATE INSTRUCTION

Differentiated instruction is a way of providing instruction so that all students have multiple options for learning the information that is presented. It is based on the theory that instructional approaches should vary in response to individual and diverse student needs and preferences (Tomlinson, 2014). In other words, rather than expecting students to adapt to a static curriculum, differentiated instruction adjusts the curriculum and the way information is presented. This differentiation accounts for individual student skills and interests and helps students understand information and make sense of concepts. As a result, all students benefit, including those who are advanced in a particular area and those who are struggling. In essence, the idea is to maximize each student's learning and growth.

Differentiated instruction can best be viewed as a learning cycle involving ongoing decision making. That is, the process involves continually assessing and evaluating student progress and learning and adjusting instruction accordingly. Table 5.4 shows the basic components of the assessment and instructional adjustment process (e.g., Tomlinson, 2014). To craft relevant and meaningful instruction, teachers should have information about each particular student (Acosta-Tello & Shepherd, 2014). One important area is the student's background knowledge and readiness for learning particular content. Examples of areas that may affect learning and should be considered are language issues (e.g., Is the student a second language learner? Does the student have receptive language delays?), academic and skill level (e.g., Can the student read at grade level? Does the student have the skills needed to complete the task at hand?), and behavior (e.g., Does the student lack self-regulation skills that might impede learning?). Assessment of these variables needs to be ongoing so that instruction can be regularly adjusted in response to new information.

Table 5.3. Examples of small-group activities

Activity	How to implement	Example
Group round	Moving around the group, each student is given an opportunity to say something.	Each student has 3 minutes to describe his or her favorite part of a book.
Buzz groups	Students partner with a neighbor to discuss their own answers, and then the larger group reconvenes and discusses the answers.	Students have 1 minute to describe how they found the solution to a mathematics problem.
Snowball or pyramid groups	Students partner with their neighbor for discussion (buzz group), then neighboring groups are sequentially paired to form larger groups of four, then eight; representatives from each group present the smaller group's discussion to the larger group.	Partners discuss the question of whether slavery was the main issue in the beginning of the Civil War. As groups are paired, they compare their beliefs about events that led to the Civil War. Finally, representatives from large groups report on all of the ideas generated.
Fishbowl groups	Groups are divided in two, forming an inner group for discussion or role-play, and an outer group to observe. After a period of observation and a debrief session, the roles may be switched.	Students extend their ideas of the personalities of characters in a book by role-playing their responses to teacher-developed scenarios. Observers discuss their beliefs about the accuracy of the role-play. Then the groups switch roles and repeat the role-play, observation, and discussion.
Crossover groups	Students are divided into groups for an initial discussion. The groups are then divided again into new subgroups to maximize the amount of information crossover.	Each student in the class is given a paper denoting potential group membership (e.g., A1, A2, B1, B2). Identical letters are grouped to discuss potential essay responses on a study guide. Subsequently, identical numbers are paired to discuss those responses and generate additional ideas.
Circular questioning	Each group member asks a question to another group member, who briefly answers the question. Then the next person in the circle asks a question. The exercise is complete when everyone has asked a question. The facilitator can wrap up the session by summarizing questions and responses.	Students question one another about a book they have read for language arts class.
Horseshoe groups	Small groups are arranged around tables, and each table is arranged in horseshoe fashion around the teacher. This allows the teacher to move between lecturing and interactive small-group activity.	Students select a topic of choice for a small-group science experiment. The teacher describes the steps in conducting a science experiment. After each step, each small group discusses how the step applies and the procedures it will use to carry out its specific experiment.

Table 5.4. Components of differentiated instruction

Student characteristics to consider
Readiness
Interests
Learning style
Ways teachers can differentiate instruction
Content
Process
Product

Source: Tomlinson (2014).

In addition to background and readiness, the students' interests should be considered, as we describe in the section that follows. A student's preferred activities and hobbies can be incorporated into teaching and instruction. To understand students' interests, teachers should regularly talk to them about their outside activities.

Once teachers have an understanding of the students in their class, they can begin to differentiate instruction to meet individual student needs. The strategies for differentiating instruction fall into three broad categories: content, process, and product. *Content* refers to what is taught. The general content of instruction should address the same skills for all students, but differentiation can occur in the complexity of the content or the manner in which students gain access to the content. For example, when multiplication is studied, some students may be learning single-digit facts while others are learning to solve multiple-digit problems.

The second category of differentiation is process, which includes how students are taught and how they learn. This is where interests and learning preferences are particularly important. Students are inspired to study topics in which they are interested. For example, they might be given a choice of genre in reading or the opportunity to create a story around a person or activity of interest. In addition, instruction can be designed and differentiated to match the way that students best learn a particular skill (e.g., through individual explicit instruction, working with a partner or in a small group, using manipulatives, using the computer or other media). Flexible groupings are commonly used whereby teachers can introduce instruction, then break students into groups for intensive individual instruction or form larger groups to extend the concept by completing projects or other activities.

The third category, product, includes the way in which students demonstrate what they have learned. Products are critical because they allow teachers to evaluate the acquisition of material and further differentiate instruction for optimal student learning. Assessments can range from formal to informal and include a variety of outcomes and forms of preferred student expression (e.g., tests, interviews, surveys, projects, papers, oral reports, service projects). Menus of options for students are useful, and teacher-selected and student-selected products can be balanced, depending on the topic and goal (e.g., students need to learn a particular response format for standardized tests). Such assessments will reflect varying degrees of difficulty and means of evaluation (e.g., scoring procedures). There are numerous publications and books that describe specific strategies for designing and managing differentiated instruction that should be consulted for more detail (e.g., Tomlinson, 2005).

Finally, some argue that it is important to understand each student's preferred learning style (Manolis, Burns, Assudani, & Chinta, 2013). Perhaps the most common model is one developed by Kolb (1984). This model categorizes students into four learning styles. Divergent learners prefer to "feel and watch" and perform best in circumstances that require generating ideas, such as brainstorming. The assimilating style includes students who prefer watching and who approach learning logically, performing well when material is presented in an organized and clear format. The converging approach is characterized by "doing and thinking," and students with this learning style excel at problem solving and experimenting with new ideas. Finally, students with the accommodating learning style prefer "doing and feeling," learning well with hands-on experiences and relying on instinct rather than logical analysis.

There are a number of learning style inventories commercially available (e.g., Kolb, 2005). However, we caution readers that research on learning styles is mixed, with some research showing that other variables (e.g., outside of class study, belief about efficacy) may play a larger role in learning than style differences (e.g., Adams & Bush, 2013). Furthermore, much of the research has been conducted with older students (e.g., college age) and may not be applicable to younger students (Bhatti & Bart, 2013).

INCORPORATE STUDENT INTEREST

As we noted in the description of differentiated instruction in the previous section, incorporating student interest into academic instruction can increase student engagement and motivation (Kern & Clemens, 2007; Koller, Baumert, & Schnabel, 2001). Student interests can be incorporated into assignments and activities in a number of ways. First, topics of student interest can be the focus of an assignment. For instance, in language arts, students can write stories or essays about their interests or activities. Social studies projects can be based on family history or the local community. Student interests can also be indirectly incorporated into assignments. For example, the content of word problems can include situations pertaining to students in class (Hinton & Kern, 1999) or handwriting practice can consist of writing a letter to a friend (Kern & Clemens, 2007).

Another way to increase student interest in academics is to connect instruction to students' real-world experiences. For example, a science unit on recycling can include review of procedures for recycling in the local community or even going to visit a recycling center (Kern, Bambara, &

Fogt, 2002). Similarly, a persuasive essay might pertain to a community issue, such as construction that is being debated or candidates for a mayoral race.

Finally, student interests can be reflected in the curriculum by offering choices. Curricular choice can be provided in numerous ways, including allowing students to select the task or activity they complete, the sequence in which they complete activities, the materials they use to complete activities, the partner(s) they work with on an assignment, the location where the assignment is completed, or when the assignment is completed. Chapter 9 contains additional information on student interest and choice making, as well as examples for implementation.

INCREASE ACTIVE STUDENT ENGAGEMENT

Although it is important that students are engaged during instruction, there are different levels of student engagement. Broadly, students can be engaged either passively or actively. Passive engagement occurs when students are attending to a task by listening (usually during a lecture) but not actively participating. Although passive engagement is preferred to nonengagement, it is difficult to determine the extent to which students are absorbing the material when they are passively engaged. That is, a student might show all the signs of being fully engaged in a teacher's lecture by facing the teacher, making eye contact, and leaning in a forward body pose while at the same time thinking about an event upcoming that evening. The point is that educators can never be sure students are paying attention and learning the material they are presenting if the students are passively engaged. Therefore, it is important to keep students actively engaged as much as possible.

Active student engagement means that students are participating in activities rather than simply sitting and listening. The following ancient Chinese proverb illustrates the concept of active engagement: "Tell me, I forget. Show me, I remember. Involve me, I understand." In fact, research shows that when teachers increase the number of opportunities for active student engagement in their classrooms, students achieve better academically and disruptive classroom behavior is decreased (e.g., Sticher et al., 2009; Sutherland & Wehby, 2001). Furthermore, these results have accrued with students with and without disabilities (e.g., Haydon et al., 2010; Horn, 2010; Sutherland & Wehby, 2001).

There are several strategies for keeping students actively engaged. One is choral responding, which requires that all students in a class orally respond in unison to a teacher question or prompt. After the teacher poses a question or prompt, there should be a brief delay (e.g., a few seconds) to allow students "think time" before responding. Then, the teacher provides a cue (e.g., clap, finger snap, statement such as "everyone") for students to respond. When first introducing choral responding, it is important to conduct a brief instructional session to introduce the strategy and have students practice the procedures. Choral responding is best used when the response is brief (e.g., a number, one to three words) and there is a single correct answer. Examples include orally stating the answer to a math problem (e.g., the answer to "What is 5 times 12?"), the main character of a book, or reading words from flashcards. Responses can also be nonverbal, such as thumbs up for true and thumbs down for false.

Another strategy for keeping students actively engaged is through the use of response cards. Each student is given a card or set of cards that can be used to display answers to a question or problem. Response cards can be preprinted with responses (e.g., true/false, yes/no) or blank cards on which students write their responses. For written responses, laminated cards or small whiteboards are ideal because they can be reused. The procedure with response cards is the same as choral responding with respect to posing a question, allowing wait time, and prompting a response; students simultaneously display their written response, which the teacher can quickly scan for accuracy. After response cards are displayed, the teacher should state the correct response, particularly if not all student responses are accurate. Preprinted response cards (true/false or yes/no) can be used in response to questions or test items (e.g., James Buchanan was the 15th president, Matilda is the main character in the book). Blank cards or whiteboards can be used to record almost any brief response (e.g., math problems, spelling words, types of molecules, historical dates, chemical compounds).

USE A BRISK PACE

Pacing refers to the rate or speed of instruction during a lesson as well as progress through the curriculum. It is not uncommon for teachers to find that they have spent far too much time on one activity, leaving insufficient time for another. Instructional pacing is very important—if it is too fast, students will become lost, but if it is too slow, they will be bored. Pacing must match the needs of the learner; however, generally, a brisk rate of instruction has been demonstrated to maximize instruction while maintaining student interest (Tomlinson, 2005). In addition, teachers must keep in mind the broad curricular goals in order to adequately cover the content.

A few strategies can help teachers with pacing. First, having materials prepared and readily accessible reduces downtime (and behavior problems). In addition, a timer can serve as a reminder to both the teacher and students that there is a schedule that needs to be maintained. The timer can be used to allocate time to each activity as well as transitions. Also, maintaining the goal of a lesson is critical for proceeding through instruction at a brisk pace. Unnecessary diversions interfere with the instructional flow and student learning. Students should be allowed ample time to answer questions that are posed; however, too much delay results in student disengagement. A general rule is to wait 3–5 seconds for a response. Although teachers tend to wait only 1–2 seconds, a slightly longer wait time has been demonstrated to increase the length and depth of student responses and the number of unsolicited responses, including those from students who tend to struggle with material (e.g., Rowe, 1987). In other words, a slightly longer wait time actually helps to keep students engaged. For particularly challenging concepts, partner or group discussion prior to responding will help to maintain a quick pace.

When students are expected to complete group or individual work, visually displayed instructions help to maintain the instructional pace. This is particularly helpful with multistep tasks or new activities. For example, students can refer to a PowerPoint list of steps to complete a math problem or components of a paper. This decreases the downtime required when a teacher is moving from group to group to explain directions. Teachers must constantly check for student understanding, as we have noted many times in this chapter. Lack of student understanding can dramatically slow even a well-planned lesson. Finally, transitions that are brief and orderly maintain student engagement and reduce problem behaviors (remember, an extra minute for each transition can translate into hours and hours of lost learning each year).

PROVIDE EXPLICIT INSTRUCTION

How children best learn has been extensively studied and written about. Several decades of research support the value of instruction that is presented in a systematic and step-by-step fashion, which is characteristic of explicit instruction (Rosenshine, 1986; Sawyer, Graham, & Harris, 1992). Explicit instruction involves a sequence of supports that gradually moves from extensive teacher involvement to minimal teacher involvement (e.g., Boyles, 2001). This process results in a high likelihood that students will master academic concepts and skills.

Explicit instruction begins with setting the stage for learning. This involves explaining to students what they are going to learn and why it is important (often referred to as *anticipatory set*). Other valuable aspects of preparing for learning are ensuring that instruction considers student background knowledge, linking upcoming learning to previous learning, and connecting instruction to students' interests. This is followed by a clear explanation of what is expected. In this phase, students are told the specific steps that are needed to accomplish a task or activity. Dividing a task into multiple small steps makes it simple, clear, and easy to understand. Next is teacher modeling of the task. Rather than simply explaining how to do a task, the teacher demonstrates or shows students how to complete the task by performing it in the exact way that will be expected of the student.

Teacher modeling or demonstration of a task is followed by guided practice. This involves students performing the task while the teacher checks for understanding and provides corrective feedback, if necessary. After students are able to perform the task correctly with teacher guidance, the next step is independent practice. Students are only ready for independent practice when the teacher is fairly sure they understand the steps of the new skill and will be highly successful. This phase allows teachers to be sure that students can perform without teacher support. Finally, teachers must continuously assess acquisition, both formally and informally, to determine whether and what type of reteaching is needed (described in the section that follows). We recommend readers refer to the many textbooks, articles, and web sites that provide extensive information and examples of explicit instruction (e.g., Archer & Hughes, 2011).

RETEACH IF NEEDED

Reteaching skills that students have not sufficiently acquired is a task often overlooked by teachers. With increased pressure to meet annual yearly progress goals, prepare students for standardized testing, and attend to Common Core and other standards, rushing through the curriculum sometimes seems imperative. Unfortunately, students who have not developed good foundational skills struggle academically throughout their school years. Reteaching is an essential component of instruction that is necessary to ensure student learning and future progress.

Determining when reteaching is needed requires frequent monitoring of student progress, as we described above. When a student has not met the predetermined goal or cutoff to indicate mastery, the first step is to determine what errors the student is making and why. Error analysis allows reteaching to be focused and efficient. This requires deconstructing a task into progressive steps and determining what skills the student lacks on that progression. For more information on error analysis strategies, see, for example, Ferris (2006) and Montague (1992).

It is also important to consider a new or different instructional approach when reteaching. If a student did not acquire a skill when it was originally taught, an alternative teaching method is often helpful. For instance, if a student did not understand how to complete a math problem following teacher modeling, using manipulatives to illustrate the concept might be helpful.

SUMMARY

There is a close link between academics and student behavior, and good instruction is the first step in avoiding problem behaviors. Furthermore, well-planned instruction increases student engagement and learning. Effective instruction begins with a solid curriculum with clear expectations. As we described in this chapter, a number of instructional strategies can be incorporated into lessons to enhance student engagement and increase student interest and motivation. Finally, careful monitoring of student skill acquisition (both formal and informal) is critical to determining when reteaching is needed. Ensuring all students have mastered the curriculum provides them with the foundational skills they will need to continue to make progress throughout their school career.

Self-Reflection

1. Identify your academic expectations.
2. Describe how you use a motivating curriculum in the classroom. Identify how you can use additional motivational techniques.
3. Describe how your teaching methods are diverse. In what ways can you improve?
4. Describe how you differentiate your instruction. Identify ways you can improve and better personalize your instruction.
5. Describe ways you incorporate areas of student interest into your classroom. Identify additional ways you can encourage student interests.
6. Describe how you encourage active student engagement. Identify ways you can promote additional engagement.
7. Describe the pace of your classroom. In what ways do you work at a brisk pace? How can you improve this pace for all students?
8. Describe how you give explicit instruction. Identify ways this can be improved.
9. Describe how you reteach materials. Identify ways you can improve.

REFERENCES

Acosta-Tello, E., & Shepherd, C. (2014). Equal access for all learners: Differentiation simplified. *Journal of Research in Innovative Teaching, 7*, 51–57.

Adams, J.D., & Bush, B.V. (2013). The relationship between supplemental instruction leader learning style and study session. *Learning Assistance Review (TLAR), 18*(2), 51–65.

Archer, A.L., & Hughes, C.A. (2011). *Explicit instruction: Effective and efficient teaching.* New York, NY: Guilford Press.

Bhatti, R., & Bart, W.M. (2013). On the effect of learning style of scholastic achievement. *Current Issues in Education, 16*(2), 1–6.

Boer, H.D., Bosker, R.J., & Van der Werf, M.P.C. (2010). Sustainability of teacher expectation bias effects on long-term student performance. *Journal of Educational Psychology, 102*, 168–179.

Boyles, N.N. (2001). *Teaching written response to text: Constructing quality answers to open-ended comprehension questions.* Gainesville, FL: Maupin House.

Farley, C., Torres, C., Wailehua, C.T., & Cook, L. (2012). Evidence-based practices for students with emotional and behavioral disorders: Improving academic achievement. *Beyond Behavior, 21*(2), 37–43.

Ferris, D.R. (2006). Does error feedback help student writers? New evidence on the short-and long-term effects of written error correction. In K. Hyland & F. Hyland (Eds.), *Feedback in second language writing: Contexts and issues* (pp. 1–104). New York, NY: Cambridge University Press.

Haydon, T., Conroy, M.A., Scott, T.M., Sindelar, P.T., Barber, B.R., & Orlando, A.M. (2010). A comparison of three types of opportunities to respond on student academic and social behaviors. *Journal of Emotional and Behavioral Disorders, 18*, 27–40.

Hayling, C.C., Cook, C., Gresham, F.R., State, T., & Kern, L. (2008). An analysis of the status and stability of the behaviors of students with emotional and behavioral difficulties: A classroom direct observation study. *Journal of Behavioral Education, 17*, 24–42.

Hinnant, J.B., Brien, M.O., & Ghazarian, S.R. (2009). Longitudinal relations of teacher expectations to achievement in the early school years. *Journal of Educational Psychology, 101,* 662–670.

Hinton, L.M., & Kern, L. (1999). Increasing homework completion by incorporating student interest. *Journal of Positive Behavior Interventions, 1,* 231–241.

Horn, C. (2010). Respond cards: An effective intervention for students with disabilities. *Education and Training in Autism and Developmental Disabilities, 45,* 116–123.

Imeraji, L., Antrop, I., Sonuga-Barke, E., Deboutte, D., Deschepper, E., Bal, S., & Roeyers, H. (2013). The impact of instructional context on classroom on-task behavior: A matched comparison of children with ADHD and non-ADH D classmates. *Journal of School Psychology, 51,* 487–498.

Johnson, J.P., Livingston, M., Schwartz, R.A., & State, J.R. (2000). What makes a good elementary school? A critical examination. *Journal of Educational Research, 93*(6), 339–348. Retrieved from http://www.jstor.org/stable/27542288

Kern, L., Bambara, L., & Fogt, J. (2002). Classwide curricular modification to improve the behavior of students with emotional and behavioral disorders. *Behavioral Disorders, 27,* 317–326.

Kern, L., & Clemens, N. (2007). Antecedent strategies to promote appropriate classroom behavior. *Psychology in the Schools, 44,* 65–75.

Kolb, A.Y. (2005). *The Kolb Learning Style Inventory* (Version 3.1) [2005 technical specifications]. Boston, MA: Hay Resource Direct.

Kolb, D.A. (1984). *Experiential learning: Experience as the source of learning and development* (Vol. 1). Englewood Cliffs, NJ: Prentice-Hall.

Koller, O., Baumert, J., & Schnabel, K. (2001). Does interest matter? The relationship between academic interest and achievement in mathematics. *Journal of Research in Mathematics Education, 32,* 448–470.

Manolis, C., Burns, D.J., Assudani, R., & Chinta, R. (2013). Assessing experiential learning styles: A methodological reconstruction and validation of the Kolb Learning Style Inventory. *Learning and Individual Differences, 23,* 44–52.

Montague, M. (1992). The effects of cognitive and metacognitive strategy instruction on the mathematical problem solving of middle school students with learning disabilities. *Journal of Learning Disabilities, 25*(4), 230–248.

Rosenshine, B. (1986). Synthesis of research on explicit teaching. *Educational Leadership, 43*(7), 60–69.

Rowe, M.B. (1987). Wait time: Slowing down may be a way of speeding up. *American Educator, 11*(1), 38.

Russell, S.J. (1997). The role of curriculum in teacher development. In S.N. Friel & G.W. Bright (Eds.), *Reflecting on our work: NSF teacher enhancement in K-6 mathematics* (pp. 247–254). Lanham, MD: University Press of America.

Sawyer, R.J., Graham, S., & Harris, K.R. (1992). Direct teaching, strategy instruction, and strategy instruction with explicit self-regulation: Effects on the composition skills and self-efficacy of students with learning disabilities. *Journal of Educational Psychology, 84*(3), 340–352.

Scott, T.M., Hirn, R.G., & Alter, P.J. (2014). Teacher instruction as a predictor for student engagement and disruptive behaviors. *Preventing School Failure: Alternative Education for Children and Youth, 58,* 193–200.

Sticher, J.P., Lewis, T.J., Whittaker, T.A., Richter, M., Johnson, N.W., & Trussell, R.P. (2009). Assessing teacher use of opportunities to respond and effective classroom management strategies: Comparison among high- and low-risk elementary schools. *Journal of Positive Behavior Interventions, 11,* 68–81.

Sutherland, K.S., & Wehby, J.H. (2001). Exploring the relationship between increased opportunities to respond to academic requests and the academic and behavioral outcomes of students with EBD. *Remedial and Special Education, 22,* 113–121.

Tomlinson, C.A. (2005). Quality curriculum and instruction for highly able students. *Theory into Practice, 44*(2), 160–166.

Tomlinson, C.A. (2014). *Differentiated classroom: Responding to the needs of all learners* (2nd ed.). Alexandria, VA: Association for Supervision and Curriculum Development.

6

Promoting Student Social Skills

Socially competent behavior is important in order for students to profit from instruction and succeed in later life (Wentzel & Looney, 2007). In this chapter, we address the importance of directly teaching social skills and provide guidance for embedding social skills instruction within the daily curriculum. We touch upon developmental differences in students' social skills and factors influencing students' social acceptance. We also review a strategy, known as *template matching*, to assist students in gaining social competence and describe a problem-solving approach for improving students' conflict-resolution skills. Finally, we provide examples of commercially produced resources for improving social skills in schools.

DEVELOPMENTAL DIFFERENCES IN CHILDREN'S SOCIAL SKILLS

Students who are cooperative, follow rules and expectations, pay attention in class, and get along with others are better equipped to benefit from instruction (Gresham & Elliott, 2008) and appear more likely to achieve success in and outside of school (Wentzel, 2009). Children in early grades (kindergarten through third grade) tend to make significant growth in social skills (Lamont & Van Horn, 2013), which has important implications for their future success. For example, Caprara, Barbaranelli, Pastorelli, Bandura, and Zimbardo (2000) found that teacher ratings of third-grade students' prosocial behavior were better predictors of eighth-grade academic achievement than was students' academic achievement in third grade.

It is hypothesized that children need different social skills as they mature and develop in school. Younger children need to listen, ask for help, say "please" and "thank you," ignore distractions, share, and make friends.

As they grow older, other skills come into play: expressing feelings, dealing with anger, exercising self-control, responding to teasing, accepting consequences, avoiding conflicts, initiating conversations, dealing with peer pressure, and solving problems. McGinnis (2012) described critical social skills for elementary and secondary students in her Skillstreaming series (see Tables 6.1 and 6.2). Differences in skills at these different ages underscore the need to tailor social skills training to students' development. In addition, strategies for skill training differ for elementary, middle school, and high school students. In general, teachers can be more direct with recommendations for social skills in younger students (e.g., "You have a very nice smile. Why don't you smile more when you enter new groups?"), whereas the approach with older students should be more subtle (e.g., "Sometimes teenagers do better when they smile often when entering a new group."). Adapting social skills instruction to focus on critical skills matched to students' developmental level will assist students of all ages to meet external demands and expectations.

CONSIDERATIONS WHEN TEACHING SOCIAL BEHAVIOR

Just as teaching specific academic skills leads to competence in content subject areas, teaching specific social skills leads to students' social competence (McFall, 1982). Consequently, the direct teaching of social skills for students with persistent behavioral problems in schools emerges as an important agenda. When teaching social skills, several considerations should be kept in mind.

First, it is important to recognize that behavior is influenced greatly by the social context within which it occurs. People behave differently in different social contexts. A person's behavior at the baseball park when his or her favorite player hits a home run differs (in terms of the behavior itself and its intensity, duration, and frequency) from the same person's behavior in the public library. Teachers need be mindful of this important consideration and, therefore, understand that social behavior is best taught in the context in which it occurs. Recognition of the relationship between social context and behavior reinforces an important lesson about the teaching of social skills; namely, teaching social skills in natural contexts (i.e., the actual social environment in which the skill is expected and appropriate to occur) is more effective than teaching social skills in isolation.

Teachers and school staff can conceptualize the teaching of social skills as a universal intervention, one that is appropriate for all students during every social interaction across the day. Teachers and school personnel should view every social interaction as a prospective mini-skills instruction and an opportunity to either teach new skills or to shape and reinforce existing skills. Keep in mind that it is not productive for teachers to deemphasize or remove academics from the classroom agenda in an attempt to "teach" behavior first (get the behavior under control before introducing academics). This is because teachers and other school staff should clearly convey that

Table 6.1. Key social skills for elementary-age children

Classroom survival skills	
Listening	Offering help to an adult
Asking for help	Asking a question
Saying thank you	Ignoring distractions
Bringing materials to class	Making corrections
Following instructions	Deciding on something to do
Completing assignments	Setting a goal
Contributing to discussions	
Friendship-making skills	
Introducing yourself	Offering help to a classmate
Beginning a conversation	Giving a compliment
Ending a conversation	Accepting a compliment
Joining in	Suggesting an activity
Playing a game	Sharing
Asking a favor	Apologizing
Skills for dealing with feelings	
Knowing your feelings	Dealing with your anger
Expressing your feelings	Dealing with another's anger
Recognizing another's feelings	Expressing affection
Showing understanding to another's feelings	Dealing with fear
Expressing concern for another	Rewarding yourself
Skill alternatives to aggression	
Using self-control	Problem solving
Asking permission	Accepting consequences
Responding to teasing	Dealing with an accusation
Avoiding trouble	Negotiating
Staying out of fights	
Skills for dealing with stress	
Dealing with boredom	Accepting no
Deciding what caused a problem	Saying no
Making a complaint	Relaxing
Dealing with losing	Dealing with group pressure
Being a good sport	Dealing with wanting something that isn't yours
Dealing with being left out	Making a decision
Dealing with embarrassment	Being honest
Reacting to failure	

From *Skillstreaming the Elementary School Child: A Guide for Teaching Prosocial Skills (3rd Edition),* by Ellen McGinnis, Champaign, IL: Research Press, 2012. Permission to adapt granted by Research Press.

Table 6.2. Key social skills for adolescents

Beginning and advanced social skills	
Listening	Giving a compliment
Starting a conversation	Asking for help
Having a conversation	Joining in
Asking a question	Giving instructions
Saying thank you	Following instructions
Introducing yourself	Apologizing
Introducing other people	Convincing others
Skills for dealing with feelings	
Knowing your feelings	Expressing affection
Expressing your feelings	Dealing with fear
Understanding the feelings of others	Rewarding yourself
Dealing with someone else's anger	
Skill alternatives to aggression	
Asking permission	Standing up for your rights
Sharing something	Responding to teasing
Helping others	Avoiding trouble with others
Negotiating	Keeping out of fights
Using self-control	
Skills for dealing with stress	
Making a complaint	Responding to persuasion
Answering a complaint	Responding to failure
Being a good sport	Dealing with contradictory messages
Dealing with embarrassment	Dealing with an accusation
Dealing with being left out	Getting ready for a difficult conversation
Standing up for a friend	Dealing with group pressure
Planning skills	
Deciding on something to do	Gathering information
Deciding what caused a problem	Arranging problems by importance
Setting a goal	Making a decision
Deciding on your abilities	Concentrating on a task

From *Skillstreaming the Adolescent: New Strategies and Perspectives for Teaching Prosocial Skills (3rd Edition),* by Ellen McGinnis, Champaign, IL: Research Press, 2011. Permission to adapt granted by Research Press.

being in school is primarily about learning; stopping instruction to focus on behavior may explicitly or implicitly convey to students that learning is less important. Furthermore, delaying academic instruction to focus on social skills will put students with social problems behind their peers academically, creating an additional problem.

Teachers can embed social skills instruction throughout the day by providing frequent descriptions of expected behavior and praising students who are exhibiting that behavior. Another way that social skills can be embedded throughout the day is by providing students with preprompts of behavior that is expected prior to each new activity. For example, Ella had great difficulty transitioning from activity to activity, and it took 10–15 minutes for her to calm down and attend to academics after morning circle, recess, lunch, and specials. This transition difficulty resulted in as much as an hour of lost instructional time each day. Her teacher solved this problem by pulling her aside during the transition, explaining the behavioral expectations when she returned to her desk (e.g., "You need to walk directly to your desk and sit down, take out your reading book, and begin reading where you left off yesterday."). If teacher prompting is insufficient, students can repeat the instructions (e.g., "When circle time is over, I need to go directly to my seat."). Students can also be taught to self-instruct during the transition (initially aloud, but quickly moving to doing so silently). For example, a student might repeat, "First I walk straight to my desk, then I get out my book, then I begin reading" during the transition.

A second consideration when teaching social behavior is the quality of the relationship between the teachers and students. Research suggests that students learn better from teachers who care about them (Berry & O'Connor, 2010; Noddings, 1992; Wentzel, 1997). This is especially true for students who experience social and academic problems and who may be at risk for dropping out (Muller, 2001). Caring takes many forms. Teacher empathy, consistency, and persistent encouragement of independence and decision making within the classroom are just some of the ways teachers show care and contribute to students' willingness to engage in school and aspire to achieve (Aspy & Roebuck, 1977; McNeely, Nonnemaker, & Blum, 2002). For example, Ms. Macintosh worked with an eighth-grade student, Will, who had experienced frequent moves as a member of a military family. He had entered her school in November and seemed disinterested in schoolwork, relationships with peers, or extracurricular activities. Ms. Macintosh shared with Will that she had also grown up in a military family and had experienced frequent moves that were very hard for her. Simply sharing this information and empathizing with Will and his situation resulted in him lighting up and seeming more comfortable around her, and also set the stage for her to make specific recommendations to him on increasing his involvement with peers. It also set up Ms. Macintosh to be Will's ally, which was important to him as she made connections with the school psychologist about concerns regarding what appeared to be anxiety symptoms he was presenting.

MEETING THE UNWRITTEN DEMANDS OF SCHOOL

All situations in school, both academic and nonacademic, involve rules that students must follow to be socially successful. As mentioned in Chapter 4, teachers should have explicit expectations for their classrooms and frequently reinforce students for following those expectations. Some students, especially those with social, emotional, and behavioral problems, have trouble following expectations. They find it particularly challenging to navigate unwritten or "tacit" rules of particular situations, such as expectations related to appearance and situations such as athletics, lunch, transitions between classes, and free and recreational time. For example, the unwritten rules for classroom transitions may be to stroll in a casual manner but not too slowly, talk to a few people along the way, smile a few times, make eye contact briefly but attentively, and so forth. Students who lack social competence often struggle to understand and apply these unwritten social rules. The following sections offer strategies for teaching students how to recognize, learn, and follow the nuances of social rules, including those who struggle with social skills and social awareness.

EMBEDDING SOCIAL SKILLS INTO ONGOING INSTRUCTION

Teachers should treat the teaching of social skills as a universal intervention. This means that they will need to develop creative ways for integrating explicit social skills instruction into their daily lessons. A good way to begin is by reviewing behavioral expectations before planned activities across the day. The review of social expectations may be brief but should consist of a clear and concise recitation of the specific behavioral expectations students should perform to achieve success. The expectations should be stated in terms of the behaviors students can perform (versus the behaviors the teacher does not wish to see; see Chapter 2). For example, the teacher should state, "Ask Keith if you can play," rather than "Don't grab toys from Keith." Similarly, as students are about to make a transition to another class down the hall, the teacher might remind students to "Line up with an arm's length between classmates," rather than stating "No pushing." Setting clear expectations prior to the activity is an excellent way to cue students to specific social behaviors that will lead to their success in that activity.

In addition to stating clear expectations, teachers should keep in mind that every social interaction is a potential "teachable moment" wherein a student's response in a social encounter is an opportunity for teaching new social behaviors (acquisition deficits) or shaping and reinforcing existing social behaviors (performance and fluency deficits) (Gresham, 1981, 1995). Students who already know the expectations are reminded of them. Students who are not fluent in the expectations are cued to the appropriate social responses. When social errors occur, gently correcting awkward or inappropriate social behaviors gives students new information (alternative responses) about how to better meet teacher expectations in the future and serves to improve students' overall social competency.

The quality of teachers' error correction can have a large impact on students' motivation and future responses. When students make responding errors in social interactions, teachers should strive for a business-like, non-threatening response to first alert students to the error and then provide additional information or cues on how to respond correctly next time (e.g., quietly stating, "James, Lauren is still using the computer. Please wait until she is finished with her game, then you can have a turn."). Just as important, teachers should refrain from using sarcasm when correcting social errors (e.g., "Nice interrupting, James.") and should avoid correcting students' social behavior in front of their peers. Teachers should monitor error rates and analyze students' errors for patterns. A pattern of similar errors under similar conditions may indicate a skill deficit that requires reteaching. For example, Andrew repeatedly interrupts when other students are speaking because he does not have the skill of entering a conversation appropriately. When Andrew responds as suggested (or prompted by the teacher) in the future, his teacher recognizes the correct response and provides reinforcement. This can be done simply with words (e.g., "Nice job taking turns speaking, Andrew.").

Universal social skill instruction that uses clear definitions of acceptable and unacceptable behavior, similar language in terms of expectations, and prompts and corrections across settings is likely to enhance generalization of skills.

FACTORS INFLUENCING SOCIAL SKILLS

Students' social skills are enhanced or compromised by appearance and skills such as eye contact, social distance, and mannerisms, known as *molecular* skills (Bellack, 1979). For many students, these skills need to be taught as well.

Social Appearance

Students often make judgments about one another based on appearance. Outdated, unusual, or unclean clothing can often engender negative treatment from peers. Although it may be difficult to approach students or their parents about appearance, avoiding this discussion will in all likelihood result in continued peer problems. With younger students, conversations about students' appearance can be held with parents and guardians. For example, a teacher might approach a parent in the following way: "Thank you, Ms. Blalock, for coming in. I enjoy Cody in my class. Overall, he is doing fine, and I value his sense of humor. I have noticed that his peers sometimes tend to avoid him. At times students have teased him about the clothes he wears. The other day, he wore a T-shirt to school that had a red heart around the word 'Hogwarts.' The other children teased him and called him a 'wart head,' a 'wart hog' and a few other things. Has he mentioned those incidents to you?" This type of discussion can prompt parents to become more vigilant about monitoring what their children wear to school and help them intervene to promote more appropriate choices.

Teachers of middle and high school students, in particular, should have direct, private, and supportive conversations on appearance with their students. For example, the teacher might say, "Jane, I really appreciate your leadership in the class. I have noticed that some days you seem well groomed and ready for school, and other days you seem disheveled and your clothes seem wrinkled and sometimes unclean. May I ask if things are okay at home? I hope you don't mind me bringing this up, but I want you to know that I want the best for you here at Ridge Middle School." Depending on the direction of this interaction, the teacher could then discuss differences in clothing and appearance on good days as opposed to challenging days, get a sense of whether the student has adequate clothing, and begin to generate ideas about ways to be helpful (e.g., discreetly obtaining donations of clothing for the student in her size).

When children come to school dirty and unkempt, teachers (with the support of school mental health staff) should contact the parent or guardian, seek to understand what is going on, and generate ideas with them on ways to promote better student hygiene. In some circumstances, children coming to school consistently dirty and unkempt is a sign of neglect and/or abuse, and appropriate steps need to be taken to ensure the safety and appropriate care for the child (e.g., involving local child protective services).

Molecular Social Skills

Molecular social skills contribute to children's social competence. Such skills include eye contact, body distance and orientation (being the right distance away and orienting the body toward the individual they are interacting with), latency of speech (waiting an appropriate amount of time after another person talks), duration of speech and content (saying something that makes sense and that is not too brief or too long), use of hand motions when speaking (making natural fluid motions versus jerky or no movements), and avoiding rude or unusual behavior or mannerisms (interrupting, making comments or gestures inappropriate to the situation). These skills can be taught just as other skills through modeling, prompting, and reinforcement. In the following section, we suggest additional approaches to teaching social skills.

THE TEMPLATE MATCHING STRATEGY

Template matching is an easy-to-use strategy to enhance students' appearance and improve molecular skills such as eye contact, social distance, and mannerisms. In template matching, the student identifies particular situations that are challenging for him or her (e.g., making a transition between classes). Next, within those situations the student identifies a peer who does reasonably well and then covertly observes the peer (without staring), noting particular aspects of appearance and behavior. For example, he or she might take note of what the student was wearing, how the student walked, what type of eye contact the student made, who the student talked with, how loud and long the student's speech was, and how the student entered and left social situations. Teachers and staff members can help students generate specific events they should observe based on their social challenges. Students are then encouraged to model the behavior of the targeted peer. Template matching can help students display social behaviors that are associated with likeability and are appropriate to the context and setting.

Ms. Macintosh used the template matching strategy with Judy, an eighth-grade student who seemed very shy and reluctant to interact with other peers. She asked Judy to stay after school one day and conveyed concern about her limited social relations in a very supportive way (i.e., "Judy, it seems like you are not interacting with other students in my class very much. Can I help in any way?"). Judy confided that she was somewhat nervous around other students, especially when joining in on new activities, and really did not know how to do this. Ms. Macintosh asked Judy to name two other girls in the class who did pretty well in these social situations, and Judy named Amy and Sarah. Ms. Macintosh then encouraged Judy to observe those two girls in a nonobvious way, in the situations that were challenging for her, and to note the behaviors they displayed and the general styles or strategies they used in these situations. Ms. Macintosh then met again with Judy to discuss her observations. Ms. Macintosh encouraged her to try some of the things she observed and provided verbal encouragement for doing so, and Judy began to come out of her shell.

PROBLEM SOLVING TO ADDRESS ONGOING SOCIAL PROBLEMS

There are many paradigms for solving problems. The problem-solving process we describe here is based on the work of Glasser (1968) and assumes students have input into their learning and are held responsible for their (mis)behaviors. The problem-solving process is an alternative structure for resolving conflicts or correcting misbehaviors that typically result in office disciplinary referral (ODR). The purpose of problem solving is to resolve issues and return students as quickly as possible to the instructional setting based on the assumption that teaching is a better intervention than punishment and that students are better off in class engaged in the curriculum than sitting in a principal's office. For students who make repeated errors or create disturbing episodes, especially in instances in which the teacher believes the student already possesses the required social skill, individual problem-solving sessions may be conducted.

There are four steps to the problem-solving process: 1) problem identification, 2) prevention, 3) action plan, and 4) commitment to the plan (also see alternative problem-solving frameworks presented in Chapter 11). Each of these steps is described in the following subsections.

Problem Identification

For problem identification, the student identifies the issue that resulted in the problem behavior, reviews the expectations governing the behavior, and accepts responsibility (ownership) for the behavior. The adult uses the opportunity to probe for more details about the incident, asking, "What caused you to become so upset?" In addition, the adult reviews the expectations and the rationale behind them and emphasizes the importance of conforming to reasonable expectations.

Prevention

After the student has identified the problem, he or she is asked to identify a replacement behavior he or she could have used instead of the problem behavior. The student is prompted to describe and forecast how use of the replacement behavior could prevent similar problems in the future. Teachers should not be surprised if naming a replacement behavior is difficult, especially for students with histories of problem behaviors in school, but teaching positive, functionally equivalent replacement behaviors as substitutes for problem behaviors is important (Maag, 2005). The adult may also prompt the student to articulate replacement behaviors by saying, "What could you have done to avoid the problem?" Finally, the adult asks about things the teacher might do differently next time to help the student manage his frustration and contain his anger.

Development of an Action Plan

The third phase entails developing an action plan that specifies particular behaviors the student will engage in the next time a similar situation arises. Essentially, the action plan is a statement of behavioral expectations and begins with the words, "Next time." For example, the student might state, "Next time I want the iPad and my classmate is using it, I will ask her when she will be finished. I will ask if I can use it after she is finished. I will then find something else to do until she is finished." Action plan steps can include a number of different options (e.g., "I will ask my classmate to share" or "I will ask my teacher for assistance") but should be simple and concise, using few words and listing specific behaviors the student could perform.

Commitment

The final step in the problem-solving process is commitment. Commitment occurs when the student acknowledges his or her obligation to abide by the plan that he or she and the adult just worked together to create. It consists of the student's affirmation that he or she sees the plan as a reasonable series of action steps that will result in a different (and better) way of handling frustration and anger in the future. The adult reviews the action plan with the student, asking, "Are you able to do these steps? Great, then when we go back to class I would like you to show me." When the student is calm and can orally repeat the steps of the plan, he or she is escorted to class to implement the plan now in place.

After Problem Solving

When the student returns to the classroom after problem solving, the teacher should be accepting and welcoming, stating, for example, "I am happy you've chosen to rejoin the class." There are important roles the teacher will play regarding the action plan. The teacher and the adult involved in problem solving with the student should meet briefly to review the plan, determine the modifications and supports needed to prevent escalations in the future, and decide how to teach the student appropriate responses to deal with frustration.

Using problem solving in a challenging situation permits the teacher and the student to arrive at a better understanding of the specific problem (problem identification), identify mutually agreeable solutions (prevention and action plan), and become motivated (commitment) to implementing a plan. An advantage of the problem-solving process is that any adult in the school setting—principal, vice principal, teacher, or classroom aide—can conduct problem-solving sessions. Problem solving deals with the "here and now." The sessions should be brief in nature. Problem solving allows students to sit with a caring and respectful adult, share their perceptions of the problem situation, and participate in the development of a reasonable plan for succeeding in school. The latter point may be especially important for students with histories of school adjustment problems who often believe they are punished unfairly without the ability to explain their perceptions of the problematic situations. Just as important, the process is designed to return the students back to class better equipped to deal with frustration in the future. Moreover, it holds students accountable for their behaviors and makes them responsible for following through with a plan they helped develop. Finally, it is contextual. It teaches students alternative, more appropriate social behaviors to use in the very setting in which problematic situations occur. Doing so provides another strategy for embedding social skills instruction in the school curriculum.

Problem-Solving Example

The following case study illustrates application of the problem-solving process. Ethan, a student in Mr. Daniels' math class, became extremely frustrated when a peer, Andrew, would not agree to play the game he chose during free time. Shortly after free time began, Ethan began to take and hide pieces of the game Andrew was playing. As free time continued, Ethan started to destroy toy pieces, eventually leaving the room and slamming the door behind him. When Ethan was located, he was directed to meet with the school counselor, Mrs. Simmons, and engage in problem solving.

Mrs. Simmons began by asking Ethan to explain the problem (problem identification). He had some difficulty at first, stating, "Andrew wasn't being fair." Mrs. Simmons guided him to think about how the problem started, and he was able to describe that he and Andrew wanted to play different games. She also led him to describe specifically why this made him angry. He claimed that there weren't many games he enjoyed and, even though he liked playing with Andrew, Ethan didn't like the games Andrew chose because he wasn't good at them.

In the next phase, prevention, Mrs. Simmons and Ethan discussed what he could do in the future, rather than becoming destructive and leaving the room, when a similar situation arose. Ethan suggested that he could ask for the teacher's help to resolve the problem. Mrs. Simmons agreed this was a good approach for the time being until Ethan could learn to resolve the problem without adult assistance.

The next step was to develop an action plan. Ethan's specific plan needed to describe the specific actions he could perform when frustrated to help minimize the occurrence of the problem behavior in future similar situations. In Ethan's situation, his action plan referred to the specific peer and interaction that was problematic, because he rarely had problems with other peers and needed specific guidance on interacting with Andrew. In addition, Mrs. Simmons and Ethan discussed the exact nature of "negotiation or deciding to play with someone else." For example, they talked about deciding when it would be better to play alone. Ethan's action plan was simple and straightforward:

1. Return to class and reenter quietly.
2. Negotiate with Andrew to play a game that I select, watch while Andrew plays with other kids so I can learn the rules of games I do not like, choose to play with another classmate, or play alone at my desk.
3. The next time I get frustrated, I will raise my hand to ask for the teacher's help to resolve the problem rather than leave the room without permission.

Finally, during the last step, commitment, Ethan agreed that he could follow the steps in the action plan when he and Andrew could not agree on a game to play together. He repeated the plan to Mrs. Simmons and described situations when he might need to use the plan. Mrs. Simmons then escorted him back to class.

Mrs. Simmons communicated Ethan's action plan to Mr. Daniels. In this situation, it was important for Mr. Daniels to know that Ethan now had a plan that encouraged him to raise his hand for teacher assistance when negotiating difficult social situations, and also to know the courses of action (watch, choose another classmate, or play alone) available to Ethan to resolve the problem. This also allowed Mr. Daniels to look for patterns of social errors, note when Ethan perceived (whether accurately or not) a social situation was not going his way, and prompt Ethan to use his action plan rather than becoming frustrated and attempting to gain control and escape the situation by leaving the room.

We also note a number of other preemptive steps that Mr. Daniels could take in the future. Knowing Ethan's triggers for anger and frustration, Mr. Daniels will say to the whole class prior to free time, "We have a limited number of games to play in the classroom during free time. I expect you to share. If you need help negotiating what to do, please raise your hand and I will help you." He also will privately say to Ethan, "Free time is sometimes difficult for you. Remember, if you get angry or frustrated, all you have to do is raise your hand and ask for help."

Initially, Ethan may not be able to independently recognize his mounting anger, and it will be necessary for Mr. Daniels to become more assertive and privately direct Ethan to use his action plan: "Ethan, I would like you to think about your options. If Andrew doesn't want to play, you can ask another classmate to play or play alone at your desk." If Ethan is observed following his action plan and does so appropriately, the teacher might say at the end of class, "Ethan, I am very proud of you for following through with your plan. I know free time has been a difficult period for you in the past. I can tell you're really trying to do well."

CLASSWIDE SOCIAL SKILLS INTERVENTIONS

There are a few social skills interventions or programs that teachers can readily implement classwide, particularly in classes in which there are numerous students with interaction problems. We describe three such programs—the Good Behavior Game, the PAX Good Behavior Game (PAX GBG), and the Strong Kids™ programs—that have research to support their effectiveness.

The Good Behavior Game

The Good Behavior Game (Barrish, Saunders, & Wolf, 1969) is an approach for managing classroom behaviors that rewards students for appropriate behavior during instructional times. Several studies have demonstrated the game to be an effective means of increasing appropriate behavior, leading to endorsement by the Institute of Medicine's Report on the Prevention of Mental, Emotional, and Behavior Disorders (National Research Council, 2009), which indicated that this strategy was one of the most influential prevention approaches that teachers can implement. The original version used a response-cost paradigm in which students received "demerits" for breaking a publicly posted classroom rule. We recommend a newer version in which the teams can earn bonus points to offset demerits (Rathvon, 2008).

When setting up this approach, the first step is to identify times during the school day or activities that are particularly problematic, when the game would be beneficial (e.g., during teacher lecture when students tend to be inattentive). At the middle or high school level, this might mean a particular class. Next, specific behavior that will earn merits is operationally defined. For example, if supporting peers during a collaborative small-group activity is the focus of an intervention, it could be operationally defined as moving close to the peer appearing to need help, commenting on what he or she is doing (e.g., saying, "That problem was hard for me. Is it hard for you too?"), and offering to help (e.g., saying, "Can I show you how I figured out how to do that?").

The next step is to determine the criteria for receiving a merit (e.g., five incidents of positive peer interactions during a period, raising hands with no more than two call outs in a period), how often students will receive merits (e.g., every 10 minutes, at the end of the class period), and how often students can exchange merits for rewards (e.g., at the end of the class period, at the end of the day, weekly). For classes with high rates of problem behaviors, rewards will need to be frequent at the start of the program. Merits can be monitored with tallies on the board or cards given to the students, which are collected and counted at the end of specific time intervals. Rewards or privileges (e.g., extra free time) should be provided for earning a predetermined number of merits.

As we described in Chapter 4, the Good Behavior Game procedures can be modified by dividing the class into two teams and allocating merits to a team for any appropriate behavior displayed by one of its members. This variation has been successfully used with adolescents (e.g., Kleinman & Saigh, 2011), illustrating the versatility of the intervention.

The PAX Good Behavior Game

The PAX GBG is a set of evidence-based strategies for increasing self-regulation and cooperation and decreasing unwanted behaviors in classrooms as well as in the school at large. PAX stands for peace, productivity, health, and happiness and represents the traits students aspire to achieve in their classrooms throughout the year. The teacher works with the students to establish common expectations and a shared language about classroom behavior. For example, using actual examples from PAX GBG, *kernels* are brief and effective strategies that help students do well, such as cueing students that a transition is about to occur, making reinforcers more personal by using notes to individual students, and creating fun competition, such as timing tasks and calling out times of winning teams. Negative and unwanted behaviors are called *spleems,* a nonsense term used to objectively refer to the occurrence of problem behaviors without the negative connotations or personal reactions among students when misbehaviors are more directly labeled (e.g., yelling, arguing, fighting). Overall goals for the game are to increase positive behaviors by getting into the spirit of the game (and competing against other teams of students) and earning rewards (which are often playful and student-conceived, such as being able to tap a pencil on a desk for 30 seconds) while reducing negative behaviors, or spleems.

The teacher first applies kernels in the classroom. Once kernels are integrated successfully into classroom activities (e.g., students begin to show enthusiasm for activities that are timed and competitive), the game is played among two to five teacher-selected heterogeneous teams that are changed routinely. During the game, the teacher identifies, counts, and records all unwanted behavior (spleems) without using names and also points out PAX (peaceful, productive, healthy, happy) behaviors that occur. At the end of the game, the teams with three or fewer spleems are rewarded with a prize in the form of an activity (often silly, as previously described) such as a minute of dancing around or a 10-second giggle fest. Initially, the game is played for only a few minutes at a time (e.g., 1–2 minutes with younger students), but as students improve at the game, it is played for longer periods of time as well as during different activities (e.g., hallway, lunches, study hall, recess) and times of the day. The PAX GBG is an evidence-based practice for use in schools, as reported by the National Registry of Evidence-based Programs and Practices (NREPP) of the Substance Abuse and Mental Health Services Administration (SAMHSA).

Strong Kids Programs

The Strong Kids programs (see http://www.brookespublishing.com/resource-center/book-series/strong-kids-curricula) have evidence for improving social and emotional skills in children. The Strong Kids programs are brief and practical socioemotional learning curricula appropriate for Pre-K children and students Kindergarten through Grade 12. Strong Start is for use with students Pre-K through Grade 2, Strong Kids is designed for students in Grades 3–8 and includes versions for both elementary and middle school students, and Strong Teens is designed for high-school students in Grades 9–12. The Strong Kids programs may be used effectively with high-functioning, typical, and at-risk youth, as well as with students with emotional and behavioral disorders, in a variety of settings. They may also be adapted and modified for use with specific cultural groups.

COMMERCIALLY AVAILABLE, EVIDENCE-BASED SOCIAL SKILLS PROGRAMS

As mentioned previously, the NREPP program of SAMHSA is an excellent resource for evidence-based programs that promote positive functioning in children and adults. Presently, more than 325 programs are listed, with more than half of those programs targeting children and adolescents. When the search terms *social skills* and *school* were used, 47 programs were identified. Many of those programs are manualized interventions, meaning that the steps for implementation are delineated; however, implementers may have considerable work to do before, during, and following sessions, such as preparing for individual or group meetings, organizing supplemental materials, and choosing questions and situations that will enhance the relevance of and interest in skill training (Schaeffer et al., 2005). Table 6.3 lists examples of those programs by grade level. The programs listed and described in Table 6.3 are taken directly from the NREPP web site and, consonant with the focus of this chapter, emphasize strategies for improving students' social competence within the school setting.

SUMMARY

Social skills play an important role in how well students adjust to school and succeed both academically and socially. Teachers can enhance the social skills of their students by establishing positive relationships with them

Table 6.3. Examples of evidence-based school-age social skills programs

Program	Grade level	Description
Elementary school programs		
Al's Pals: Kids Making Healthy Choices	Preschool–grade 1	Al's Pals: Kids Making Healthy Choices is a school-based prevention program that seeks to develop socioemotional skills such as self-control, problem solving, and healthy decision making in children in preschool, kindergarten, and first grade.
Early Risers "Skills for Success"	Grades 1–5	Early Risers "Skills for Success" is a multicomponent, developmentally focused, competency-enhancement program that targets 6- to 12-year-old elementary school students who are at high risk for early development of conduct problems, including substance use.
Lesson One: The ABCs of Life	Preschool–grade 6	Lesson One: The ABCs of Life is a universal, school-based intervention designed to integrate social competency skills with academics in prekindergarten through grade 6. Grounded in the theory of social and emotional competence, Lesson One prepares children with the basic skills they will need throughout their lives to make healthy decisions; avoid violence, bullying, and other risk-taking behaviors; and achieve personal and academic success.
Open Circle	Kindergarten–grade 5	Open Circle, a curriculum-based program for youth in kindergarten through grade 5, is designed to strengthen students' social and emotional learning skills related to self-awareness, self-management, social awareness, interpersonal relationships, and problem solving and to foster safe, caring, and highly engaging classroom and school communities.
Project KIND (Keys to Improvement Necessary for Development)	Kindergarten	Project KIND is a life-skills curriculum designed for kindergarten students to increase their school success by promoting social, emotional, and behavioral skills.
Promoting Alternative THinking Strategies (PATHS); PATHS Preschool	Preschool–grade 5	PATHS and PATHS Preschool are school-based preventive interventions for children in elementary school or preschool. The interventions are designed to enhance areas of socioemotional development such as self-control, self-esteem, emotional awareness, social skills, friendships, and interpersonal problem-solving skills while reducing aggression and other behavior problems.
Schools And Families Educating Children (SAFEChildren)	Grades 1–5	SAFEChildren is a family-focused preventive intervention designed to increase academic achievement and decrease risk for later drug abuse and associated problems such as aggression, school failure, and low social competence.
Second Step	Preschool–grade 8	Second Step is a classroom-based social skills program for children ages 4 to 14 that teaches socioemotional skills aimed at reducing impulsive and aggressive behavior while increasing social competence.
Social Skills Group Intervention (S.S. GRIN)	Grades 3–5	S.S. GRIN 3–5 is a social skills curriculum for children in grades 3–5 who have immature social skills relative to peers, are being rejected and teased by peers (e.g., experiencing bullying and victimization), or are socially anxious and awkward with peers.
Steps to Respect: A Bullying Prevention Program	Grades 1–5	Steps to Respect: A Bullying Prevention Program is a schoolwide intervention designed to prevent bullying behavior and counter the personal and social effects of bullying where it occurs by promoting a positive school climate.

From National Registry of Evidence-based Programs and Practices. (n.d.). *Descriptions of evidence-based school-age social skills programs.* Rockville, MD: U.S. Department of Health and Human Services, Substance Abuse and Mental Health Services Administration; reprinted by permission.

Program	Grade level	Description
Middle and high school programs		
Capturing Kids' Hearts Teen Leadership Program	Middle school–high school	The Capturing Kids' Hearts Teen Leadership Program, a curriculum-based intervention for middle and high school youth, is designed to improve students' emotional well-being and social functioning, including improving communication with parents, reducing feelings of loneliness and isolation, improving self-efficacy, and minimizing problem behaviors.
The Challenging Horizons Program (CHP)	Middle school–high school	CHP is a school-based set of interventions for middle or junior high school students with attention-deficit/hyperactivity disorder. Building on behavioral and cognitive theories about the nature of the disorder, CHP aims to provide a safe learning environment enhanced by supportive counseling relationships between students and staff.
Hip-Hop 2 Prevent Substance Abuse and HIV (H2P)	Middle school–high school	H2P is designed to improve knowledge and skills related to drugs and HIV/AIDS among youth ages 12–16 with the aim of preventing or reducing substance use and risky sexual activity as well as anxiety and depression in childhood, adolescence, and adulthood.
Multilevel programs		
CAPSLE: Creating a Peaceful School Learning Environment	Kindergarten–grade 12	CAPSLE, a schoolwide climate change intervention for students in kindergarten through 12th grade, is designed to reduce student aggression, victimization, aggressive bystander behavior, and disruptive or off-task classroom behaviors.
Cool Kids Child and Adolescent Anxiety Management Program	Grade 1–high school	Cool Kids addresses anxiety disorders in children and adolescents ages 6–18 years. With a focus on teaching anxiety management skills, the manualized program includes sessions on identifying anxious thoughts, feelings, and behaviors (psychoeducation); challenging anxious thoughts (cognitive restructuring); approaching avoided situations or events (exposure); and using additional coping skills such as systematic problem solving, social skills, assertiveness skills, and effective strategies for dealing with teasing and bullying.
Cross-Age Mentoring Program (CAMP) for Children with Adolescent Mentors	Grades 4–12	CAMP for Children With Adolescent Mentors links high school students, typically in grades 9–11, with younger students in grades 4–8 in a mentor–mentee relationship, with the goal of benefiting both mentors and mentees.
FRIENDS Program	Grade 1–adult	The FRIENDS Program is a cognitive behavioral intervention that focuses on the promotion of emotional resilience to prevent, or intervene early, in the course of anxiety and depression in childhood, adolescence, and adulthood.
Michigan Model for Health	Kindergarten–high school	The Michigan Model for Health is a comprehensive and sequential health education curriculum that aims to give students ages 5–19 years (grades K–12) the knowledge and skills needed to practice and maintain healthy behaviors and lifestyles.
Project ACHIEVE	Preschool–high school	Project ACHIEVE is a comprehensive school reform and improvement program for preschool through high school (students aged 3–18 years) that focuses on students' academic, socioemotional or behavioral, and social skills outcomes; schoolwide positive behavioral support systems and school safety; positive classroom and school climates; the community climate; and community and parent outreach and involvement.
Safe School Ambassadors (SSA)	Grades 1–12	The SSA program is a bystander education program that aims to reduce emotional and physical bullying and enhance school climate in elementary, middle, and high schools. The program recruits and trains socially influential student leaders from diverse cliques and interest groups within a school to act as "ambassadors" against bullying.

(continued)

Table 6.3. *(continued)*

Program	Grade level	Description
Say It Straight (SIS)	Grade 1–adult	SIS is a communication training program designed to help students and adults develop empowering communication skills and behaviors and increase self-awareness, self-efficacy, and personal and social responsibility.
Social Skills Group Intervention–High Functioning Autism (S.S. GRIN-HFA)	Grades 1–12	S.S. GRIN-HFA is designed to improve social behaviors in children with high-functioning autism spectrum disorders by building basic behavioral and cognitive social skills, reinforcing prosocial attitudes and behaviors, and building adaptive coping strategies for social problems such as teasing or isolation.
The 4Rs (Reading, Writing, Respect & Resolution)	Kindergarten–grade 8	The 4Rs is a universal, school-based curriculum that integrates social and emotional learning into language arts for children in kindergarten through grade 8.
Too Good for Drugs (TGFD)	Kindergarten–grade 12	TGFD is a school-based prevention program for kindergarten through 12th grade that builds on students' resiliency by teaching them how to be socially competent and autonomous problem solvers.
Too Good for Violence (TGFV)	Kindergarten–grade 12	TGFV is a school-based violence prevention and character education program for students in kindergarten through 12th grade. It is designed to enhance prosocial behaviors and skills and improve protective factors related to conflict and violence.

and teaching and prompting appropriate peer and adult interactions. Like academic and behavioral skills, teachers should directly teach social skills, especially in natural contexts. In addition, many commercial resources are available to teachers that offer structured approaches for promoting positive social skills in students.

Self-Reflection

1. Are the social skills expectations in the different environments throughout your school or a school you have visited clear to students? Were expectations for social skills taught?
2. Identify times or activities throughout the day when the students in your class or a class you have visited have the most difficulties with social skills. Describe ways you can embed social skills instruction during these and other times.
3. Identify a particular student in your class or a class you have visited who has social problems due to appearance or molecular skills. Describe how you can use template matching to help the student improve his or her appearance or molecular skills.
4. Identify a student you have taught who would have benefitted from problem solving. In what ways could you have used it with the student? With what other student behavior problems could it be used?
5. Review the Good Behavior Game, the PAX Good Behavior Game, and the Strong Kids program. What are similarities and differences? Which of these approaches to social skill instruction would offer the best fit with your personal philosophy and teaching style?

REFERENCES

Aspy, N.D., & Roebuck, F.N. (1977). *Kids don't learn from people they don't like.* Amherst, MA: HRD Press.

Barrish, H.H., Saunders, M., & Wolf, M.M. (1969). Good behavior game: Effects of individual contingencies for group consequences on disruptive behavior in a classroom. *Journal of Applied Behavior Analysis, 2*(2), 119–124. doi:10.1901/jaba.1969.2-119

Bellack, A.S. (1979). Behavioral assessment of social skills. In A. Bellack & M. Hersen (Eds.), *Research and practice in social skills training* (pp. 75–104). New York, NY: Springer.

Berry, D., & O'Connor, E. (2010). Behavioral risk, teacher–child relationships, and social skill development across middle childhood: A child-by-environment analysis of change. *Journal of Applied Developmental Psychology, 31*(1), 1–14. doi:10.1016/j.appdev.2009.05.001

Caprara, G.V., Barbaranelli, C., Pastorelli, C., Bandura, A., & Zimbardo, P.G. (2000). Prosocial foundations of children's academic achievement. *Psychological Science, 11,* 302–306.

Glasser, W. (1969). *Schools without failure.* New York, NY: Harper & Row.

Goldstein, A.P., & McGinnis, E. (1997). *Skillstreaming the adolescent: New strategies and perspectives for teaching prosocial skills* (Rev. ed., Vol. 1). Champaign, IL: Research Press.

Gresham, F.M. (1981). Social skills training with handicapped children: A review. *Review of Educational Research, 51,* 139–176.

Gresham, F.M. (1995). Best practices in social skills training. In A. Thomas & J. Grimes (Eds.), *Best practices in school psychology* (pp. 1021–1030). Washington, DC: National Association of School Psychologists.

Gresham, F.M., & Elliott, S.N. (2008). *Social skills improvement system: Rating scales.* San Antonio, TX: Pearson Assessments.

Kleinman, K.E., & Saigh, P.A. (2011). The effects of the Good Behavior Game on the conduct of regular education New York City high school students. *Behavior Modification, 36,* 95–105. doi:10.1177/014544551039221

Lamont, A., & Van Horn, M. (2013). Heterogeneity in parent-reported social skill development in early elementary school children. *Social Development, 22*(2), 384–405. doi:10.1111/sode.12023

Maag, J.W. (2005). Social skills training for youth with emotional and behavioral disorders and learning disabilities: Problems, conclusions, and suggestions. *Exceptionality, 13,* 155–172.

McFall, R. (1982). A review and reformulation of the concept of social skills. *Behavioral Assessment, 4,* 1–35.

McGinnis, E. (2011). *Skillstreaming the adolescent: New strategies and perspectives for teaching prosocial skills* (3rd ed.). Champaign, IL: Research Press.

McGinnis, E. (2012). *Skillstreaming the elementary school child: A guide for teaching prosocial skills* (3rd ed.). Champaign, IL: Research Press.

McGinnis, E., & Goldstein, A.P. (2003). *Skillstreaming in early childhood: New strategies and perspectives for teaching prosocial skills.* Champaign, IL: Research Press.

McNeely, C.A., Nonnemaker, J.M., & Blum, R.W. (2002). Promoting school connectedness: Evidence from the National Longitudinal Study of Adolescent Health. *Journal of School Health, 72*(4), 138–146.

Muller, C. (2001) The role of caring in the teacher–student relationship for at-risk students. *Sociological Inquiry, 71,* 241–255.

National Registry of Evidence-based Programs and Practices. (n.d.). *Descriptions of evidence-based school-age social skills programs.* Rockville, MD: U.S. Department of Health and Human Services, Substance Abuse and Mental Health Services Administration.

National Research Council. (2009). *Preventing mental, emotional, and behavioral disorders among young people: Progress and possibilities.* Washington, DC: National Academies Press.

Noddings, N. (1992). *The challenge to care in schools: An alternative approach to education.* New York, NY: Teachers College Press.

Rathvon, N. (2008). *Effective school interventions: Evidence-based strategies for improving student outcomes.* New York, NY: Guilford Press.

Schaeffer, C.M., Bruns, E., Weist, M.D., Stephan, S.H., Goldstein, J., & Simpson, Y. (2005). Overcoming challenges to evidence-based interventions in schools. *Journal of Youth and Adolescence, 34,* 15–22.

Wentzel, K.R. (1997). Student motivation in middle school: The role of perceived pedagogical caring. *Journal of Educational Psychology, 3,* 411–419.

Wentzel, K. R. (2009). Peer relationships and motivation at school. In K Rubin, W. Bukowski, & B. Laursen (Eds.), Handbook on Peer Relationships (pp. 531–547). New York, NY: Guilford.

Wentzel, K.R., & Looney, I. (2007). Socialization in school settings. In J. Gruesec & P. Hastings (Eds.), *Handbook of socialization: Theory and research* (pp. 382–403). New York, NY: Guilford Press.

7

Preparing for Intensive Intervention

In the first section of this book, we introduced the concept of a tiered approach to intervention. We described one specific tiered approach in Chapter 2, school-wide positive behavior support (SWPBS), because the procedures for implementation have been clearly articulated in the literature and there is growing research evidence that it results in reductions in student problem behavior and emerging evidence that it may improve student academic performance as well (Horner, Sugai, & Anderson, 2010). In addition, it is aligned with our philosophy that behavior needs to be taught and students should be treated with respect and dignity. We described both Tiers 1 and 2 in Chapter 2, noting that some students require more intensive intervention than is offered by Tiers 1 and 2. However, Tier 3 intervention requires a great deal more effort than either Tiers 1 and 2 because a functional behavioral assessment (FBA) must be conducted in order to develop an intervention. Furthermore, the resulting intervention is individualized and fairly time-intensive to implement. In this chapter, we discuss preliminary considerations to make sure Tier 3 is needed. In addition, we describe a procedure for intensifying a Tier 2 intervention that can be used prior to Tier 3. Finally, we offer guidance on how to assess resources in preparation for implementing Tier 3 intervention.

DETERMINING THE NEED FOR TIER 3 INTERVENTION

Tier 3 intervention requires a great deal more time, effort, and, sometimes, additional personnel and fiscal resources than interventions at Tier 1, Tier 2, or even classwide interventions. It is therefore important to first determine whether a student truly needs intensive Tier 3 intervention before launching into it. In some situations, the severity of a student's behavior indicates an immediate need for intensive Tier 3 intervention. For example, there are students who injure animals, bring weapons to school, or purposefully start fires. In addition to these "externalizing" behavioral problems, other students have experienced serious trauma and are unable to focus on school or are severely depressed and/or anxious to the point of having great difficulty functioning. Other students present real risk of self-harm. Emotional and behavioral challenges such as these indicate urgent need of intensive (and most likely ongoing) intervention, often involving close collaboration with other systems such as mental health (see Barrett, Eber, & Weist, 2013). Because it is highly unlikely that Tier 1 or 2 interventions would provide adequate support, Tier 3 intervention must be immediately implemented.

Fortunately, teachers infrequently encounter students with these types of serious behavior problems. More often, students engage in less serious, yet persistent, behavior problems. For instance, Spaulding et al. (2010) examined office disciplinary referrals (ODR) from 1,510 schools nationwide. In their comprehensive study, the majority of students in elementary school received ODRs for fighting (32.4%), followed closely by defiance (29%). However, by the time students reached middle school, they were most frequently sent to the office for defiance (31%), followed by disruption (18%). Among high school students, ODRs occurred most frequently for defiance (24.2%) and tardiness (24%), followed by truancy (21.3%). In fact, violations across all grade levels for weapons, arson, bomb threats, drugs, or alcohol each represented less than 1% of ODRs. These data suggest that, in general, teachers most frequently encounter student defiance rather than more serious school violations that would indicate an immediate need for Tier 3 intervention.

Determining the need for and appropriateness of a Tier 3 intervention involves answering a series of questions that will help determine whether a more intensive intervention is required (Figure 7.1). The first question to be asked is, "Is problem behavior pervasive among many students in my classroom?" This question is important for two reasons. First, if several students in a classroom are exhibiting ongoing problem behaviors, this may indicate that a classwide intervention is the place to start, rather than developing several more intensive interventions for individual students. That is, it is likely that there are classroom structures (e.g., expectations), procedures (e.g., routines), or instructional delivery (e.g., format, pace, engagement) that need to be introduced or tightened up to address the misbehavior of the students. This approach also is aligned with the data indicating that only a small percentage (1%–5%) of students (i.e., one or two in a classroom at most) should need intensive intervention. Second, when an individualized support plan is implemented in a classroom with problem behavior across a number of students, optimal outcomes are unlikely. Specifically, when a student has a history or propensity to engage in problem behaviors, it is difficult

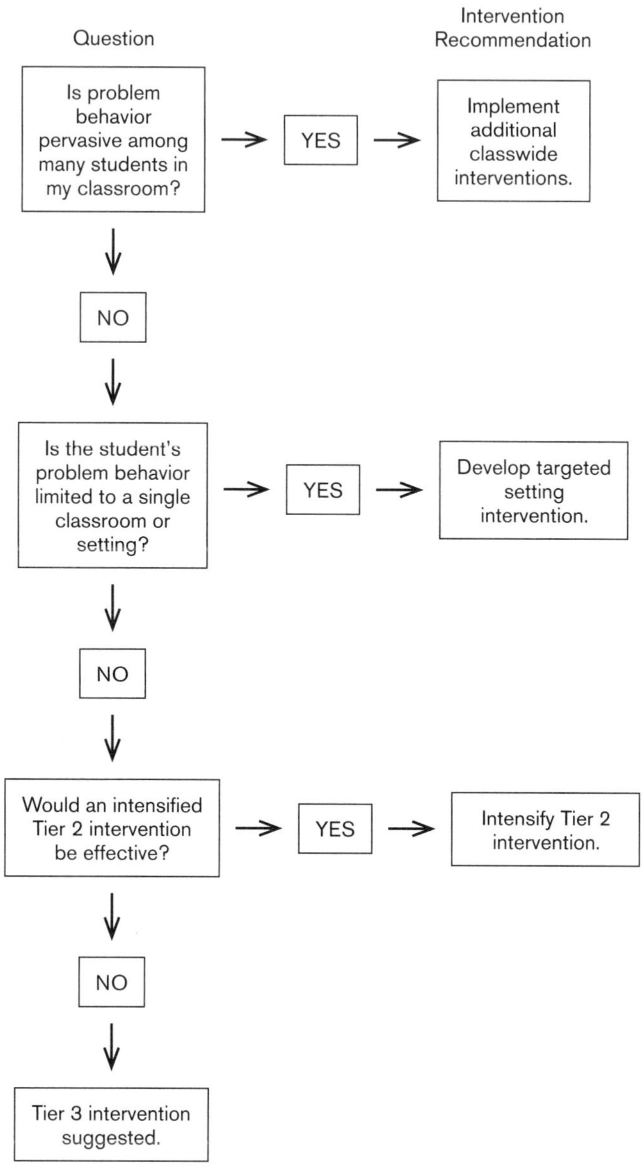

Figure 7.1. Assessing the need for Tier 3 intervention.

to eliminate those problems amid peers with similar problems. Thus, an examination of classwide behavior provides the best launching point.

The following case study illustrates the efficiency of using a classwide intervention to manage the behavior of students in an elementary classroom versus implementing multiple Tier 3 interventions. We were called to assist with the management of an elementary special education classroom for six students with emotional and behavioral disorders. The teacher reported that the students were consistently unable to stay on task and complete their lessons. They engaged in acting-out behaviors, including getting out of their seats, calling out, cursing, and physical aggression. Given the extended duration of the behavior problems, the teacher was experiencing anxiety and personal frustration (and sleepless nights) and was questioning her ability to handle the job.

In an effort to support the teacher, additional resources had been expended for the classroom, including increased supervisory support, funds for rewards, and additional aide support, bringing the ratio of adults to students to 1:1. Despite these efforts and expenditures, the level of serious behavior remained unabated, as evidenced by a high rate of acting out and aggressive behavior resulting in physical restraints (88) and episodes of seclusion time-out (210) within the first 66 days of school.

At this point, our team was asked to assess the classroom environment and develop supports that would benefit all students in the class. Our first step was to examine the classroom environment (see Chapter 3) using direct observation and brief interviews with the staff. In addition, we reviewed the students' disciplinary records; in this case, the frequency of serious problem behaviors that resulted in incidents of physical restraints and seclusion time-outs across the day. Regarding the latter, we tallied the instances of restraint and seclusion by each subject (and time) period on the classroom schedule, noting when and under what conditions the incidents took place. This allowed us to identify periods of the day that were most problematic. Furthermore, our observations and interviews allowed us to identify specific general components (classroom routines and procedures) in need of improvement. As a result of our data collection, three classwide components were identified for modification: 1) modifying the classroom behavior management system (including the point sheet), 2) simplifying the schedule, and 3) strengthening instructional routines, including actively teaching classroom expectations and acknowledging students positively when they follow the expectations.

As a first step, we changed the point sheet. Although the classroom already used a point sheet, nonacademic periods were excluded from the rating system, and students were evaluated using a 0 or 1 scale. In addition, each student's point sheet contained different goals and expectations, which made it difficult for the teacher and aides to evaluate students consistently. We recommended changing the point sheet in three ways. First, we included additional periods for evaluation on the point sheet so that students were monitored and evaluated at all times throughout the day. Second, rather than list individual student goals on the point sheet (which resulted in variation across students), we created five classroom goals on every child's point sheet matching the five schoolwide expectations. We hypothesized that having the same goals across all students promoted the use of common language among all classroom staff. A teacher's verbal intervention with one student would prompt other students as well. For example, when the teacher prompts one student to "follow directions the first time," other students are cued too because they share the same goal. Third, we changed the student rating on the point sheet from a two-point rating to a three-point rating from 0 to 2, with 0 = Did not meet expectations, 1 = Close to expectations, and 2 = Met expectations. This change removed the effect of all-or-none evaluation, allowing for a middle rating of 1, which gave students some hope for earning points even if they failed to follow the expectations perfectly during the period.

Second, we changed the classroom schedule. Noting that most problem behaviors occurred just after morning recess (beginning of language arts class) and immediately after lunch recess (beginning of math class), we inserted a short 5-minute break after the morning recess and included a small snack and a brief 10-minute "quiet time" break after lunch recess during which the teacher read a story. In addition, we divided the longer 60-minute academic periods in language arts and math into two shorter periods so that students could earn points after each shorter period, allowing them time to stretch and change activities between the sessions. Finally, we reordered the class schedule using the Premack principle (Rabian, 2005), which suggests that people are more likely to perform an activity if they know it will be followed by a more desirable activity. For example, a schedule can be arranged so that a challenging subject such as language arts or math is followed by easier preferred subjects such as read-aloud, social skills, art, or science activities.

As a final change, we addressed classroom instructional routines. All staff were taught to do three important things. First, they should review the classroom expectations before each period, specifically instructing students how to succeed during the period, even during less structured periods such as opening, recess, and lunch. Next, they should evaluate student performance privately and individually at the end of each class using the point sheet, telling each child how well he or she met the classroom expectations and providing feedback on ways to improve his or her performance (if needed) in the following period. Finally, they should minimize attention to low-level misbehaviors during class and focus instead on acknowledging students for the positive and appropriate behaviors they showed within the class period.

One final change was suggested regarding instructional procedures. We asked the teacher to write the schedule of class activities on the blackboard, allowing students to see the sequence of events to occur during the lesson. We surmised that this technique would enable students to anticipate a preferred lesson format, if the present one was not preferred, and prevent them from attempting to escape the present activity. In addition, the teacher was encouraged to change from a passive, worksheet-dominated teaching format to an active and participatory format so as to increase students' interest and engagement.

As the teacher implemented these changes, within a relatively brief period of time, student behavior began to improve. Within the first 30 days of the classwide intervention, serious problem behavior resulting in the need for physical restraint dropped from an average of 1.29 restraints per day to

0.29 per day. Episodes of seclusion time-out decreased from an average of 3.18 per day to 0.93 per day. During the last 22 days of school, there were no restraints or episodes of seclusion time-out recorded. As important, within 7 weeks of the classwide intervention, the four instructional aides were deemed unnecessary and removed from the classroom, saving significant fiscal resources for the school. This case study highlights the efficiency and effectiveness of classroom interventions.

A second question to consider when determining the need for Tier 3 intervention is, "Is the student's problem behavior limited to a single classroom or setting?" When a student has serious and intransigent behavior problems, those problems generally are seen across settings. For example, Marika has difficulty with anger management and exhibits problem behavior in multiple situations and settings (e.g., when provoked by a peer, when unable to complete a challenging task, when she realizes she has forgotten an assignment). Similarly, it is hypothesized that Jessie's behavioral symptoms (e.g., uncommunicative, incomplete work, general withdrawal from school) stem from underlying depression and can usually be seen throughout the school day. Marika's and Jessie's behaviors across multiple settings suggest substantial problems that usually warrant Tier 3 intervention.

On the other hand, when behavior problems are limited to a single class or situation, it is likely that an intervention can be identified and developed that targets the isolated issue. For instance, Ranger is constantly tardy to biology class and receives ODRs once or twice a week. His gym teacher noted that he is the last one to leave the gym class, which is scheduled just before biology class, and appears stressed while attempting to organize his belongings. Ranger's lack of organization is one of his behavioral symptoms of Attention Deficit Hyperactivity Disorder (ADHD). To address this isolated problem, a plan was developed to excuse him a few minutes early from gym, allowing extra time for him to shower, change clothing, organize his belongings, and get to class on time. As illustrated in Ranger's situation, brief interviews and a quick review of ODRs can serve as a starting point for assessing whether behavior problems are localized to one setting or manifested across settings and determining whether a Tier 3 intervention is required.

A third question to ask when evaluating the need for Tier 3 intervention is, "Would an intensified Tier 2 intervention be effective?" If Tier 2 interventions can be modified so that they offer a different type or more intensive support, the need for a Tier 3 intervention is obviated. We describe the specific procedures for intensifying interventions later in this chapter, in the section titled Intensifying Tier 2 Interventions.

Tier 3 interventions are expensive in terms of time, effort, and resources, and sometimes just are not necessary. Educators are wise to give careful thought before rushing to develop complex and costly interventions. Answering the three questions posed in this section will help determine the appropriateness of moving to a Tier 3 intervention. If the answer to each of the three questions is "No," then it is likely that Tier 3 intervention is needed.

RULING OUT COMMON CAUSES OF BEHAVIORAL PROBLEMS

Prior to implementing Tier 3 intervention, there are a few common problems frequently associated with problem behavior that should be considered. Because there are often ready solutions to these problems, a comprehensive functional assessment-based intervention (i.e., Tier 3) may not be necessary. In Chapters 4, 5, and 6, we described numerous strategies that address behavioral, instructional, and social concerns. Although we will not reiterate the strategies in this chapter, we will revisit and highlight important considerations teachers can take into account to rule out the more common causes of behavior problems prior to embarking on Tier 3 intervention.

The first common cause of behavior problems is a mismatch between student skill level and assigned work. The school day is comprised of a large number of academic demands. Pressure imposed by federal legislation (commonly known as the No Child Left Behind Act of 2001 [PL 107-110]) to meet state academic standards and improve student performance on standardized tests has left many children behind. Teachers feel compelled to move briskly through the curriculum in order to cover the breadth of content that will appear on the state tests, leaving little time for reteaching or for creating meaningful curricular modifications and adaptations for students who might benefit from them. As a result, students who have not mastered basic or prerequisite skills fall further and further behind (Gilbertson, Duhon, Witt, & Durfene, 2008).

The gap between a student's academic skills and the expectations of a prescribed curriculum is problematic. That is, problem behaviors often arise when students are asked to complete material that exceeds their skill level or, in the case of some students, when they are asked to complete material they perceive as exceeding their skill level (i.e., they may have the skills to succeed but lack the confidence to move forward). To address this problem, some schools have begun to implement Tier 2 academic interventions that provide focused skill practice, reducing the need for Tier 3 intervention. Thus, it is time-efficient to examine the match between student skill and academic requirements and identify available supports before initiating a Tier 3 intervention. After all, the increased academic supports would likely be part of a Tier 3 comprehensive support plan eventually.

A second common cause of behavior problems is insufficient adult support. Students need and benefit greatly from adult guidance throughout their school years, from early childhood through adolescence. However, home circumstances prevent many students from receiving sufficient support and guidance (e.g., a single parent working two jobs, parents with mental health challenges). As we describe in Chapter 11, mentoring programs allow students to connect with an adult at school who provides guidance and can assist in identifying additional supports that may benefit the student. A great deal of research has shown a number of positive outcomes from mentoring programs (e.g., DuBois, Holloway, Valentine, & Cooper, 2002; McQuillin, Terry, Strait, & Smith, 2013). We recommend that every school establish a mentoring program and use it as a preventive approach before serious problem behaviors occur. In addition, students who are not responsive to Tier 2 intervention may benefit from mentoring. Additional information about mentoring and related programs can be found in Chapter 11.

A third common cause of behavior problems is student social skill deficits. There is much evidence that school-age students would benefit from additional social skill instruction. For example, as we earlier noted, research has shown that fighting with peers is the most common reason that elementary-age students receive ODRs (Spaulding et al., 2010). Although fighting becomes less frequent as children age and learn to control their impulses during problematic peer-to-peer interactions, social skill difficulties remain a problem in schools. This can be seen in many forms of problematic interactions plaguing schools, such as bullying and relational aggression (Young, Boye, & Nelson, 2006). In our work with high school students via a large-scale study through the Center for Adolescent Research in the Schools (CARS), we conducted a development phase to identify interventions that would benefit secondary students with social, emotional, and behavioral problems. Staff in all participating schools (approximately 20) reported that social interaction skills were a fundamental deficit and recommended that all students receive intervention in this area (Kern et al., 2015). We suggest that teachers consider whether students would benefit from strategies to improve social interactions prior to considering Tier 3 intervention. In Chapter 6, we describe a number of approaches that can be used at school or embedded into classroom routines to address this important issue. By generating broad solutions to common behavior problems in schools, the time and effort of developing assessment-based (Tier 3) interventions can be reduced, and many more students will benefit from interventions that are less intensive to implement.

INTENSIFYING TIER 2 INTERVENTIONS

In Chapter 2, we described the most common Tier 2 interventions associated with SWPBS. In recent years, educators have begun to explore ways to modify standard Tier 2 interventions to achieve better student outcomes. This approach has been referred to as an "adapted intervention framework" (e.g., Wehby & Kern, 2014). Using this approach, adaptations can be made to interventions either before they are implemented (based on previous knowledge of a student's needs) or after they are implemented (based on student responsiveness to an intervention) (Kern & Wehby, 2014).

The idea of adapting effective interventions has been used with success in other fields. In drug treatment, for example, because of the varied response to treatment programs, adaptations have been made to improve the outcomes of individuals with addiction problems. To illustrate, Marlowe et al. (2008) applied an adaptive algorithm with participants required to appear in a misdemeanor drug court. Adaptations were made to both the frequency of court hearings and the number of case management sessions they received based on a prespecified criterion that was linked to each participant's performance (e.g., history of drug use, frequency of relapses). The adaptations allowed intervention to be quickly delivered for lapses before they developed into serious problems. Participants in the adaptive framework had greater improvements in drug abstinence compared with participants who received typical drug court intervention without adaptations.

In recent years, a few studies have illustrated how adaptations can be made to Tier 2 interventions to increase their effectiveness. Check In Check Out (CICO), as we mentioned in Chapter 2, is the most commonly used Tier 2 intervention (e.g., Mitchell, Stormont, & Gage, 2011). Swoszowski, McDaniel, Jolivette, and Melius (2013) implemented CICO with four students, ages 7–9, who exhibited behavior problems. The standard CICO protocol was implemented in which students 1) "checked in" with a staff member at the start of each school day and were provided a CICO point sheet, 2) received feedback and scores for behavior on their point sheet at the end of each class period, 3) "checked out" with a staff member at the end of the school day to review their behavior ratings, 4) brought their point sheets home after school (in this case, to a residential setting), and 5) returned their signed point sheet to school staff the following day. Three of the four students responded well to the intervention, demonstrating reductions in off-task behavior. The fourth student, however, did not respond to the intervention. Thus, an adaptation was made in which a midday "check-in" was added. The additional check-in improved the intervention effects, resulting in reductions in off-task behavior. This study illustrated that increasing the intensity of an intervention can be an effective adaptation approach.

There is also evidence suggesting that consideration of behavioral function may help to determine whether an intervention is likely to be effective. That is, an effective adaptation may involve selecting an intervention that is well matched to the function a behavior serves (e.g., Campbell & Anderson, 2008; March & Horner, 2002). As we describe in Chapter 8, problem behavior almost always serves a purpose, which is to obtain something desirable (e.g., peer or adult attention, a preferred item or activity) or to escape or avoid something undesirable (e.g., a task, a person). A comprehensive FBA is recommended for students who require Tier 3 intervention (see Chapter 8). For students with behavior problems that are less complex and serious, function can sometimes be presumed using less intensive procedures, such as a teacher interview. McIntosh, Campbell, Carter, and Dickey (2009) used a simple interview method to identify behavioral function of 34 students in grades 1–5 receiving the Tier 2 intervention CICO. Teachers were administered the Functional Assessment Checklist for Teachers and Staff (FACTS; March et al., 1999), a semistructured interview designed to generate a hypothesized function of problem behavior. Subsequently, they examined the effectiveness of CICO in relation to behavioral function. They found that students who engaged in problem behavior to gain attention responded significantly better to CICO than students who engaged in problem behavior that served an escape function. This makes intuitive sense because CICO provides students with attention during morning and afternoon check-ins, at the end of each class period when teachers provide students feedback on their behavior, and at home when a parent or care provider reviews their daily performance. As the study illustrated, a simple and quick interview can help providers identify interventions that are likely to be effective, an adaptation made prior to implementing intervention.

Thus, the literature on adapted interventions suggests that at least two factors have emerging research support and might be considered either prior to implementing a Tier 2 intervention or when a student fails to respond to Tier 2. One is to adapt the intensity of the intervention based on either student characteristics or responsiveness to the standard Tier 2 protocol. For instance, students with high-frequency or persistent problem behaviors may benefit from a more intensive intervention. The frequency of check-ins when using CICO or the frequency of social skills instruction can easily be adjusted. Intervention intensity also can be increased in other ways, such as providing periodic in-vivo prompts to engage in appropriate social skills or providing more frequent social skills sessions.

The second factor to be considered for adapting Tier 2 interventions relates to behavioral function. Specifically, interventions can be designed that match the hypothesized behavior function. For example, increasing the attention a student receives (CICO, mentoring) may be best matched to students with problem behavior that serves an attention function, while other interventions (Tier 2 academic interventions such as skill practice) may be better suited for students with an escape function.

Although few adaptations have been described in the literature, the options are innumerable. One adaptation is modifying or intensifying the type or amount of reinforcement that is provided to a student. For example, periodic free time might be provided throughout the day, rather than solely at the end of the day, for meeting preestablished behavior goals. Tangible reinforcement can be modified so that reinforcers better match a student's personal preference or the amount of reinforcement a student receives can be increased.

To date, a limitation in the adaptive intervention framework literature is that specific procedures to determine when and how adaptations should be made have not been clearly articulated. Nonetheless, the literature provides some guidance about the likelihood that common interventions will be effective (e.g., CICO) based on function as well as how to make adaptations. This guidance, coupled with the fact that teachers and school-based practitioners often have excellent clinical judgment regarding an intervention's promise for a particular student, is bound to help determine when and what type of adaptation will be useful.

IDENTIFYING AVAILABLE RESOURCES

Because students who are nonresponsive to Tier 2 intervention usually have multiple and complex needs, intervention also must be comprehensive and multicomponent (see Chapter 8). In addition, interventions based on individual student needs vary tremendously. A withdrawn student with depression requires a very different intervention than a student with problem behaviors related to academic skill deficits. Thus, an array of intervention options must be available to students, preferably in the school setting but also accessible in the community if school resources are limited.

Evidence-based interventions that address most of the difficulties students experience can be provided by school-based practitioners and do not require specialized expertise. For example, cognitive behavioral therapy, the most effective intervention for depression, can be provided by a school psychologist, counselor, or even a teacher with sufficient training or support (e.g., Hilt-Panahon, Kern, & Divatia, 2007). Similarly, school-based practitioners routinely provide instruction in social skills. Sometimes, however, resources are not available to provide an intervention. A student may have needs (e.g., experiencing an eating disorder) that exceed the expertise of school staff and require a specialized provider. A useful process to evaluate resource availability and needs in both the school and community is resource mapping (Adelman & Taylor, 2006).

The process of resource mapping can take many forms (e.g., asset mapping, environmental scanning) and has long been used to identify supports available in the community to ensure resources are aligned with policies. However, the process is not typically used in a systematic way in school settings. As a result, resources are frequently misused or underused, particularly in middle and high schools (e.g., Kern et al., 2015). Further, resources available in the school and community are usually not well coordinated, making access to services difficult and inefficient for families. In this section, we provide information about how resource mapping can be implemented in the school setting and recommend extending the process to the community so that the full complement of resources available to students and families can be identified and future goals can be established relevant to both the school and community.

The purpose of resource mapping is to 1) understand the full scope of existing resources, 2) ensure resources are available and deployed effectively and efficiently, and 3) identify any gaps in resources that need to be filled. Examples of resources in a school setting include the number of personnel available for counseling or social skills instruction, a variety of curricula for teaching social skills, types of academic support for students who struggle with coursework, and so forth. A primary question is whether current resources can be used differently to help meet a school's goals or whether new resources are needed. Because resource mapping can be a large undertaking, it is best to establish a team to complete the process. We recommend the task of resource mapping be assigned to the schoolwide team.

It is also important to keep in mind that resource mapping should be considered an ongoing process. That is, the process generally begins by determining what resources currently exist in a school and how they can be best coordinated. Over time, the process should evolve so that the purpose is to fill gaps by adding, enhancing, and/or redeploying resources. As this happens, resource maps will be regularly updated. A subgroup of the original team can be identified that is responsible for regular updating.

The steps for resource mapping have been described in various ways (e.g., Adelman & Taylor, 2006). We have combined a number of these steps to describe a comprehensive process, beginning with simple tasks that build over time (Table 7.1). The first step is to establish goals for resource mapping. The goals need to pertain to relevant questions at hand. When mapping services to address the needs of students with social, emotional, and behavioral concerns, the goal might be "to ensure immediate availability and ready access of evidence-based practices for 100% of students and their families with social, emotional, and/or behavioral needs." Establishing a goal will help to guide the resource mapping process.

After the goal has been established, Step 2 is to identify available people and agencies and determine their role or function. This requires listing names of people in a school or from outside agencies who provide behavioral or mental health services to students, and their general function. In addition, community resources should be identified. When starting, it is important to determine 1) the type of information that should be collected, 2) how it will be collected, 3) who is responsible for collecting it, and 4) a timeline for completion. There are many different ways to collect data, and considerations should include the ease of data collection, the team's familiarity with providers, and

Table 7.1. Steps for resource mapping

1. Establish goals.
2. Identify available people and agencies and determine their role or function.
3. Organize and analyze information.
4. Establish future goals.
5. Evaluate resources and related decision making.
6. Develop and implement an action plan.

how well services need to be understood. For example, a team member might want to conduct a personal interview with an agency with whom he or she has never worked. Similarly, a personal phone call may be warranted with individuals or organizations reporting to provide "counseling," as there are many different forms with a range of effectiveness. Some potential methods for obtaining information are questionnaires, surveys, interviews (e.g., telephone, face-to-face), focus groups, and group discussions. During this process, it is also important to keep in mind that much information may already exist and may just need to be verified. Table 7.2 provides an example of a partial resource map.

Table 7.2. Partial resource map for South Side High School

Staff role	Potential social/emotional/ behavioral support	Time spent	Other expertise
School psychologist	• Help to assess student needs • Consult with school staff and families to provide or recommend interventions (early identification of need) • Provide counseling for students and parents • Develop interventions to improve academic, social, and emotional well-being	• As needed • Ongoing • As needed • Ongoing	Trained in cognitive behavioral therapy (CBT)
School counselors (three)	• Provide counseling for students and parents • Oversee scheduling for all students • Assist with college and career counseling • Work with students, staff, families, and members of the community • Provide small-group or individual support	• As needed • Quarterly • Ongoing • Ongoing • Ongoing	Dr. Tucker trained in schoolwide positive behavior support
Transition coordinator	• Assist with college and career counseling • Connect staff and families with outside services	• Ongoing • Ongoing	
Social worker	• Provide peer mediation • Help to identify at-risk students • Assist families with community referrals • Provide crisis intervention	• As needed • Ongoing • As needed • As needed	
Behavior specialist	• Chair student assistance program (SAP) • Assist with schoolwide positive behavior support implementation • Provide information on accessing community services	• As needed • Ongoing • Ongoing	Expertise in functional behavioral assessment
Satellite social worker	• Conduct evaluations • Provide small-group or individual counseling • Assist families with referrals or refer families for additional services	• As needed • As needed • As needed	

The third step is to organize and analyze information. This involves specifying programs, activities, and services that exist within and outside of the school in a useful way. The initial list developed in Step 2 can be sorted into meaningful categories. One way to sort is to align with the tiered support provided within the SWPBS framework. Table 7.3 offers an example of a partial list sorted in this way. After this process has been completed, overlaps, gaps, and needs can be identified with respect to the school's goal.

Step 4 is to establish future goals. During this step, the team assesses the current status of resources and determines goals for the future. Table 7.4 shows an example of a partial analysis to identify overlaps, gaps, and resulting future goals based on the information gathered.

Table 7.3. Example of resource mapping Step 3: Categories of programs, activities, and services in a school

CURENT PROGRAMS, ACTIVITIES, AND RESOURCES

SCHOOL: Emerson Middle School
DATE: September 19, 2015

Category	Programs, activities, services	Time allocated	Future goals
Tier 1	• Schoolwide Tiger Bucks • Peer buddies • Cross-age tutoring • Welcoming committee • Service learning • School jobs • Drug and alcohol prevention • School clubs • Counseling drop-in	• Embedded in day • 30 minutes/week • 30 minutes daily, after school • 30 minutes/month, as needed • Embedded in academics • N/A • 1 hour quarterly • 30 minutes weekly • 4 hours daily	1. Determine reasons for counseling drop-ins and implement preventive programs.
Tier 2	• Social skills groups • Check In Check Out • Academic skills groups • Individual counseling	• 30 minutes, 3 times per week • 20 minutes daily • 30 minutes, 3 times per week • 2 hours daily	1. Add academic skill groups. 2. Intensify Tier 2 programs. 3. Decrease individual counseling and replace with cognitive behavioral therapy (CBT) and problem-focused groups.
Tier 3	• Individual support plans • Check & Connect • CBT groups • Wraparound		1. Develop strategies to increase family engagement. 2. Increase number of CBT groups and make available to all students.
Parent engagement and support	• Parent newsletter • Parenting workshops • School garden • PTA • Social worker contact		1. Identify ways to increase number of parents involved.

Table 7.4. Partial analysis of resources at Emerson High School

Emerson High School
Resource Mapping

GOAL: To ensure immediate availability and ready access of evidence-based practices for 100% of students and their families with social, emotional, and/or behavioral needs

Overlaps	Gaps	Future goals
Multiple school staff conducting individual counseling and crisis management	Lack of preventive strategies; services conflict with student schedules	Increase number of social skills and cognitive behavioral therapy (CBT) groups; make groups available before and after school; increase flexible schedules.
Many skilled staff working on scheduling	Insufficient skilled resources to provide mental health services	Identify other individuals (e.g., school volunteers) to complete scheduling, allowing staff with mental health training to provide mental health services.
Resources not deployed adequately	All Tier 3 resources are devoted to students with disabilities; few resources are available for Tier 3 students who do not have a disability.	Expand Tier 3 to include all students; identify screening procedure to better identify nondisabled Tier 3 students.
Lack of coordination with community resources	Community services are not readily accessible to students and families.	Provide after-school bus service to Schilling Community Health Center and other providers.

The fifth step is to evaluate resources and related decision making. After there is consensus about future goals, the available resources must be examined as well as the process for decision making. This involves translating existing efforts, as well as needs, into dollar expenditures and/or time commitments onto a spreadsheet. We often find that resources in a school are used inefficiently or there are overlaps in resources and that resources can be reallocated without additional expense. The decision-making process related to resources also needs to be understood. That is, the team needs to be clear about who determines whether programs will be established, maintained, or discontinued. Also, it is important to understand who makes decisions about allocating resources. This process will entail reviewing policies to ascertain the use of resources both inside and outside of the school. Through this process, it may be evident that policy changes are needed to accomplish consensual goals. In addition, this information is critical for developing an action plan.

Step 6 is to develop and implement an action plan. Table 7.5 shows an example of a partial action plan based on the information gathered about South Side High School. The action plan is based on broad and specific goals. After an action plan is developed, it is critical to communicate the contents of that plan to the school staff and other relevant stakeholders (e.g., community service providers, community members). The final action plan should delineate the action or task to be completed, who is responsible for

Table 7.5. Example of partial action plan for South Side High School

Action	Person responsible	Target date for completion	Timeline for review
Determine how staff schedules can be rearranged to provide before- and after-school groups.	Mrs. Lu	November 1	Monthly
Initiate more groups in place of individual counseling and crisis management.	Mrs. Lu	First group November 1; gradually increase across school year	Monthly
Increase flexible schedules.	Mr. Thomas	Next year	Fall
Identify alternative personnel to do scheduling to free time of school counselors so they can provide mental health services.	Mr. Daniels	December 15	January (spring schedule)

carrying out the task or action, the timeline or deadline for completing the action, and the timeline for periodically reviewing the progress.

It is important to note that resource mapping should not focus exclusively on the people, programs, and resources in the school, or on programs paid for by the school or district, but should also include people and programs working collaboratively with the school, such as community mental health clinicians (Weist, 1997; Weist, Lever, Bradshaw, & Owens, 2014) as well as relevant community programs and resources. In this regard, an evolving resource guide of available community programs or resources can be invaluable to school staff in assisting students and families in making connections to these programs or resources, and can also help the school to avoid duplicating work that has been already done.

SUMMARY

Because intervention at Tier 3 is labor- and time-intensive, it is worthwhile to evaluate whether it is truly needed. In this chapter, we reviewed broad considerations to guide teachers in determining the need for Tier 3, including the pervasiveness of problem behaviors in a classroom, where and when a student's problem behaviors occur, and whether a variation of Tier 2 intervention might offer sufficient support. We also reviewed common causes of problem behavior (e.g., work difficulty, lack of adult support, social skills deficits) that should be considered and are more easily addressed in Tier 2 rather than implementing Tier 3 intervention.

In addition, prior to jumping into Tier 3 intervention, an emerging strategy is to intensify Tier 2 intervention. Although the specific ways that Tier 2 intervention can be intensified to address a student's needs are not yet clearly delineated, examples are beginning to appear in the body of literature that provide guidance for practitioners.

Finally, we described a process of resource mapping to identify available resources and how they are being used within and outside of school settings. We have found that resources within schools and through collaborating community programs are not well utilized. Often, responsive strategies are put into place when students are experiencing a significant problem (e.g., crisis management, drop-in counseling), but few resources are allocated to preventing those problems (e.g., social skills groups, cognitive behavior therapy to prevent depression or anxiety). Also, we have found that schools provide many services that are not evidence-based, and students fail to improve. Thus, we strongly encourage resource mapping as a starting point to evaluating how the social, emotional, and behavioral needs of all students can be met.

Self-Reflection

1. Describe a student in your school (or develop a hypothetical example) who needs intensive Tier 3 behavior support. What specific behaviors indicated the need for Tier 3 intervention?
2. What Tier 2 interventions are in place in the school where you work or have visited? Describe ways in which they could be intensified.
3. How easy is it to identify the full scope of available resources for students with social, emotional, or behavioral problems in the school where you work or have visited?
4. Describe how you could go about resource mapping in the school where you work or have visited.
5. How easy is it to identify the full scope of available community resources for students with social, emotional, or behavioral problems?
6. Describe how you could go about resource mapping in your community.

REFERENCES

Adelman, H., & Taylor, L. (2006). Mapping a school's resources to improve their use in preventing and ameliorating problems. In C. Franklin, M.B. Harris, & P. Allen-Meares (Eds.), *The school services sourcebook: A guide for social workers, counselors, and mental health professionals* (pp. 977–990). New York, NY: Oxford University Press.

Barrett, S., Eber, L., & Weist, M.D. (2013). *Advancing education effectiveness: An interconnected systems framework for positive behavioral interventions and supports (PBIS) and school mental health.* Center for Positive Behavioral Interventions and Supports (funded by the Office of Special Education Programs, U.S. Department of Education). Eugene: University of Oregon Press.

Campbell, A., &, Anderson, C. (2008). Enhancing effects of targeted interventions with function-based support. *Behavioral Disorders, 33*(4), 233–245.

DuBois, D.L., Holloway, B.E., Valentine, J.C., & Cooper, H. (2002). Effectiveness of mentoring programs for youth: A meta-analytic review. *Journal of Community Psychology, 30*(2), 157–197.

Gilbertson, D., Duhon, G., Witt, J.C., & Durfene, B. (2008). Effects of academic response rates on time-on-task in the classroom for students at academic and behavioral risk. *Education and Treatment of Children, 31,* 153–165.

Hilt-Panahon, A., Kern, L., & Divatia, A. (2007). School-based interventions for students with or at-risk for depression: A review of the literature. *Advances in School Based Mental Health Promotion, 1,* 32–41.

Horner, R.H., Sugai, G., & Anderson, C.M. (2010). Examining the evidence base for school-wide positive behavior support. *Focus on Exceptional Children, 42*(8), 1–14.

Kern, L., Evans, S.W., Lewis, T.J., State, T.M., Weist, M.D., & Wills, H.P. (2015, April 9). CARS comprehensive intervention for secondary students with emotional and behavioral problems: Conceptualization and development. *Journal of Emotional and Behavioral Disorders.* Advance online publication. doi: 10.1177/1063426615578173

Kern, L., & Wehby, J. (2014). Using data-based individualization to intensify behavioral interventions: Implementation example. *Teaching Exceptional Children, 46,* 45–53.

March, R.E., & Horner, R.H. (2002). Feasibility of contributions of functional behavioral assessment in schools. *Journal of Emotional and Behavioral Disorders, 10,* 158–171.

March, R.E., Horner, R.H., Lewis-Palmer, T., Brown, D., Crone, D.A., & Todd, A.W. (1999). *Functional assessment for teachers and staff (FACTS).* Eugene, OR: Author.

Marlowe, D.B., Festinger, D.S., Arabia, P.L., Dugosh, K.L., Benasutti, K.M., Croft, J.R., & McKay, J.R. (2008). Adaptive interventions in drug court: A pilot experiment. *Criminal Justice Review, 33*(3), 343–360.

McIntosh, K., Campbell, A.L., Carter, D.R., & Dickey, C.R. (2009). Differential effects of a tier two behavior intervention based on function of problem behavior. *Journal of Positive Behavior Interventions, 11,* 82–93.

McQuillin, S.D., Terry, J.D., Strait, G.G., & Smith, B.H. (2013). Innovation in school-based mentoring: Matching the context, structure and goals of mentoring with evidence-based practices. *Advances in School Mental Health Promotion, 6*(4), 280–294. doi:10.1080/1754730X.2013.832009

Mitchell, B.S., Stormont, M., & Gage, N.A. (2011). Tier two interventions implemented within the context of a tiered prevention framework. *Behavioral Disorders, 36*(4), 241–261.

No Child Left Behind Act of 2001, PL 107-110, 115 Stat. 1425, 20 U.S.C. §§ 6301 *et seq.*

Rabian, B. (2005). Premack principle. In M. Hersen, J. Rosqvist, A. Gross, R. Drabman, G. Sugai, & R. Horner (Eds.), *Encyclopedia of behavior modification and cognitive behavior therapy: Volume 1: Adult clinical applications volume 2: Child clinical applications volume 3: Educational applications.* (Vol. 2, pp. 967–969). Thousand Oaks, CA: SAGE Publications. doi: http://dx.doi.org/10.4135/9781412950534.n2094

Spaulding, S.A., Irvin, L.K., Horner, R.H., May, S.L., Emeldi, M., Tobin, T.J., & Sugai, G. (2010). Schoolwide social-behavioral climate, student problem behavior, and related administrative decisions empirical patterns from 1,510 schools nationwide. *Journal of Positive Behavior Interventions, 12*(2), 69–85.

Swoszowski, N.C., McDaniel, S.C., Jolivette, K., & Melius, P. (2013). The effects of Tier II Check-in/Check-out including adaptation for non-responders on the off-task behavior of elementary students in a residential setting. *Education and Treatment of Children, 36*(3), 63–79.

Wehby, J., & Kern, L. (2014). Intensive behavior intervention: What is it, what is its evidence base, and why do we need to implement now? *Teaching Exceptional Children, 46,* 38–44.

Weist, M.D. (1997). Expanded school mental health services: A national movement in progress. In T.H. Ollendick & R.J. Prinz (Eds.), *Advances in clinical child psychology* (Vol. 19, pp. 319–352). New York, NY: Plenum Press.

Weist, M.D., Lever, N., Bradshaw, C., & Owens, J. (2014). *Handbook of school mental health: Research, training, practice, and policy* (2nd ed.). New York, NY: Springer.

Young, E.L., Boye, A., & Nelson, D. (2006). Relational aggression: Understanding, identifying, and responding in schools. *Psychology in the Schools, 43,* 297–312.

8

Conducting a Functional Behavioral Assessment

In Chapter 1, we introduced the concept of tiered support. As we discussed, implementation of tiered interventions will reduce the need for an intensive Tier 3 intervention. Some students, however, engage in significant and intensive behavior problems that put them at significant risk of harming themselves or others and/or are likely to interrupt their learning or the learning of others. In these situations, Tier 3 intervention should be immediately considered. In addition, students who do not respond sufficiently to Tier 1 or 2 interventions will need an intensive, individualized, assessment-based intervention offered at Tier 3.

In this chapter, we describe the process of FBA. Because it is time-consuming to complete an FBA and develop a related intervention plan, it is not a feasible approach to apply to more than a small percentage of the school population. However, for students who need Tier 3 intervention, FBA-based interventions hold many advantages over interventions that are not assessment-based. In this chapter, we offer a rationale for conducting an FBA. We then describe a step-by-step approach for completing an FBA.

THE PURPOSE OF A FUNCTIONAL BEHAVIORAL ASSESSMENT

When a student has not responded satisfactorily to interventions implemented at Tiers 1 and 2 or when behavior problems are severe from the start, an individualized support plan is needed. Usually, these students have complex needs that cannot be supported through more generic types of interventions. Aidan, a 12-year-old, is an example of a student with complex needs who requires intensive intervention. Risk factors contributing to Aidan's difficulties include a single parent who works two jobs, requiring that Aidan is alone unsupervised after school, a family history of depression, and intelligence in the low average range. In addition, Aidan has difficulties with sustained attention, putting him behind academically. Finally, he has a long history of significant problem behaviors in the classroom that have resulted in both in-school and out-of-school suspensions. Not only have these suspensions caused him to fall further behind academically, but he also has learned that he can avoid or escape work that he abhors by causing problems in the classroom.

For students like Aidan, an individualized and intensive support plan is greatly beneficial for several reasons. First, an FBA can identify specific variables in the environment that contribute to problem behavior. In Aidan's case, the FBA will help his teachers determine what activities and events are associated with problem behavior that might be modified or eliminated. In addition, the FBA can identify consequences that follow problem behavior that may reinforce that behavior (i.e., contribute to it continuing). For Aidan, it is likely that suspension is contributing to, rather than decreasing, his problems. Second, an FBA also determines skills that a student needs to be successful in the future. Aidan will undoubtedly need instruction in a number of skills over the long term to ensure that his problem behavior will be eliminated, including intensive academic skill instruction, instruction in self-control strategies when he is feeling frustrated and angry, and instruction in a successful method to solicit help from others when he experiences work that he is unable to complete. Third, an FBA can identify broad supports that may benefit a student. For instance, it may be that Aidan would benefit from a mentor who could monitor his academic and behavioral progress, brainstorm how to address issues that arise, provide ongoing encouragement, and be available should Aidan need an adult in whom to confide. In the next sections, we provide a step-by-step description of how to complete an FBA (see Table 8.1 for an overview).

Table 8.1. Steps for conducting a functional behavioral assessment

Step 1: Build an individualized behavior support team.

Step 2: Identify, prioritize, and define problem behaviors.

Step 3: Conduct a functional behavioral assessment.
- Conduct adult interviews.
- Complete a student interview.
- Complete direct observations.

Step 4: Analyze and summarize the data.
- Display the direct observation data in graphic or tabular format.
- Compare all sources of data for consistency.
- Determine whether team is confident that antecedents and responses have been accurately identified.

Step 5: Formulate hypothesis statements.

Source: Kern, Childs, Dunlap, Clarke, & Falk (1994).

CONDUCTING A FUNCTIONAL BEHAVIORAL ASSESSMENT

There are five steps to complete an FBA. Each step should be conducted in sequential order. The result of the five-step process is hypotheses that link directly to the behavior support plan, described in Chapter 9.

Step 1: Build an Individualized Behavior Support Team

Chapter 2 described the purpose, agenda, and composition of collaborative school teams for implementing SWPBS. A team process also is used when individual support is needed for many of the same reasons, including developing a vision for the student, monitoring the student's data, establishing procedures for completing the FBA and developing the support plan, and supporting one another. Individual student-centered teams often share membership with school-based teams because of members' expertise in the area of behavior support. However, additional or alternative team members may be included if particular expertise is needed to fully support a student or if particular individuals have an interest in participating on the team.

When selecting team membership, parents or other direct care providers should always serve as team members. With respect to additional team members, Thousand and Villa (2000) suggest considering three questions (see Table 8.2). The first is, "Who has the expertise needed to best address the student's specific concerns?" A student might have mental health issues, for example, that would benefit from the expertise of the school counselor. Similarly, academic problems may indicate the need for a reading specialist on the team, or health problems may necessitate including the school nurse. The second question is, "Who will be affected by the team's decisions?" For example, paraprofessionals often implement the support plan, so their input is critical. In addition, the value of including the student himself or herself on the team (particularly older students) has been increasingly understood. Students often contribute important information that cannot be gained from other sources, regarding variables that influence their problem behavior as well as their preferences (Kern, Dunlap, Clarke, & Childs, 1994). In addition, support plans for older students usually consider long-term goals and post-school needs, for which student input is critical. Finally, a third question is, "Who has a vested interest in participating on the team?" For example, a student's mentor might request membership on the team because he or she

Table 8.2. Important questions when identifying individual support team members

- Who has the expertise needed to best address the student's specific concerns?
- Who will be affected by the team's decisions?
- Who has a vested interest in participating on the team?

From Thousand, J.S., & Villa, R.A. (2000). Collaborative teaming: A powerful tool in school restructuring. In R.A. Villa & J.S. Thousand (Eds.), *Restructuring for caring and effective education: Piecing the puzzle together* (2nd ed., p. 259). Baltimore, MD: Paul H. Brookes Publishing Co.; adapted by permission.

has a close relationship with the student and a genuine interest in how the student fares.

After the team is established, a team leader should be identified. This is generally a member with the most expertise in the process (e.g., behavior specialist, SWPBS team leader). The team leader schedules and leads team meetings, organizes and oversees completion of the FBA process, and generally manages the data collected.

Step 2: Identify, Prioritize, and Define Problem Behaviors

After team membership has been determined, the next step is to identify, prioritize, and operationally define "target behaviors" that need intervention. Team members often have different opinions about behaviors they view as problematic. For example, a teacher might find interrupting as highly problematic, while other team members do not consider it a high priority in the scope of an individual's repertoire of problem behavior. Thus, it is important that all team members agree on the behaviors that should be targeted and prioritized for intervention.

When prioritizing problem behaviors for intervention, team members should consider the seriousness of a student's behavior with respect to the harm or damage caused. This means that it is important to intervene with destructive behaviors first, followed by disruptive behaviors (Janney & Snell, 2000). Destructive behaviors include any behavior that could be harmful to the student himself or others. Examples include self-injury (e.g., head banging, cutting, ongoing use of illegal substances), physical aggression, and bringing weapons to school (Bambara, 2005). Disruptive behaviors, while not putting the student or others in immediate danger, generally interfere with ongoing activities, learning, and/or social relationships. Examples of disruptive behaviors include engaging in tantrums, refusing to complete work, threatening others, and destroying property. Distracting behaviors are a third priority. These problem behaviors may cause minor property damage or interfere with social acceptance (e.g., self-stimulatory behavior, scribbling on one's art project). The team may also want to consider addressing "internalizing" behaviors such as depression and anxiety, which are often not destructive, disruptive, or distracting to others, but nonetheless are associated with significant problems in school adjustment and achievement. Figure 8.1 shows questions to guide the process of prioritizing problem behavior.

After target behaviors have been identified, they should be operationally defined. A clear and unambiguous definition facilitates communication among team members and others and allows the behavior to be measured in order to evaluate intervention effectiveness (Miltenberger, 2005). At this point, the operational definition should simply provide an objective description of the behavior and not speculate about cause. Table 8.3 provides examples of operational definitions. As illustrated, the behaviors defined can be observed and measured. Additional description of the components of an operational definition can be found in Chapter 10.

Intervention Priorities

Student: ______________________ Problem behavior: ______________________

First priority: Destructive behaviors

- ❑ Is the behavior harmful or life threatening (e.g., aggression, cutting, self-injury)?

IF NO

Second priority: Disruptive behaviors

Is the behavior

- ❑ Destroying materials (e.g., breaking objects)?
- ❑ Interfering with learning of student or others (e.g., yelling or cursing during class)?
- ❑ Causing problems with social relationships (e.g., threatening others)?
- ❑ Preventing participation in important events or activities (e.g., making inappropriate gestures that result in office referrals)?
- ❑ Likely to become harmful or life threatening?

IF NO

Third priority: Distracting behaviors

Is the behavior

- ❑ Impeding social acceptance (e.g., withdrawing, failing to interact, engaging in self-stimulatory behavior)?
- ❑ Affecting the student's image (e.g., drawing inappropriate pictures on papers)?
- ❑ Causing minor damage to materials (e.g., writing on desk)?
- ❑ Likely to become disruptive?

Figure 8.1. A process for prioritizing problem behavior for intervention purposes. (From Janney, R., & Snell, M.E. [2000]. *Teachers' guides to inclusive practices: Behavioral support.* Baltimore, MD: Paul H. Brookes Publishing Co; adapted by permission.)

Step 3: Conduct a Functional Behavioral Assessment

With the target behaviors identified and operationally defined, team members can then plan to conduct an FBA. The general purpose of an FBA is to collect information about immediate environmental events that may be contributing to the occurrence of problem behavior. In addition, broad information is gathered about past (e.g., trauma, drug use) or present events (e.g., health issues) that may help to fully understand the behavior or suggest additional interventions that are needed.

The information obtained through an FBA helps teams create a plan that relies on a variety of strategies to reduce problem behavior and build adaptive and prosocial skills. Specifically, rather than simply providing a

Table 8.3. Examples of operational definitions

Aggression: Hits, kicks, or attempts to hit or kick another individual
Property destruction: Causes damage to property, such as breaking, tearing, or damaging materials
Inappropriate social interactions: Makes derogatory or demeaning statements to another individual (e.g., calls a peer "stupid," states that a peer cannot read well)

consequence after problem behavior occurs, interventions can be developed that 1) prevent problem behavior from occurring and 2) teach new skills. In addition, team members and school personnel can identify responses that are unlikely to reinforce the problem behavior. This type of individualized and comprehensive intervention plan has a much greater likelihood of reducing problem behavior over the long term than traditional consequence-only plans (e.g., Newcomer & Lewis, 2004). The activities described in the following subsections comprise an FBA.

Conduct Adult Interviews The first activity when beginning an FBA is to conduct interviews. An advantage of interviews is that they take less time than other forms of information gathering (e.g., direct observation). Also, information can be obtained that is not accessible through other methods (e.g., cannot be directly observed). Finally, interviews provide information that assists with the remainder of the FBA, such as identifying when behavior problems are most and least frequent. Such information points to where future observations should occur.

It is important to conduct interviews with each adult who may either have past or present information about the student and his or her problem behavior. To expedite the process, the interview can be completed as part of a team meeting. However, when completed as a group, it is important to consider and record each team member's input and opinion, because the FBA is in the early phase and it is premature to rule out any potential source of information. If the team knows ahead of time that a student engages in several different types of problem behaviors across settings or that team members have different opinions about the student and his or her problem behavior, another option is to have each team member independently complete the interview, then collectively discuss each person's responses at the team meeting. If the interview is completed during a team meeting, individual interviews should also be conducted with every individual who either could not attend the meeting (e.g., a parent) or is not a team member. The functional assessment interview (Figure 8.2) contains the most critical information that should be considered when conducting the FBA and developing the individualized support plan.

Section A of the functional assessment interview identifies the student's strengths, which may be incorporated into a support plan. For example, if Jill has a talent for art or particularly enjoys it, the team may want to make sure that each semester her schedule includes an art class to increase her overall life satisfaction and provide her with a sense of accomplishment. Section B simply reiterates the behaviors that were prioritized as targets for intervention. Section C solicits information about broad concerns that may be directly or indirectly influencing problem behavior and long-term adjustment. Here, consideration of internalizing behaviors is important. These include reactions to common life events such as personal or family member serious illness, parental divorce or the death of family members or

FUNCTIONAL ASSESSMENT INTERVIEW

Student name: ______________________ Grade: _______ Age: _______ Sex: ______

Date of interview: ______________________ Interviewer: ______________________

Respondents: ______________________

STEP 1: IDENTIFY TEAM MEMBERS

______________________ ______________________

______________________ ______________________

______________________ ______________________

STEP 2: CONDUCT A FUNCTIONAL ASSESSMENT INTERVIEW

A. Student profile

List three positive characteristics the student brings to school that can be capitalized on:

1. ______________________
2. ______________________
3. ______________________

B. Target behaviors

Provide an operational definition for each target behavior. The behavior should be described in a way that it can be observed by others and measured.

Example: Aggression consists of hitting others, biting others, and kicking others. Attempts to hit, bite, or kick others are also considered aggression.

1. ______________________
____
2. ______________________
____
3. ______________________
____
4. ______________________
____

C. Broad concerns

Check any issue that may be contributing to behavior problems or should be addressed in a behavior support plan.

- ❑ Student experienced traumatic event (e.g., death, major illness, parent divorce, shooting).
  Explain: ______________________
- ❑ Student has health or physical concerns (e.g., depression, anxiety, allergies, sleep problems, recurring illness).
  Explain: ______________________
- ❑ Student has academic problems.
  - ❑ Reading fluency
  - ❑ Reading comprehension
  - ❑ Math
  - ❑ Writing
  - ❑ Class participation
  - ❑ Organizational skills
  - ❑ Study skills

Source: Dunlap, Kern-Dunlap, Clarke, and Robbins (1991).

Figure 8.2. Functional Assessment Interview.

(continued)

Figure 8.2. *(continued)*

- ❑ Student has social problems.
  - ❑ Difficulties with peers
  - ❑ Difficulties with adults
  - ❑ Problems initiating social interactions
  - ❑ Problems responding to social initiations of others
  - ❑ Misinterprets intentions of others
  - ❑ Difficulties dealing with provocations
- ❑ Student has poor overall quality of life.
  - ❑ Access to few preferred activities
  - ❑ Few or no friends
  - ❑ Lack of positive role models

D. Events associated with problem behavior

Setting events:

What distant events may be associated with the target behaviors (e.g., sleep difficulties, academic problems, medications, allergies, social problems, pain, hunger)?

1. ______________________________
2. ______________________________
3. ______________________________
4. ______________________________
5. ______________________________

Antecedent events:

What immediate event predicts when the behaviors are likely and not likely to occur?

Antecedent	Most likely to occur	Least likely to occur
Time of day		
Setting		
People		
Activity		
Aspect of task (e.g., difficulty)		
Level of attention		
Wants item		
Other		

Responses to problem behavior or maintaining consequences

What immediately follows the problem behavior that may reinforce the continuation of the target behavior (e.g., escape from task or situation, teacher attention, peer attention)?

Check each that occurs:	Indicate rank (most to least frequent)
❑ Gets out of work (e.g., avoids work, gets assistance with work)	________
❑ Gets adult attention	________
❑ Gets peer attention	________
❑ Obtains activity	________
❑ Obtains item	________

Source: Dunlap, Kern-Dunlap, Clarke, and Robbins (1991).

E. Schedule review

List the student's daily schedule and the academic area or activity presented during that time. Rate the probability that the behavior will occur during the indicated time or activity.

Time, period, activity	Typical problem behavior(s) (#1 or #2 from above)	Probability of problem behavior (low, medium, high)	Typical triggering antecedent(s)	Typical maintaining consequence(s)
		L M H		
		L M H		
		L M H		
		L M H		
		L M H		
		L M H		
		L M H		
		L M H		
		L M H		
		L M H		

F. What might work to reduce problem behaviors? What has not worked in the past?

Describe any interventions that have been successful or have not been successful.

____

____

____

____

____

____

____

G. Summary

Complete the chart below by transferring information gathered in parts A, B, C, and D.

Setting events (slow triggers)	Antecedents (fast triggers)	Problem behavior(s)	Responses	Perceived function

Source: Dunlap, Kern-Dunlap, Clarke, and Robbins (1991).

(continued)

Figure 8.2. *(continued)*

Specific hypothesis formation: Use the information above to answer the questions below to develop a specific hypothesis about the function of the behavior.

Given the circumstances when (setting event) ____________________

and ____________________

when (antecedent) ____________________

____________________ *occurs*

the student does (problem behavior) ____________________

____

in order to (function) ____________________

____

To what degree of accuracy do you think you have identified the setting events, antecedents, and function of the problem behavior?

Not Very Confident				*Very Confident*
1	2	3	4	5

Source: Dunlap, Kern-Dunlap, Clarke, and Robbins (1991).

significant others, and the experience of depression and anxiety. In addition, students may experience serious traumatic events, such as being victims of abuse and/or neglect or witnessing or experiencing violence. These events can lead to depression and anxiety and in some cases, more serious reactions such as posttraumatic stress disorder (PTSD), which is discussed in Chapter 12.

Other issues, such as allergies, sleep problems, and recurring illnesses (e.g., asthma, ear infections), may be amenable to intervention or, if not, a support plan can be designed that considers these issues (see Chapter 9). Academic problems also can play a role in student problem behavior, given the reciprocal relationship in these domains (e.g., academic success promotes positive behavior; positive behavior promotes academic success). However, regardless of their association to problem behavior, deficits should be addressed for continued long-term success. An additional issue suggested in section C is social difficulties, which are often related to problem behavior. This is particularly important given the long-term implications of more serious social and behavioral problems, including increased risk of dropout, incarceration, and constrained employment (see Ialongo et al., 1999). It is important to specify the type of difficulty the student is having, because intervention effectiveness is enhanced when specific skills are targeted.

Finally, information should also be obtained on overall quality of life. A poor quality of life, often associated with a student's multiple problems in social, emotional, behavioral, and academic domains, has been implicated as an important variable contributing to problem behavior (Sacks & Kern, 2008). On the other hand, major variables that contribute to a positive quality of life are family nurturance and support, positive relationships with other adults, involvement in enriching activities (e.g., extracurricular, spiritual, sports), positive peer relations, self-regulation skills, and school competencies (O'Connell, Boat, & Warner, 2009; also see Chapter 11 for a discussion on protective factors for children and youth).

Unlike section C, which examines broad variables, section D obtains information about specific events that directly and immediately influence the occurrence of problem behavior. Although such information will be obtained through direct observation, there are several reasons these data should be considered in the interview as well. First, when team members agree that problem behaviors occur only during particular times of the day, during specific activities, or with certain people, times when observations need to occur are greatly narrowed. Another reason this information should be solicited through the interview is that some behaviors are not readily subject to direct observation, and information about the occurrences of these behaviors depends on the knowledge of team members. This is particularly true with older students, who can become adept at hiding problem behavior. For example, a behavior such as cutting, which becomes more frequent in adolescence, may be difficult to directly observe, particularly when the student engages in the behavior privately and keeps the results hidden with clothing. However, a particular team member, such as the student's mother, may have knowledge about when she has observed fresh cuts, scratches, or wounds on her son or daughter, which can provide valuable information for identifying an appropriate intervention. That is, if the student's mother reports that she has frequently observed self-inflicted wounds on her student around test time at the end of each semester, when the student is given excessive amounts of homework, when the student is having difficulty with friends, or during other busy, potentially stressful times, this can provide clues as to when and why the student might feel particularly distressed and anxious.

There are three specific types of information obtained in section D of the interview, each pertaining to events closely related to the problem behavior. These include setting events, antecedent events, and responses. *Setting events* are events that do not directly cause a behavior problem but increase the likelihood that problem behavior will occur. For example, although Alisha finds her morning academic work challenging, she generally will complete it without incident. However, roughly twice a week, she refuses to complete her work and, if prompted by her teacher, Mr. Crandall, to begin working, she begins to have a tantrum. Alisha's mother informed Mr. Crandall that Alisha was having difficulty getting along with her older sister, and sometimes morning fights led to intensive screaming matches. Alisha's mother and Mr. Crandall began to share daily notes about Alisha's fights at home and her work completion at school. These notes helped Mr. Crandall identify fights at home as a setting event for problem behavior at school: specifically, failure to complete morning assignments. As a result, Mr. Crandall incorporated interventions into Alisha's plan that focused on strategies her mother could use at home to eliminate fights. Another intervention in the plan included providing Alisha an activity that was calming and relaxing prior to her academic routine on mornings following a fight. As the example illustrates, the presence of setting events can usually be suspected when problem behaviors occur inconsistently and in the presence of particular antecedents. Other common setting events noted in section D include lack of sufficient sleep, illness, allergies, social problems, pain, and hunger.

In addition to setting events, information also is obtained about antecedents. *Antecedents* are events that immediately precede or trigger the problem behavior. Common antecedents listed in section D are time of day (e.g., morning, just after lunch, end of day), setting (e.g., classroom, gym, hallways, bus, noisy atmosphere, crowded atmosphere), people present (e.g., particular teacher, paraprofessional), activity (e.g., math, reading, independent seatwork, exercise, free time), aspect of the task (e.g., level of difficulty, written assignment), level of attention (e.g., teacher working with other students and attention insufficient), and access to item (e.g., preferred activity or item). Other events should also be noted that the interviewee believes are antecedents to problem behavior, such as a change in the student's typical routine or schedule or a teacher providing corrective feedback on errors.

The third type of specific information that is collected is others' responses to problem behavior. It is important to record responses to problem behavior because events that follow problem behavior generally tend to cause the problem to continue. That is, when a response that follows behavior results in something desirable for the student (i.e., reinforces the behavior), the behavior will continue or be maintained by the response. This cycle may not always be evident, because teachers tend to view certain responses as universal punishers. For example, a common response to problem behavior is to send a student to the principal's office, a consequence that would be distressing for most students. Consider, however, the student who has a history of failure with academic tasks. Sending that student to the office may be much less punishing to him or her than struggling through an academic assignment that he or she does not understand and expects to fail. Thus, information on responses allows teams to 1) determine whether a response may be reinforcing problem behavior and 2) identify a way to respond that is unlikely to be reinforcing.

After setting events, antecedents, and responses are identified, the team can begin to speculate about the function of behavior. There are two broad reasons that problem behaviors occur. The first is to escape or avoid something (providing negative reinforcement). In this case, the response allows the student to get out of something undesirable. For example, sending a student outside of the classroom or to the office may allow him or her to escape a difficult assignment. If this consequence is delivered following each incident of misbehavior, the team might hypothesize that behavior serves an escape function. Similarly, when a student begins to have a tantrum, the teacher may immediately come to assist the student with his or her work. Although the assistance has been delivered with good intentions, the teacher has taught the student that a tantrum can produce assistance, which allows the student a form of escape from the original assignment.

A second broad function of problem behavior is to gain something, either attention (adult or peer) or an item or activity. For example, although the class rules require raising a hand to be called on, Cooper constantly blurts out. Because he is quite humorous, his peers cannot help but laugh at his antics. In spite of his teacher's efforts to punish him by deducting points, Cooper finds the peer attention highly reinforcing. Thus, his problem behavior serves an attention function (i.e., gains him peer attention). Maykala's problem behavior illustrates the function of gaining an activity. Maykala has autism and limited communication skills. She uses a picture card system and has learned to request a few items. When she is asked to make a transition from certain preferred tasks to other less preferred activities, Maykala frequently uses the card to request more time with the preferred activity. Staff members generally try to honor her request for more time by allowing her one additional minute with the preferred item before she makes a transition to the next task. However, she has started to become aggressive when she cannot have additional time with an activity. This pattern of behavior has allowed her support team to conclude that her problem behavior functions to obtain preferred activities.

After information has been obtained via interview, the team may choose to complete a schedule review (section E). Section E can be completed based on variables most relevant to the student's problem behavior. For example, if a student's problem behavior occurs only during class time, the left column (time, period, activity) can reflect his or her class schedule. If, however, problem behavior does not seem to coincide with academic classes, general activities (e.g., morning transition, recess, lunch) or specific within-class activities (e.g., teacher lecture, group work, independent seatwork) can be listed. This activity guides teams in identifying when behavior occurs most frequently and when it occurs least frequently. Rather than conducting observations throughout the school day, teams can select specific time periods both when behavior occurs at a high rate and when behavior rarely occurs.

Section F prompts teams to consider interventions that have or have not worked in the past. This information can save teams a great deal of time and effort. However, it is important to discuss how the intervention was implemented. Potentially effective interventions may appear ineffective if not implemented as designed for a sufficient length of time.

Conduct a Student Interview Student interviews contain much of the same information as adult interviews. That is, they attempt to ascertain when and why students have problem behaviors. It is worthwhile to solicit information from students themselves for several reasons. First, students have access to information that may not be available to adults. For example, many behaviors are not subject to observation by adults, such as internalizing problems (i.e., feeling depressed or anxious), clandestine behaviors (e.g., bullying, drug use, cutting), or problems outside of school. In this case, students may provide information that is critical to the success of a support plan. In addition, students often have a unique perspective about their own behavior and are able to generate ideas or changes that could reduce problem behaviors. For instance, we once worked with Gerry, a student attending an urban high school, who was failing all of his academic classes because he did not complete his homework. He informed us that he is teased relentlessly among his social group if he carries a backpack around school. Upon further inquiry, we found that students did not carry backpacks because all assignments were posted in electronic format. Gerry, however, did not have a computer at home to access assignments. This information allowed us to make arrangements with his family to permit him time each night at the public library to use a computer to access his homework. An example of a student interview form can be found in Figure 8.3.

Complete Direct Observations In addition to administering interviews, it is also critical to conduct direct observations. Direct observations document antecedents and responses when problem behavior occurs rather

FUNCTIONAL ASSESSMENT INTERVIEW

Student name: ____________________ Grade: _____ Age: _____ Sex: _____

Date of interview: ____________________ Interviewer: ____________________

Section I: Rate how often you have problem behaviors in the following subjects by circling the corresponding number.

Subject	Not at all		Some-times		Very much
Reading	1	2	3	4	5
Math	1	2	3	4	5
Spelling	1	2	3	4	5
Handwriting	1	2	3	4	5
Science	1	2	3	4	5
Social studies	1	2	3	4	5
English	1	2	3	4	5
Physical education	1	2	3	4	5
Computers	1	2	3	4	5
Art	1	2	3	4	5
Other:	1	2	3	4	5
Other:	1	2	3	4	5
Other:	1	2	3	4	5

Section II: Answer the following questions for each subject rated 3, 4, or 5 above.

1. Why do you have problems in ____________________?
(subject)

____
____
____

2. What changes could be made so you would have fewer problems?

____
____
____

3. Why do you have problems in ____________________?
(subject)

____
____
____

Source: Kern, Dunlap, Clarke, and Childs (1994).

Figure 8.3. Student Functional Assessment Interview.

(continued)

Figure 8.3. *(continued)*

4. What changes could be made so you would have fewer problems?

____

____

____

5. Why do you have problems in ____________________?
(subject)

____

____

____

6. What changes could be made so you would have fewer problems?

____

____

____

Source: Kern, Dunlap, Clarke, and Childs (1994).

than relying on recollection, as is the case with interviews. Thus, they are generally considered more accurate than interviews. Even when teams believe in the accuracy of interviews, direct observation is important in confirming the information obtained from interviews.

Direct observations serve two purposes. The first is to identify events that immediately surround problem behavior. The second is to determine events that occur when problem behavior is absent. Thus, the team should identify times of the day when problem behavior occurs at a high frequency and when it occurs at a very low frequency or does not occur. It is likely that this information was generated through the functional assessment interview (sections D, F, and G) or in the student interview.

During direct observations, the observer collects information on antecedents, problem behavior, and responses to the problem behavior. There are numerous formats available to facilitate data collection, but all collect essentially the same information. The particular format should be determined by the observer's preference. For example, some people prefer to take detailed notes describing events that surround the problem behavior. The ABC Report Form (Figure 8.4) organizes information by time, antecedent, behavior, and consequence, and provides space for the observer to write descriptions in each category (e.g., Kern, O'Neill, & Starosta, 2005).

Other individuals prefer to use a checkbox format (Figure 8.5), particularly if behavior is high-frequency or the observer has competing responsibilities that preclude time for detailed notes (e.g., Kern et al, 2005). In addition, in situations wherein team members are fairly confident that they accurately identified setting events, antecedents, and the function of problem behavior during the interview process, a checklist may be sufficient, because the primary purpose in that situation is to confirm the interview information.

Sufficient observations of problem behavior need to be conducted to identify a clear pattern. Unless problem behavior is serious (e.g., aggression, self-injury, major disruption), observation of 15–20 occurrences is generally recommended. However, if data indicate that antecedents and responses are highly consistent, fewer observations may be required. Alternatively, if data are inconsistent and no clear patterns emerge, additional observations will be needed. It is also important to note that data need to be as specific as possible. For example, data indicating that Aidan engages in problem behavior during math are helpful but not sufficient for developing a behavior support plan. Beyond knowing that math is problematic for Aidan, it is also important to understand the specific assignments or activities that are problematic. For instance, it may be that he is fine during lecture, math games, and computer activities, but problem behavior occurs when he is given an independent assignment that he cannot easily complete. In Aidan's case, knowing that problem behavior occurs during difficult independent assignments will greatly facilitate the selection of specific supports matched to his difficulties.

ABC REPORT FORM

Name: ______________________________ Date/time of observation: ________________________

Place observation occurred: ____

Environmental conditions (number of students, arrangement, number of adults, etc.): ____________

____

Activities observed during observation: ____

Unusual or potentially influential conditions: ____

Time	Antecedent	Behavior	Consequence

Source: Kern, O'Neill, and Starosta (2005).

Figure 8.4. ABC Report Form.

ABC CHECKLIST

Student: Teacher: Date:

9:00–9:30 Subject: ______________		
No problem behaviors observed ❑		
Setting: Independent 1:1 Small group Whole group Other:		
ANTECEDENT	BEHAVIOR	CONSEQUENCES
❑ Told to stop or start an activity	❑ Noncompliance with stopping or starting an activity	❑ Redirection
❑ Working independently	❑ Attempting to gain teacher attention	❑ Preferred item or activity
❑ Given a multistep direction	❑ Noncompliance with direction(s)	❑ Encouragement
❑ Repeating a direction	❑ Minor disruptive behavior	❑ No response
❑ Denial of preferred item or activity	❑ Aggression	❑ Help
❑ Other:	❑ Other:	❑ Time out
		❑ Other:

9:30–10:00 Subject: ______________		
No problem behaviors observed ❑		
Setting: Independent 1:1 Small group Whole group Other:		
ANTECEDENT	BEHAVIOR	CONSEQUENCES
❑ Told to stop or start an activity	❑ Noncompliance with stopping or starting an activity	❑ Redirection
❑ Working independently	❑ Attempting to gain teacher attention	❑ Preferred item or activity
❑ Given a multistep direction	❑ Noncompliance with direction(s)	❑ Encouragement
❑ Repeating a direction	❑ Minor disruptive behavior	❑ No response
❑ Denial of preferred item or activity	❑ Aggression	❑ Help
❑ Other:	❑ Other:	❑ Time out
		❑ Other:

10:00–10:30 Subject: ______________		
No problem behaviors observed ❑		
Setting: Independent 1:1 Small group Whole group Other:		
ANTECEDENT	BEHAVIOR	CONSEQUENCES
❑ Told to stop or start an activity	❑ Noncompliance with stopping or starting an activity	❑ Redirection
❑ Working independently	❑ Attempting to gain teacher attention	❑ Preferred item or activity
❑ Given a multistep direction	❑ Noncompliance with direction(s)	❑ Encouragement
❑ Repeating a direction	❑ Minor disruptive behavior	❑ No response
❑ Denial of preferred item or activity	❑ Aggression	❑ Help
❑ Other:	❑ Other:	❑ Time out
		❑ Other:

Source: Kern, O'Neill, and Starosta (2005).

Figure 8.5. ABC Checklist.

(continued)

Figure 8.5. *(continued)*

10:30–11:00 Subject: ______ No problem behaviors observed ❑ Setting: Independent 1:1 Small group Whole group Other:		
ANTECEDENT	BEHAVIOR	CONSEQUENCES
❑ Told to stop or start an activity ❑ Working independently ❑ Given a multistep direction ❑ Repeating a direction ❑ Denial of preferred item or activity ❑ Other:	❑ Noncompliance with stopping or starting an activity ❑ Attempting to gain teacher attention ❑ Noncompliance with direction(s) ❑ Minor disruptive behavior ❑ Aggression ❑ Other:	❑ Redirection ❑ Preferred item or activity ❑ Encouragement ❑ No response ❑ Help ❑ Time out ❑ Other:
11:00–11:30 Subject: ______ No problem behaviors observed ❑ Setting: Independent 1:1 Small group Whole group Other:		
ANTECEDENT	BEHAVIOR	CONSEQUENCES
❑ Told to stop or start an activity ❑ Working independently ❑ Given a multistep direction ❑ Repeating a direction ❑ Denial of preferred item or activity ❑ Other:	❑ Noncompliance with stopping or starting an activity ❑ Attempting to gain teacher attention ❑ Noncompliance with direction(s) ❑ Minor disruptive behavior ❑ Aggression ❑ Other:	❑ Redirection ❑ Preferred item or activity ❑ Encouragement ❑ No response ❑ Help ❑ Time out ❑ Other:
11:30–12:00 Subject: ______ No problem behaviors observed ❑ Setting: Independent 1:1 Small group Whole group Other:		
ANTECEDENT	BEHAVIOR	CONSEQUENCES
❑ Told to stop or start an activity ❑ Working independently ❑ Given a multistep direction ❑ Repeating a direction ❑ Denial of preferred item or activity ❑ Other:	❑ Noncompliance with stopping or starting an activity ❑ Attempting to gain teacher attention ❑ Noncompliance with direction(s) ❑ Minor disruptive behavior ❑ Aggression ❑ Other:	❑ Redirection ❑ Preferred item or activity ❑ Encouragement ❑ No response ❑ Help ❑ Time out ❑ Other

Source: Kern, O'Neill, and Starosta (2005).

Step 4: Analyze and Summarize the Data

After interviews and direct observations have been completed, the next step is to analyze and summarize the data in a way that facilitates intervention development. Specifically, the data will be examined to identify patterns as well as consistencies across data sources (e.g., adult interviews, student interview, direct observation data). It is often the team leader who organizes the data so that they are easy to interpret.

To summarize direct observation data, the setting events, antecedents, and responses to problem behavior should be displayed in graphic or tabular format. To illustrate, we introduce Damien, a middle school student with a history of aggression toward his peers. During the current school year, his aggression escalated and, in spite of Tier 2 intervention, his aggression did not decrease. Therefore, an FBA was conducted. Figure 8.6, Figure 8.7, and Figure 8.8 show direct observation data collected for Damien, displayed in graphic format. The data can be examined to detect patterns across observations. As Figure 8.6 shows, aggression occurs most frequently during morning meeting, recess, transition, and lunch. Few or no occurrences were observed during academics or special classes (e.g., gym, art, library, computers). Additional information displayed in Figure 8.7 shows that Damien's aggressions are most frequently directed at a particular peer (Josiah). Figure 8.8 provides further detail, showing that the specific antecedent to aggression is a belittling or derogatory comment, most commonly made by Josiah.

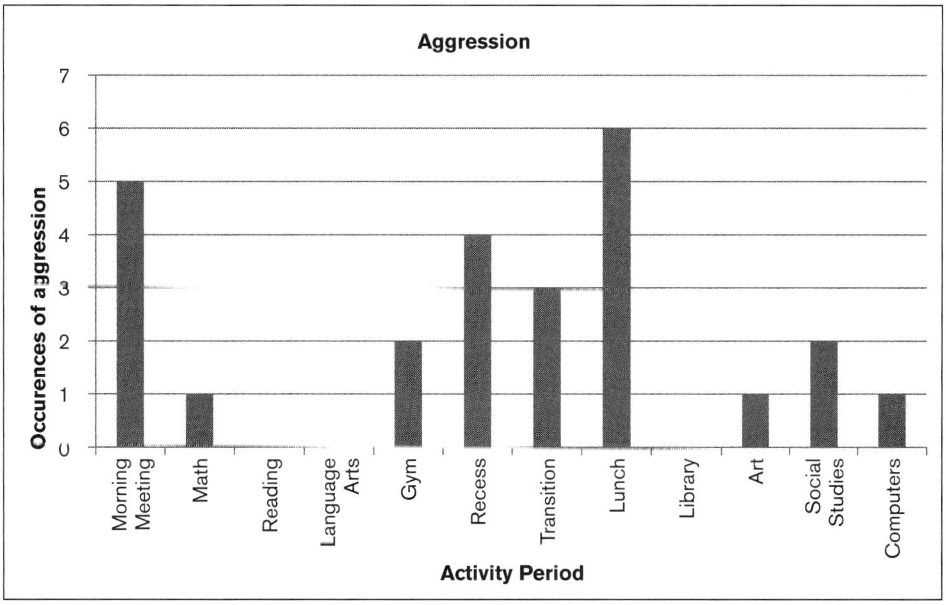

Figure 8.6. Damien's graphed direct observation data showing the frequency of aggression during activities throughout the day.

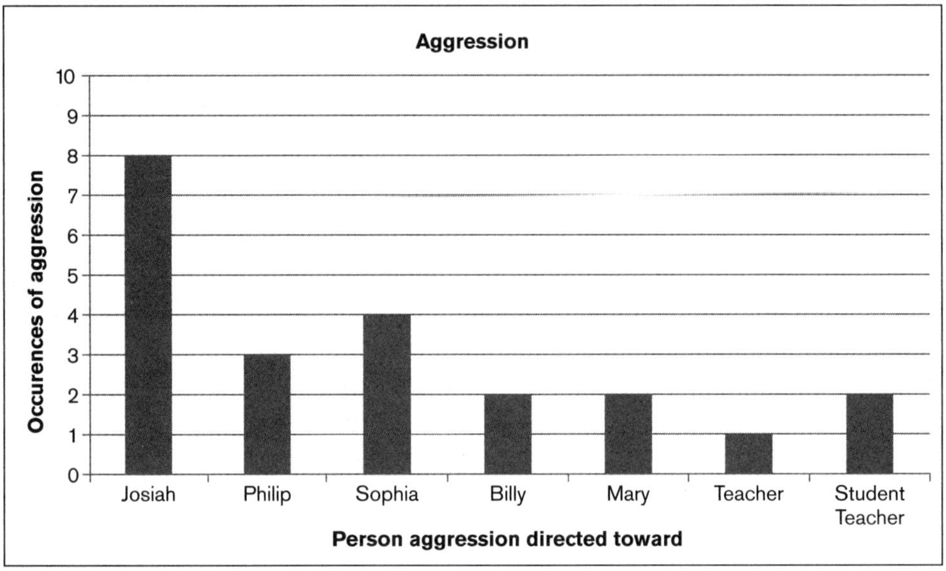

Figure 8.7. Graphic display showing target of Damien's aggressions.

Peyton, a fifth-grade student in elementary school, exhibited problem behaviors that were nonresponsive to the Tier 2 intervention known as CICO (described in Chapter 2). Subsequently, the intervention was intensified (Chapter 7) so that she received a midday check-in, in addition to the morning and afternoon check-ins. Peyton continued to engage in an unacceptable rate of problem behavior, so Tier 3 was initiated. Direct observation data collected during the FBA for antecedents and responses

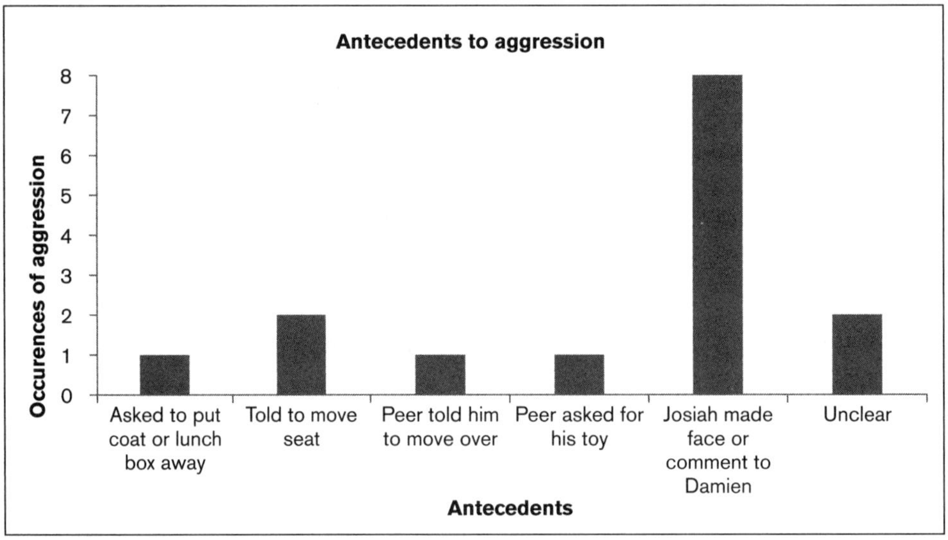

Figure 8.8. Graphic summary of antecedents to Damien's aggressions.

Table 8.4. Summary of Peyton's occurrences of problem behavior in table format

Activity	Number of times observed	Occurrences of problem behavior	Notes
Math	12	7	Five behavior problems observed during timed multiplication assessments. One problem behavior occurred during practice for state standardized assessment.
Reading	12	5	All behavior problems occurred during fluency assessments.
Spelling	12	2	Both problem behaviors occurred during weekly spelling test.
Science	5	1	Peer said something (could not hear).
Gym	6	1	Upset from previous class and refused to participate.

to Peyton's problem behavior are summarized and displayed in Tables 8.4 and 8.5. The tables are organized by frequency, from greatest to least. As Table 8.4 shows, initial data indicate that Peyton's problem behavior occurs most frequently during math and reading, which generally resulted in being sent out of the classroom (Table 8.5). Additional data in the "Notes" column in Table 8.4 indicate that the specific antecedent was completing timed activities, such as math or reading fluency assessments.

After direct observation data are summarized, they are compared to data from the interviews and other sources (e.g., meetings, reports, record reviews). Figure 8.9 provides an example of how data can be summarized and compared. When the information collected from various sources is consistent, the team generally concludes that antecedents and responses have been accurately identified. In this case, the team can move on to hypothesis development. On the other hand, if the information gathered is not consistent and team members agree that they are not confident that antecedents and responses have been identified, additional data need to be collected. Generally, this will require collecting additional direct-observation data. These observations may target specific areas of confusion or inconsistency.

Table 8.5. Summary of teacher responses to Peyton's problem behavior in a table format

Event following problem behavior	Frequency	Notes
Sent to office	7	Teacher noted that behavior was "out of control" or appeared to be escalating.
Sent to hallway	5	Teacher sent Peyton to hallway outside of classroom to calm down.
Reprimanded	2	Both students involved in altercation during science class were reprimanded.
Called parent	1	Behavior problem occurred at end of day and parent was called to pick Peyton up.
Sent to counselor	1	Gym teacher noted that Peyton was crying and appeared agitated.

SUMMARY OF ASSESSMENT RESULTS

Student: ______________________ Date: ______________

	Direct observation	Adult interviews	Student interview	Other sources of information	Consistencies or inconsistencies
Setting events					
Antecedents to problem behavior					
Response that maintains problem behavior					

Summary:

☐ Data across all sources are sufficiently consistent and team is confident that antecedents and responses have been identified. ↓ DEVELOP HYPOTHESIS STATEMENT	☐ Data are inconsistent and team is not confident that antecedents and responses have been identified. ↓ COLLECT ADDITIONAL DATA

Figure 8.9. Summary of Assessment Results.

To illustrate, direct observation data indicated that Gina's off-task and disruptive behavior occurred most frequently during first-period algebra class, and the teacher's response usually resulted in some type of escape from the task. Therefore, her teachers believed that math was a problematic subject for Gina. On the contrary, when Gina's mother was interviewed, she indicated that Gina loved math and had always done well on tests and homework. She did not believe it was a result of the subject matter and suggested that Gina has a difficult time waking up in the morning and did not function well during early hours. Noting that problem behavior only occurred during morning math class, Ms. Barker, Gina's math teacher, agreed to allow Gina to attend her afternoon algebra class, which could be flipped with her study hall. To the teachers' surprise, Gina did very well in the afternoon class, completing her work and exhibiting no problem behavior. This provided the team sufficient data to be confident they had identified the antecedents to Gina's problem behavior and were ready to move forward with hypotheses.

Step 5: Formulate Hypothesis Statements

Many times, team members collect an abundance of data but fail to rely on those data when developing a behavior support plan. Without a link between assessment data and the support plan, there is little likelihood of identifying an effective intervention. Thus, a crucial step is to develop hypothesis statements, which will ensure there is a connection between the data gathered and the behavior support plan. In fact, the hypothesis statements should be used to guide the development of the behavior support plan. Although hypotheses can be stated in different ways, it is essential to include 1) setting events, if any have been identified; 2) the antecedent to problem behavior; 3) the problem behavior; and 4) the perceived function (Figure 8.10).

Perceived function refers to the hypothesized reinforcement for problem behavior. As we described earlier, problem behavior can be reinforced through negative reinforcement, which allows the student to escape or avoid something (e.g., task, nonpreferred activity, unpleasant interaction), or through positive reinforcement, allowing the student to gain something (e.g., attention, activity, item, stimulatory input). This is the presumed function that is included in the hypothesis statement. An example of a hypothesis statement is "When Rory has not slept well (setting event) and is given a

Specific hypothesis formation: Use the functional assessment information gathered to develop a specific hypothesis about the function of the behavior.
Given the circumstances when (setting event) ____________________ *and*
when (antecedent) ______________________________ *occurs,*
the student does (problem behavior) ______________________ *in order*
to (presumed function) ______________________________.

Figure 8.10. Hypothesis statement.

Table 8.6. Examples of hypothesis statements

- When Jim is given an assignment that takes longer than 15 minutes to complete *(antecedent),* he engages in disruptive behavior *(problem behavior)* to escape the task *(presumed function).*
- When Corey has not slept well *(setting event)* and is given a math assignment *(antecedent),* he curses and has tantrums *(problem behavior)* to escape the task *(presumed function).*
- When Jenna is in whole class instruction *(antecedent),* she yells out *(behavior)* to obtain attention *(presumed function).*
- During circle time, when another student gets an instrument during music *(antecedent),* Quanda has tantrums *(problem behavior)* to obtain access *(presumed function).*
- When Tory is asked a question *(antecedent),* he engages in self-injury *(problem behavior)* to escape interactions *(presumed function).*
- When Alex is left without anything to do *(antecedent),* he engages in hand flapping *(problem behavior)* to obtain access to sensory stimulation *(presumed function).*

lengthy writing assignment that exceeds 10 minutes (antecedent), he engages in disruption (behavior) to escape the task (presumed function)." Additional examples are provided in Table 8.6. After data-based hypothesis statements have been developed, the information that has been gathered should be adequate to develop a behavior support plan.

SUMMARY

It is important to conduct an FBA for students who engage in serious behavior problems or when behavior is intransigent and has not been responsive to interventions implemented at Tier 1 or Tier 2. The efficiency and effectiveness of support plans are greatly increased when they are based on information derived from an FBA. In this chapter, we described the process and steps for conducting an FBA. The process results in hypothesis statements, which link the information that was gathered to the behavior support plan. In Chapter 9, we describe how to build a multicomponent support plan based on the FBA.

Self-Reflection

1. Is there an individual in the school where you work or have visited who has the expertise to lead a Tier 3 team? What training is available to increase teacher skill level?
2. List student behaviors that bother you the most when you are teaching. Where do these problems fall with respect to the recommended procedures for prioritizing problem behavior described in Figure 8.1? Does your list need to be prioritized differently to address more serious student problems?
3. As we noted in this chapter, setting events are usually difficult to observe. Teachers, however, develop a good sense of when students are experiencing setting events that affect their daily performance. What types of setting events do you believe have occurred with students in your class or a class you have visited?

4. Student interviews can yield important information about a student's own problem behavior that sometimes cannot be obtained from adults. What type of information would be useful to you as a teacher that only a student could provide?
5. A common problem with functional–assessment-based support plans is that there is not a sufficient link between the assessment data and the final support plan. How can you increase the likelihood that the support plan will be based directly on assessment data?

REFERENCES

Bambara, L.M. (2005). Overview of the behavior support process. In L.M. Bambara & L. Kern (Eds.), *Individualized supports for students with problem behaviors* (pp. 47–70). New York, NY: Guilford Press.

Dunlap, Kern-Dunlap, Clarke, & Robbins (1991). In *Supporting Students with Emotional and Behavioral Problems: Prevention and Intervention Strategies* by Lee Kern, Michael P. George, & Mark D. Weist. Copyright © 2016 by Paul H. Brookes Publishing Co.

Ialongo, N.S., Wethamer, L., Kellam, S.G., Brown, C.H., Wang, S., & Lin, Y. (1999). Proximal impact of two first-grade preventive interventions on early risk behaviors for later substance abuse, depression, and antisocial behavior. *American Journal of Community Psychology, 27,* 599–641. doi:10.1023/A:1022137920532

Janney, R., & Snell, M.E. (2000). *Teachers' guides to inclusive practices: Behavioral support.* Baltimore, MD: Paul H. Brookes Publishing Co.

Kern, L., Childs, K.E., Dunlap, G., Clarke, S., & Falk, G.D. (1994). Using assessment-based curricular intervention to improve the classroom behavior of a student with emotional and behavioral challenges. *Journal of Applied Behavioral Analysis, 27,* 7–19.

Kern, L., Dunlap, G., Clarke, S., & Childs, K. (1994). Student-assisted functional assessment interview. *Diagnostique, 19,* 29–39.

Kern, L., O'Neill, R.E., & Starosta, K. (2005). Gathering functional assessment information. In L.M. Bambara & L. Kern (Eds.), *Individualized supports for students with problem behaviors* (pp. 129–164). New York, NY: Guilford Press.

Miltenberger, R.G. (2005). Strategies for measuring behavior change. In L.M. Bambara & L. Kern (Eds.), *Individualized supports for students with problem behaviors* (pp. 107–128). New York, NY: Guilford Press.

Newcomer, L.L., & Lewis, T.J. (2004). Functional behavioral assessment: An investigation of assessment reliability and effectiveness of function-based interventions. *Journal of Emotional and Behavioral Disorders, 12*(3), 168–181.

O'Connell, M.E., Boat, T., & Warner, K.E. (2009). *Preventing mental, emotional, and behavioral disorders among young people: Progress and possibilities.* Washington, DC: National Academies Press and U.S. Department of Health and Human Services, Substance Abuse and Mental Health Services Administration. Retrieved from http://dhss.alaska.gov/dbh/Documents/Prevention/programs/spfsig/pdfs/IOM_Matrix_8%205x11_FINAL.pdf

Sacks, G., & Kern, L. (2008). A comparison of quality of life variables for students with emotional and behavioral disorders and students without disabilities. *Journal of Behavioral Education, 17,* 111–127.

Thousand, J.S., & Villa, R.A. (2000). Collaborative teaming: A powerful tool in school restructuring. In R.A. Villa & J.S. Thousand (Eds.), *Restructuring for caring and effective education: Piecing the puzzle together* (2nd ed., pp. 254–291). Baltimore, MD: Paul H. Brookes Publishing Co.

9

Developing an Assessment-Based Support Plan

Throughout this book, we have discussed the way in which behavior support has evolved. In the past, behavior management focused exclusively on responses. That is, educators waited for problem behavior to occur and applied some form of consequence, usually what they believed was punishment, in the hopes that behavior problems would not return. Educators now have a much more complete understanding of the causes of problem behavior, including an appreciation that environmental events (i.e., antecedents) may trigger it and that skill deficits can limit a student from engaging in desirable alternative behavior. This greater understanding of the many events that make problem behavior more likely has led educators to recognize that behavior supports similarly need to include multiple components. In this chapter, we describe the intervention components of a comprehensive support plan.

As we discussed in Chapter 8, an FBA is appropriate for students who engage in serious behavior problems or those with behavior problems that have not responded to less intensive intervention. We described the steps for conducting an FBA, which is needed to develop a comprehensive support plan. We also introduced the hypothesis statement, which serves as a conduit for developing a behavior support plan. That is, the hypothesis statement succinctly summarizes the data that were gathered during the FBA and increases the likelihood of a link between the assessment information and the plan. Both the hypothesis statement and the specific data collected during the FBA are used to develop an individualized support plan. In this chapter, we describe components of a well-designed support plan and delineate specific interventions that prevent behavior problems, teach alternative skills, and respond to problems in a manner that supports positive behavior change. The intervention strategies are presented in relation to the behavioral function identified during the FBA.

COMPONENTS OF A COMPREHENSIVE BEHAVIOR SUPPORT PLAN

A comprehensive behavior support plan contains four types of intervention components (see Figure 9.1). The first component is setting event interventions, which address events that occur at an earlier time and increase the probability of behavior problems in the presence of particular antecedent events. The second component, antecedent interventions, is implemented prior to the occurrence of problem behavior and reduces the likelihood that problem behavior will occur. The third component, instructive interventions, teaches alternative skills that serve the same function as problem behavior and therefore will replace it. Instructive interventions also can teach general skills that will reduce problem behavior over the long term. These skills may include academic or social skills that an individual lacks or new skills to deal more effectively with challenging situations, such as coping and tolerance strategies. The fourth component of a comprehensive intervention plan is response interventions, which include strategies that decrease the likelihood of the problem behavior reoccurring.

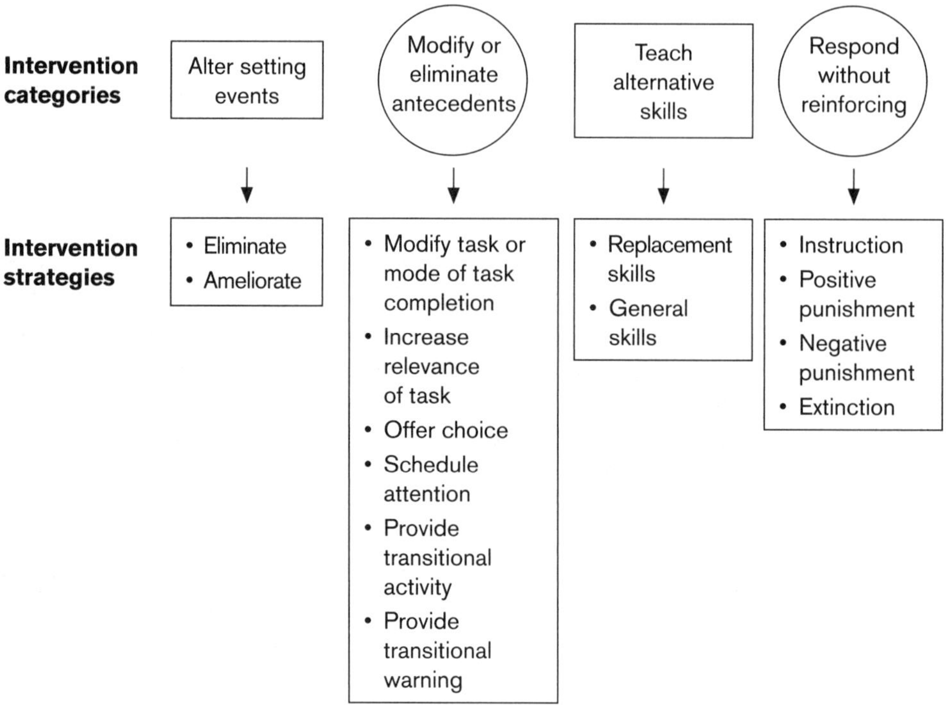

Figure 9.1. Categories of intervention.

Often, responses to problem behavior are predetermined in that they are aligned with schoolwide or classwide rules or expectations. For example, schoolwide rules may dictate that stealing results in a 1-day suspension. It is generally a good practice to have predictable consequences for infractions of the expectations. However, when it comes to intensive and persistent problem behaviors, it may be that the consequence for problem behavior inadvertently reinforces the behavior. In these situations, it is important to customize the consequences (e.g., responses) to problem behavior. In the sections that follow, we describe interventions that fall in each of the aforementioned categories.

Setting Event Interventions

As we described in Chapter 8, at times distal events make problem behavior more likely to occur. It can be difficult for teachers and school practitioners to determine what these events are because they cannot be directly observed. However, almost every teacher can recall a student who had good and bad days, and most teachers could predict the type of day it would be based on the student's entry into the classroom. Setting events are things that occur at an earlier time (i.e., not proximal to problem behavior) that increase the likelihood of problem behavior in the presence of particular antecedents. Because setting events often characterize something significantly problematic in a student's life, it is worth the effort to attempt to determine what is going on (see Chapter 8).

There are two intervention approaches to address setting events. The first is to eliminate the problematic event. For example, fatigue due to lack of sleep is a setting event that may contribute to problem behaviors at school. A sleep plan that includes regular bedtimes following a calming routine (e.g., reading) may eliminate this setting event. Another example of an intervention that eliminates a setting event is providing breakfast at the start of the school day to eliminate problem behaviors caused by hunger.

Interventions that eliminate setting events are most desirable because they remedy the problem situation. Unfortunately, setting events are often difficult to eliminate, particularly for educators who have limited or no access to events that occur outside of school. When setting events cannot be eliminated, an alternative intervention approach is to ameliorate the event in some way. This approach focuses on nullifying the effects of the setting event. For instance, if the previous example of lack of sleep cannot be successfully addressed through a sleep plan, a time could be allocated during the school day for the student to take a nap in the nurse's office (e.g., during free play or study hall) on days when he or she did not sleep well. Another option would be to structure the student's day so that core academic courses are scheduled early in the morning, when he or she is less likely to feel the effects of sleep deprivation and fatigue. Other examples of interventions that ameliorate setting events are administering medication to reduce allergy symptoms, arranging for the student to talk with a school counselor following a fight with a sibling at home or with a peer on the school bus, easing academic demands, or providing an additional brief free time period for a student to calm down on Monday mornings after a hectic weekend spent commuting to visit a parent.

Antecedent Interventions

Antecedent interventions focus on modifying events that immediately precede problem behavior, or antecedent events. There are many advantages to antecedent interventions, the primary being that they can prevent behavior problems from occurring. They also tend to be fairly fast acting, which is critical in the case of dangerous or harmful behavior. Antecedent interventions can be used in a multitude of ways to reduce problem behavior. However, in order to narrow intervention options, it is simplest to consider antecedent interventions relative to behavioral function. Thus, it is important to rely on the hypothesis statement with the presumed function to select an intervention among the examples that follow.

Antecedent Interventions for Behavior with an Escape Function A school day is largely characterized by task demands. A good match between a student's skill level and task demands is critical for productive and continued learning. Many students have difficulty meeting academic expectations because they lack prerequisite skills, have difficulty attending to their schoolwork, or do not easily acquire new or complex information. When assessment information suggests task demands are an antecedent to problem behavior, aspects of the task or the mode of task completion may be modified. Adjusting task difficulty (Kern & Clemens, 2007) is an intervention that matches academic material to a student's skill level so that he or she achieves a high rate of success. Students should achieve a high percentage of correct answers in the work they are assigned, particularly if they are completing the work independently. Academic researchers suggest that an 85%–95% rate of accuracy is desirable to ensure that students are learning new skills and not making errors that interfere with acquisition of academic material (Salvia, Ysseldyke, & Bolt, 2010). Although difficult tasks are most often associated with problem behavior, tasks that are too easy may also lead to problem behavior (e.g., Umbreit, Lane, & Dejud, 2004). Ultimately, difficulty of the task or assignment needs to match student skill level and motivation.

For students who have skills to complete a task but also find the task challenging or are unmotivated, task interspersal can reduce problem behavior (Skinner, 2002). This intervention alternates easy tasks among more difficult tasks. For example, a challenging long-division problem can be interspersed among four or five easier one-digit math problems, or several already mastered vocabulary words can be alternated with a new or difficult vocabulary word. A variation is behavioral momentum (Belfiore, Lee,

Scheeler, & Klein, 2002) in which requests to complete a series of easy tasks with high student compliance precede a request to complete a more difficult task or one with low compliance. For example, during recess, a student with difficulties making transitions might be asked to do the following: "Touch your knees, tell me your name, put your hands in the air, add two plus two, turn in a circle" prior to the request to "return to class." It is important to ensure that there is a sufficient amount of easy tasks in relation to difficult tasks to maintain student momentum and motivation.

Adjusting task length (e.g., Kern & Clemens, 2007) is another example of a simple antecedent intervention. Many students will begin a task but have a limited ability to persist with that task. Assessment data can identify tasks that are associated with initial engagement that declines over time. Rather than presenting a single long task, the task length can be adjusted, either by providing multiple brief tasks or offering periodic breaks during a lengthy assignment.

Another antecedent intervention is to modify the mode of task completion (e.g., Kern, Childs, Dunlap, Clarke, & Falk, 1994). For example, a student with fine-motor-skill difficulty might find handwriting difficult. In this case, the student can be given the option of completing his or her work on a computer rather than writing by hand. Similarly, a student with difficulty transferring oral to written language might audio record a story he or she has composed for writing class (Kern et al.).

Problem behaviors also may occur when students view tasks as irrelevant or find them mundane. Incorporating areas of student interest into the task can increase student engagement. For example, Hinton and Kern (1999) increased homework completion among inner-city middle school students by including names of classmates and meaningful scenarios into math word problems. Using similar procedures, researchers have modified handwriting assignments to replace irrelevant workbook exercises with copying instructions for video game booklets (Dunlap et al., 1993) or writing captions for a photograph book (Dunlap & Kern, 1996), both of which were hobbies or high-interest activities of students in the class.

Another antecedent intervention that has been thoroughly studied is choice making. Providing opportunities for students to assert choices appears to be effective for two reasons. First, it allows students to select a preferred option among an array of choices, increasing the reinforcing value of that assignment or activity. Second, there appears to be an innate mechanism that makes choice reinforcing. This has been demonstrated in studies showing that choice can reduce problem behaviors, even when options are nonpreferred (e.g., Kern, Mantegna, Vorndran, Bailin, & Hilt, 2001). Thus, the opportunity to make choices may be reinforcing independent from the specific choice that is made.

Choice can be provided in several different ways (Kern & Clemens, 2007). For instance, students can be provided the choice of a task or activity to complete. Choice of task sequence is another option that has the advantage of ensuring that students complete all assigned tasks. Research has also demonstrated that choice of materials to complete an assignment, such as writing instrument or electronic device (e.g., Moes, 1998), leads to greater task completion and greater compliance. Students may also be offered the opportunity to choose a partner to work with or a location in which to work (e.g., Kern, Bambara, & Fogt, 2002). Finally, giving the student the option of when to complete an assignment may also reduce problem behavior. Table 9.1 shows types and examples of choice-making opportunities.

Antecedent Interventions for Behavior with an Attention Function Students may crave attention for a variety of reasons (e.g., they receive insufficient attention at home). The structure of school settings, with students grouped for instruction and activities, generally is not organized in a way that enables ongoing attention for individual students. Therefore, antecedent interventions can be designed for those students who engage in problem behavior to gain attention. One strategy is to provide scheduled attention. This approach involves the teacher devising a schedule for providing periodic individual attention to a student when he or she is engaging in appropriate behavior. The schedule is linked to the duration of time the student is generally able to behave appropriately without attention. So, if a student yells out or disrupts the class to gain attention on average every 10 minutes, the teacher would schedule attention about every 9 minutes. It is important for the teacher to approach the student and provide individual quality attention parallel to the attention that he or she would receive by engaging

Table 9.1. Ways to provide choice

Type of choice	Procedure	Examples
Task or activity	Student selects the task or activity that will be completed.	Student selects from five different spelling tasks (ABC order, writing sentence, word search, sand writing, writing words five times). Student chooses whether to complete math, reading, or writing.
Task sequence	Student selects the order in which a series of tasks will be completed.	Student selects the order of completing flash cards, addition worksheet, and online math game.
Materials	Student chooses the materials that can be used to complete the task.	Student selects the writing instrument to complete assignment. Student chooses color of paper to complete assignment.
Partner	Student selects a classmate with whom to complete a task.	Student selects classmate to practice flashcards for science test.
Location	Student chooses where to complete a task.	Student chooses whether to complete literature assignment at desk, in reading corner, or in library.
When to complete	Student decides when to complete a task.	Student selects whether to complete task during morning or afternoon study block.

in problem behavior. For instance, the teacher might move in close proximity, pat Susanna on the back, and tell her she appreciates that she is working hard and following the classroom rules. Students also sometimes engage in problem behavior to gain peer attention. In this case, assigning the student to be a peer helper may allow him or her to appropriately gain attention from a peer.

Antecedent Interventions Linked to a Tangible Function Problem behavior sometimes occurs because students do not want to quit a preferred activity (e.g., recess, computer time) or give up a preferred object. Transitional warnings that make students aware of the upcoming transition may prevent such problem behavior. For example, a student might be told that recess will end in 1 minute. In fact, multiple transitional warnings may be more effective than a single warning (Boyajian, DuPaul, Handler, Eckert, & McGoey, 2001). For example, following a 2-minute warning with a 1-minute warning may improve transitions.

Transitional activities also may prevent problem behaviors that serve a tangible function. This can involve providing a moderately preferred transitional activity to ease the transition from a highly preferred activity to a highly nonpreferred activity. For example, a brief math bingo game or dot-to-dot counting activity could be provided when transitioning between the preferred activity of recess or lunch to the nonpreferred activity of math instruction.

Alternative Skill Instruction

The purpose of alternative skill instruction is to teach new skills, which in turn reduces problem behaviors. Problem behaviors are often the result of skill deficits, such as difficulty communicating one's needs or lack of academic skills needed to complete an assignment easily and fluently. It is critical that support plans include alternative skill instruction to 1) teach students how to achieve their immediate needs in an appropriate manner and 2) build their general skills so that problem behavior is reduced over the long term.

Here, we describe two specific types of alternative skill instruction. The first type is replacement skills, or skills that teach more adaptive, appropriate ways to achieve the same function as problem behavior. The second type is general skills, which is instruction that fills in skill deficits, thereby reducing behavior problems over the long term.

Replacement Skills Replacement skills communicate the same message as problem behavior, but in an appropriate manner. Thus, the goal of replacement skills is to teach a behavior that will take the place of the problem behavior. This is referred to as a *functionally equivalent skill* or *1:1 replacement skill.*

When identifying replacement skills, it is important to consider the effectiveness and the efficiency of the new skill. *Effectiveness* refers to the likelihood that the student will achieve the same outcome by using the alternative skill as he or she did when using the problem behavior. For example, Mr. Page has a large class of 30 biology students and tends to focus most of his attention on a few students who are high achievers and excel at biology. Therefore, Jonah, who struggles in biology, finds it difficult to obtain help by raising his hand. Instead, in frustration, Jonah either disrupts the class by talking to his peers or disengages by putting his head down and refusing to complete assignments, both of which actions allow him to escape the difficult classwork and attract a response from Mr. Page. Thus, it is important that the replacement behavior of appropriately raising his hand to ask for assistance is consistently effective in gaining help from Mr. Page. Specifically, each time Jonah raises his hand, Mr. Page must be sure to provide him assistance and discontinue approaching him and giving assistance when Jonah disrupts or disengages.

In addition, the replacement behavior must be efficient. *Efficiency* refers to the amount of effort the new skill requires to achieve the same outcome as the effort required by the problem behavior. Effort can be considered in terms of the immediacy and quality of the response to the replacement behavior. In Jonah's situation, this refers to how quickly a hand raise results in assistance from Mr. Page and whether the assistance is equivalent to that obtained through problem behavior. So, Mr. Page must provide assistance relatively quickly after a hand raise, because he generally approaches Jonah as soon as he begins to disrupt the class. In addition, Mr. Page must ensure that the assistance is equivalent to or of higher quality than that which he provides after problem behavior, because he usually offers extensive assistance after disruptive behavior in order to maintain order in the class.

Because replacement skills are linked to function, as with antecedent interventions, this intervention also relies on functional assessment information that has accurately identified the function of problem behavior. Considering behavioral function, an initial question to ask is "How do typical students get this need met?" Teaching the student a replacement skill that is consistent with the behavior of typical students will increase opportunities for the student to remain included and ensure that he or she exhibits age-appropriate and socially acceptable behavior. In classroom settings, obtaining attention or assistance usually requires hand raising and verbally requesting help or attention in a respectful way. For students who do not have verbal skills, their alternative mode of communication, such as a picture card, iPad, or vocal output device, can be used. However, it is critical that the alternative communication system includes the exact replacement skill (e.g., picture card requesting attention, vocal recording requesting "help please").

After identifying the replacement skill, the next consideration is how instruction will be provided. Teachers often think it is sufficient to simply tell students to raise their hand or interact appropriately with the assumption that because they have exhibited appropriate behavior in the past, instruction is not necessary. This conclusion is often erroneous, for several reasons, particularly for students who have intensive support needs. First, such students either have not learned appropriate skills or are unable to regularly engage in those skills when they are in emotionally stressful situations (i.e., when they are angry, frustrated, or embarrassed). Second, they almost always have a powerful history of successfully achieving the outcomes desired (e.g., escape, attention, access to activities or tangible items) by engaging in problem behavior. Therefore, teachers should assume that instruction in the new skill is required.

For students with adequate verbal communication skills, instruction should consist of describing 1) the replacement behavior, 2) the rationale for engaging in the replacement behavior, and 3) the conditions under which the replacement behavior should be exhibited. In addition, role-play is often helpful, using scenarios that are relevant to the particular student. For example, if Bianca's problem behavior occurs during circle time, the teacher can role-play sitting in a circle and raising her hand to request a brief break. Furthermore, additional in vivo instruction is usually needed as well. During circle time, Bianca's teacher can provide a prompt every 5 minutes by stating, "Remember, Bianca, if you are having difficulties staying seated quietly, you can raise your hand and ask me for a brief break."

For students who have limited verbal communication skills, analog situations may be needed to provide a sufficient number of trials to practice the replacement skill. For example, a teacher might schedule 40–50 trials, distributed throughout the day, to practice requesting an activity, food item, or break. After the student begins to independently engage in the alternative response, the number of daily trials can be decreased.

A final consideration is whether supports are needed to ensure the student uses the replacement skill. For example, raising her hand and requesting help with independent seatwork may be a part of Alicia's behavioral repertoire, but she forgets to do so when she becomes frustrated. Therefore, the teacher can provide her with a printed card that she keeps on her desktop with the words "Help please" to serve as a reminder. Similarly, Ms. Miller can provide Colin with three break cards to serve as prompts that he can take three breaks during the period when he becomes fatigued.

General Skills In addition to teaching replacement skills, a student's general skills should be considered. Intensive problem behaviors usually indicate that a student has broad deficits in communication, social skills, anger management, and/or academic competence. Therefore, building skill in these broad areas can result in the long-term prevention of behavior problems.

Results from the functional behavioral assessment (FBA) should assist in identifying areas of deficit. Additional assessments might be needed to determine specific skills that need to be addressed. For example, it might be necessary to administer reading or math assessments to identify specific skill deficits that need remediation. We will not review all of the possible interventions to teach general skills, but recommend the use of evidence-based interventions. That is, it is important to select interventions with a sufficient amount of research supporting their effectiveness. Evidence-based interventions can be found on the What Works Clearinghouse web site (http://ies.ed.gov/ncee/wwc/Publications_Reviews.aspx?f=All%20Publication%20and%20Product%20Types,1;#pubsearch).

Response Strategies

Ideally, behavior problems would be eliminated through the use of antecedent and instructional strategies. Unfortunately, this is seldom the case. Therefore, it is essential to identify a response strategy.

A response strategy is a procedure to use when problem behavior occurs. The most important consideration when selecting a response strategy is that it must not reinforce problem behavior. If the procedure provides reinforcement in the same form as that obtained from the problem behavior, it is unlikely that problem behavior will be eliminated. For example, if Adam's problem behavior during physical education results in escape from difficult social interactions required as part of a team activity and the response is to require him to sit in the bleachers, the response is actually reinforcing the problem behavior by allowing him to escape the interactions. Therefore, it is important to carefully consider what the student gains from the problem behavior and make sure that the response does not provide similar reinforcement. This may require discussion with school administrators if the response is not aligned with the school code of conduct. That is, most schools have standard responses to particular topographies of problem behavior (e.g., cursing results in detention). This may be effective for students with infrequent behavior problems. However, in order to eliminate problem behaviors that are frequent and ongoing, an alternative response must be identified that is not reinforcing.

A second consideration is that responses should not be highly punitive or stigmatizing. Attention to the use of aversive procedures in schools has increased, particularly after release of the report *School Is Not Supposed to Hurt* by the National Disability Rights Network in 2009. The report revealed the extensive use and misuse of restraint, seclusion, and other aversive procedures in schools nationwide, many times resulting in staff or student injuries and even student deaths. The report also highlighted the absence of federal laws to protect students from such procedures.

The Alliance to Prevent Restraint, Aversive Interventions and Seclusion (APRAIS) was established in 2004 with the goal of protecting children and adolescents with disabilities from highly aversive procedures. APRAIS defined highly aversive procedures in schools as those causing serious physical and psychological harm, resulting in dehumanization of anyone involved, preventing the development of respectful and supportive relationships between children and adults, and leading to segregation and exclusion (TASH, 2014). In the following sections, we discuss four strategies for responding to problem behavior that do not involve the use of unnecessary and highly aversive procedures.

Instructional Procedures Following problem behavior, a variety of responses can be delivered that instruct the student, either directly or indirectly, to engage in an alternative, more appropriate behavior. One example is to praise a student's peers for engaging in desirable behavior, pointing out the behavior of others that is expected for the student. For instance, when Ellis is off task and talking to his peers, the teacher might state, "Jenna, Thomas, and Carlos are at their seats working quietly; thank you for following instructions." Similarly, a corrective statement delivered quietly and directly to the student is often an effective way of encouraging desired behavior (e.g., "Adam, please return to your seat.").

Extinction Extinction (also referred to as *planned ignoring*) involves ignoring, or not providing a response, following problem behavior. In theory, ignoring problem behavior results in the removal of reinforcement. In other words, students generally receive some form of reinforcement from a teacher's response to the problem behavior. For example, commenting on the behavior or reprimanding the student may provide some form of attention to the student. Similarly, if a teacher assists the student with the task or provides an alternative (e.g., easier) task following problem behavior, the student may receive reinforcement in the form of escape from the original demand. In many cases, extinction or ignoring is an effective way to respond that is likely to reduce future occurrences of problem behavior, especially minor problem behavior aimed at gaining the teacher's attention (e.g., calling out, tapping pencil, leaning the chair on its two back legs).

A caution about extinction is that it is often difficult to use in school settings for several reasons. First, some behavior problems, such as those that are dangerous or highly disruptive, simply cannot be ignored. Second, when a teacher ignores a student's problem behavior, his or her classmates may get the message that the teacher does not view the behavior as a problem. This is because students are accustomed to receiving consequences (usually punishment) when they exhibit unacceptable behavior. Therefore, if a teacher intends to use extinction, it is generally best to somehow inform students. For example, she might state, "I am going to ignore talk outs when students are inappropriately trying to get my attention." At the same time, alternative behavior, such as raising one's hand to solicit the teacher's attention, can be publicly praised. A third reason that extinction can be difficult is that problem behavior often gains peer attention. If the student finds peer attention reinforcing, extinction provided by the teacher is not likely to be effective. Finally, quite often behavior increases when extinction is used. This is referred to as an "extinction burst" and occurs because the student increases the intensity or severity of the behavior in an effort to obtain a response (i.e., reinforcement) that was delivered in the past. If extinction is continuously applied, eventually the problem behavior will decrease. The risk, however, is that if the behavior escalates to a form that can no longer be ignored, the student may have learned that more serious behavior is necessary to gain the desired response. Still, extinction is often a very simple and highly effective approach for decreasing minor behavior problems.

Negative Punishment Negative punishment involves the removal of items, activities, or privileges following problem behavior. This approach is most instructive when it involves a natural consequence or one that is most likely to be imposed by nature, society, or another person. An example of negative punishment that offers a natural consequence is removing recess or free time in order for a student to complete work that was not completed during class. Conversely, a consequence that is not natural would be taking away the student's school job or removing free play and requiring the student to sit on a bench during recess.

One type of negative punishment that is used frequently in schools is time-out. This consequence, when used correctly, involves removing the student from a reinforcing activity. It is commonly misused in that a student is given time-out for engaging in problem behavior during a nonpreferred activity. For instance, when having difficultly following his teacher's math instructions, Rowan pulls toys from his desk and begins to play. His teacher sends him to time-out, a consequence that is reinforcing, allowing him to escape the difficult math assignment. When time-out is used in this manner, it potentially compounds a student's difficulties because he or she is not participating in instruction while in time-out, which may contribute to further academic difficulties. Thus, it is important to use time-out only during preferred activities where the student will be motivated to behave appropriately to avoid removal in the future.

Positive Punishment Positive punishment, the opposite of negative punishment, occurs when something undesirable is provided following problem behavior. A reprimand (e.g., "No running in the hallways") is an example of positive punishment. Other examples include a phone call to parents, requiring extra work, and detention. It should be noted that punishment (both positive and negative) sometimes angers students. Therefore, teachers should be prepared for an escalation in behavior problems.

Responding to Dangerous Behavior Procedures should be developed for students who engage in dangerous behavior. By *dangerous behaviors,* we are referring to behaviors dangerous to oneself and others, such as physical aggression, property destruction, self-injury, and serious, ongoing disruption of the learning environment. Procedures for dealing with dangerous or escalating behaviors should be included in the individualized support plans of students who may engage in such problems and should reflect information obtained through the FBA.

A key consideration to any set of procedures for dealing with escalating behavior is the safety for all concerned. When students show dangerous or aggressive behavior and are unresponsive to de-escalation efforts made by staff, procedures should be in place so that the safety of the student, other classmates, and staff is ensured. An example of a procedure for maintaining safety during episodes of escalating behavior follows:

- Quickly assess the situation. Obtain the best safety position quickly. Allow other students to move out of harm's way. Use a room-clear procedure, if indicated.
- Using a firm and calm voice, give simple directions to the student, reminding him or her what he or she should do. For example, "Sit down and take some deep breaths to get calm." Praise the student for compliance with any direction followed.
- Do not touch or grab the student! Stabilize and defuse the situation. For example, state, "I can see you are angry, but you must be safe. When you are seated, I can help you resolve the problem." Praise compliance with directions.
- Minimize conversation when the student is agitated, calmly repeating the direction using a firm voice.
- Let the student know that if he or she follows directions, serious consequences may be avoided. Allow time for the student to gain self-control.
- When the student has regained composure, a plan can be developed to resolve the issue.

When developing procedures for this section of the behavior support plan, the team should consider the following elements: 1) identify support personnel, 2) ensure safety of all students, 3) specify de-escalation procedure, 4) develop a plan for reentry, 5) document the incident, and 6) contact parent or guardian. These elements can be summarized as part of the behavior support plan (see Figure 9.2).

When procedures are in place and teachers are proficient in their implementation, the impact of a crisis can be reduced; teachers simply go to and implement a different set of procedures.

THE FINAL PLAN

What should a completed support plan look like? A number of components should be included in a comprehensive support plan that will guide team members, clarify responsibilities, and facilitate communication. The Support Plan Checklist shown in Figure 9.3 can be used to ensure the support plan is complete. As the checklist indicates, the plan needs to include an operational definition of problem behavior. In addition, general information about the functional assessment provides documentation that the plan is derived from assessment information. The hypothesis statement describes antecedents and behavioral function and links the assessment information to the interventions. The plan also should specify a behavioral goal so that

When a student shows aggressive and/or dangerous behaviors and does not respond to the efforts by staff to remain safe, the following procedures will be implemented:

1. Notify and/or call for assistance from support staff in the building. Names of support staff and contact information:

   Mrs. Coleman, Guidance Counselor, Room 117, Ext. 3334
   Mr. Jackson, Instructional Assistant, Cafeteria, Ext. 2344

2. Ensure the safety of other students by removing them to a safe area, using the Room Clear procedure. Designated area for students to use during a Room Clear: *Library or cafeteria*

   Who will supervise students during the Room Clear: *Mr. Jackson*

3. Use the following de-escalation strategies to manage the situation and assist the student to regain composure:

   Inform Bobby that you will help him resolve the situation when he is calm and seated at his desk. Remind Bobby to use a pretaught calming strategy (taking deep breaths) to regain his composure. Do not engage in conversation or respond to Bobby's attempts to control. Repeat the direction as needed, using a calm firm voice. When Bobby has regained composure and followed your direction, develop a plan for resolving the situation.

4. Develop a plan for remaining safe and returning to class. Attach to Incident Report Form.

   Next time Bobby becomes angry and upset, he will raise hand and ask for assistance or request to take some time to calm himself.

5. Document the incident using an Incident Report Form.

6. Contact parent or guardian regarding the incident. *Mr. Greene – Phone: 202-555-0171*

7. Return students to class and continue instruction.

Figure 9.2. Example of a plan for managing escalated behavior.

teams can measure progress. Multiple intervention strategies that target antecedents, alternative skills instruction, and responses should be included. In addition, it is important to describe strategies for measuring behavior change and for maintaining communication and coordination among team members throughout the process. Finally, for students who engage in dangerous behaviors, a plan should be developed to keep the student and others safe and to de-escalate serious behavior problems.

Many schools, school districts, or states have preestablished formats or templates for behavior support plans. The format is not as important as the content. However, plans are doomed to failure if they lack critical information about the target behavior, intervention strategies that teachers are responsible for implementing, procedures for evaluating behavior change, and team communication. We strongly encourage teams to expand existing templates if such information is omitted. Figure 9.4 provides an example of a completed comprehensive support plan.

SUPPORT PLAN CHECKLIST

Key components of positive behavior support plans	Yes	No	Comments
Problem behavior:			
• Defined in measurable and observable way	☐	☐	
Functional assessment:			
• Used multiple sources of information	☐	☐	
• Antecedents and function are clear	☐	☐	
Hypothesis statement:			
• Linked to assessment information	☐	☐	
• Antecedents, behavior, and function are clearly specified	☐	☐	
Behavior goals:			
• Current level of behavior	☐	☐	
• Goal and time period	☐	☐	
Intervention strategies include the following:			
• Antecedent or setting event interventions	☐	☐	
• Alternative skill instruction	☐	☐	
• Reinforcement for new behavior	☐	☐	
• Responses to problem behavior	☐	☐	
• Long-term supports	☐	☐	
• Crisis plan, if needed	☐	☐	
Monitoring and evaluation:			
• Includes a strategy for measuring behavior change	☐	☐	
• Indicates who will collect data and when	☐	☐	
Team communication and coordination:			
• Roles and responsibilities specified	☐	☐	
• Strategies for coordination are described	☐	☐	

Figure 9.3. Support Plan Checklist.

SUPPORT PLAN

Student: Noah **Date:** February 25, 2015

Team leader: Mr. Acosta

Team members: Mrs. Duffy, Mr. Tamayo, Mr. Maddox, Ms. Jaegar

Target behavior: Disruption

Definition of target behavior: Behavior that disrupts the class or interferes with work completion. This includes calling out, talking to classmates when not permitted, making any audible sounds (e.g., animal sounds, whining, yelling, banging pencil), and being out of seat and wandering around the classroom.

Current level of behavior: Averages four disruptions daily

End-of-year behavioral goal: Reduce disruptions to twice monthly

How progress will be measured: Mrs. Duffy will collect frequency data of each occurrence of disruption.

Functional assessments data collected: Interview with parent, Mrs. Duffy, and Mr. Maddox; student-assisted functional assessment interview; direct observation

Hypothesis: When given difficult math or reading assignments, Noah engages in disruptive behavior to escape the assignment.

INTERVENTIONS

Antecedent or setting event strategies	Alternative skill instruction	Response to problem behavior	Who will implement intervention? When will it be implemented?
• Adjust demand difficulty of math tasks and reading so he achieves 90% or higher accuracy. • Alter task length (provide frequent breaks and shorten activities).	• Teach Noah to ask for a break when he feels unable to focus during class; honor break request. • Tier 2 math support • Reading recovery • Reading, math practice at home	• Prompt Noah to use his break card at the first signs of problem behavior. • Provide reminders every minute to get back to work if disruption continues. • Problem-solve at end of school day.	• Mrs. Duffy will implement all interventions during math and reading.

How plan will be evaluated: Mr. Acosta will collect Mrs. Duffy's data weekly and graph the data. He will communicate progress to all team members weekly (including Noah's parents). Mr. Acosta will schedule monthly team meeting to discuss progress. If behavior is not reduced by 25% (one disruption daily), Mr. Acosta will schedule weekly team meetings to determine next steps.

Figure 9.4. Example of a completed behavior support plan for Noah.

Case Example

Our work with Dora illustrates the process for developing the FBA and support plan. Dora, a second grade student, was diagnosed as having an emotional and behavioral disorder (EBD) and attended a self-contained special education classroom in her home school. Dora was functioning approximately one year below grade level across academic areas. She had a history of aggression and disruption that was first reported when she entered preschool. Dora lived with her father, visiting her mother and two siblings every other weekend. Her parents described occasional problem behaviors at home, but far fewer in frequency than occurred at school.

Dora struck and kicked others, grabbed hair, threw objects, and destroyed materials. Her aggressive episodes often resulted in large disruptions to the classroom environment. In response, staff restrained her and physically escorted her to a separate empty room in the school. The room was located quite a distance from her classroom, so transporting her often involved dragging her while she screamed and fought. Despite numerous attempted interventions by the teaching staff, including reward systems, extinction, medication adjustments, and one-to-one instruction, Dora's aggression remained unabated. Dora's persistent and high rate of dangerous aggression and disruption resulted in a referral to the school-based behavior support team during her second grade year.

Functional Behavioral Assessment and Hypothesis Development

Our first step with Dora was to conduct a functional behavioral assessment. We began by reviewing her educational records to better understand her brief educational history. In particular, we looked at her academic performance, including test scores, across school years. Both her grades and test scores told us that she was performing below grade level academically. We also examined her history of challenging behavior and past interventions, and although we found limited information about the latter, Dora's educational records confirmed a history of problem behavior that had escalated in the current school year and had been unresponsive to intervention.

In addition to our review of school records, we distributed functional assessment interviews (see Chapter 8) to Dora's teacher, her one-to-one aide, the school principal, and Dora's psychiatrist. We conducted direct observations of Dora's performance throughout the school day. Observations were conducted across five school days with at least three observations in each subject. During observations, we collected data on antecedents to problem behavior, the type of problem behavior Dora exhibited, and the way that staff responded to problem behavior. Admittedly this was an extensive amount of direct observation, but the team agreed that the severity of Dora's problem behavior and its accompanying level of fiscal and personnel resources warranted the allocation of additional resources to ensure there was adequate and clear information that would lead to an effective support plan. We surmised that successful intervention would actually save school resources in the future.

After all data were collected, they were organized in a graphic format that allowed the team to easily see antecedents and responses to the problem behaviors. In addition, we highlighted information from each interview that we thought was important to developing a hypothesis (see Chapter 8 for details on how to summarize functional assessment information). We then reviewed the graphs and highlighted information for themes and consistencies.

The assessment information led to five hypotheses. As we noted in Chapter 8, it is common that multiple hypotheses are required to explain complex and long-standing problem behavior. The first hypothesis pertained to Dora's escape-maintained behavior and stated, "When given difficult work, Dora engages in problem behavior to escape the work." A detailed review of both interviews and direct observations indicated that because Dora's teacher was concerned about Dora's achievement of second-grade core competencies, she regularly assigned second-grade work to Dora. Furthermore, observations indicated that Dora made frequent errors on both written and oral work, which frequently preceded problem behavior.

A second hypothesis emerged from the classroom observations, which revealed that problem behavior occurred when Dora did not get something she wanted, such as being line leader, not being called on when she raised her hand, or not earning a reward based on her point system. Thus, a second hypothesis was developed stating, "When Dora does not get what she wants, she engages in problem behavior to access the item or activity."

Both interviews and direct observation data also disclosed that aggression sometimes occurred when Dora was given written work. Dora seemed to perform much better with hands-on activities or oral tasks. Thus, the following hypothesis was developed: "When Dora is given written work, she engages in problem behavior to escape the written work."

Direct observations also revealed that when Dora engaged in minor problem behavior, such as stomping her feet, making barely audible statements expressing frustration, or putting her head down, staff always intervened, usually by getting very close to Dora, attempting to calm her and get her back on task by repeatedly issuing statements and prompts (e.g., "Please continue your work," "Get yourself under control," "Take some deep breaths."). Dora responded to staff in these situations by stating "Go away" or "Leave me alone" and her behavior almost always escalated to serious aggression or disruption, with episodes often lasting as long as an hour. Consequently, we developed a fourth hypothesis stating, "When Dora engages in minor behavior problems and staff interact with her, she engages in serious behavior problems to escape staff."

Interviews also indicated that staff believed Dora engaged in higher rates of problem behavior on Mondays. Direct observations, extended across one month, supported the results of the staff interviews. Data indicated that problem behaviors were relatively more frequent on Mondays, during the first two hours of the day. Observations also indicated that she came into school from the bus agitated and complained about events that occurred with her mother and siblings during the behavioral outbursts. Thus, the final hypothesis was, "Dora engages in problem behaviors following visits with her mother (function unknown)."

Support Plan Development

Our next step was to develop a comprehensive behavior support plan with interventions that addressed each of the hypotheses. In addition, we developed supports that were designed to address broad issues and improve Dora's overall quality of life as well. Dora's support plan is shown in Figure 9.5.

SUPPORT PLAN

Student: Dora **Date:** November 25, 2015

Team leader: Ms. Elias

Team members: Ms. Taylor, Mrs. Ruiz, Mr. Jones, Dr. Graham

Target behavior: Aggression, Disruption

Definition of target behavior: Hitting, kicking, grabbing hair, throwing objects, destroying materials

Current level of behavior: Average of 2 aggressions/hour (range = 0–12/hour); average of 4 disruptions/hour (range = 0–17/hour)

End-of-year behavioral goal: No more than one aggression or disruption/hour over next 6 months, decreasing to no more than 1/day over next year

How progress will be measured: All teachers will collect frequency counts of occurrences of aggression.

Functional assessments data collected: Interviews (teacher, aide, principal, psychiatrist), direct observations

Hypothesis:

1. When given difficult work, Dora engages in problem behavior to escape the work.
2. When Dora does not get what she wants, she engages in problem behavior to get access to the item or activity.
3. When Dora is given written work, she engages in problem behavior to escape the written work.
4. When Dora engages in minor behavior problems and staff interact with her, she engages in serious behavior problems to escape staff.
5. Following visits with her mother, Dora engages in problem behaviors (function unknown).

INTERVENTIONS

Antecedent or setting event strategies	Alternative skill instruction	Response to problem behavior	Lifestyle Interventions	Who will implement intervention; when will it be implemented?
• Reduce work difficulty and amount of written work. • Rehearse not getting what she wants; provide reminders just prior to problem situations. • Decrease written work. • Ignore minor problem behaviors. • Inform school of family visits.	• Prompt to request assistance + cards. • Request brief break. • Use relaxation techniques when upset; talk with staff. • Request to be left alone.	• Ignore minor problems. • Remind Dora of expected behavior once every 5 minutes. • Point loss. • Implement crisis plan as needed.	• Peer tutoring. • Lunch bunch to develop friendships with peers. • Encourage friendships outside of school . • Join YMCA, sports team.	• All staff will implement plan. • Begin implementing plan immediately. • Coaching will be conducted by Mrs. Ruiz until staff implement with 90% integrity. • Father will implement with YMCA and sports team.

How plan will be evaluated: Conduct direct observations monthly and review point sheets weekly to examine reductions in problem behavior and determine whether trends indicate Dora will meet the end-of-year goal.

Figure 9.5. Support plan for Dora.

To address the first hypothesis, problem behavior related to difficult work, staff adjusted work demands so that Dora's assignments and instruction were on her academic level of performance as opposed to her grade level so that she could attain a high level of academic success (minimum of 95% accuracy). This intervention seemed counterintuitive to Dora's teacher, who believed that providing grade-level material was important because it would allow Dora to "catch up" to her peers and increase the likelihood of future inclusion. The teacher did not see that the challenging second-grade curriculum was a mismatch with Dora's skill levels and triggered problem behaviors that resulted in less learning and putting Dora further behind academically. The intent of providing academic tasks matched to Dora's skill level was to decrease problem behavior, enhance task engagement, and increase Dora's motivation to learn. In addition to this antecedent strategy of matching curriculum to Dora's skill levels, Dora was taught how to properly request assistance with her work when she needed help. Dora was provided with cards printed with "I need help" that she could keep at her desk and prop up when she needed assistance. These cards were intended to serve as a prompt to remind Dora to request assistance when needed and provided Dora an alternative, appropriate behavior to use when she experienced frustration over the difficulty of her work. In addition, staff provided reminders to Dora, initially every 5 minutes, to use her card to request help if needed. The verbal reminders were given less frequently after the first few periods (i.e., faded) to a reminder every 15 minutes, and eventually only when initial signs of frustration were observed.

To address the second hypothesis pertaining to problem behavior that occurred when Dora did not get what she wanted, we had Dora "pre-practice" situations that had caused difficulties in the past using appropriate social responses. These practice sessions occurred at a specified time during the school day and again just prior to the actual situation that previously resulted in problem behaviors. Simultaneously, we taught Dora to use self-talk to calm herself during these potentially difficult times. For example, Dora routinely had problems when she was not chosen as line leader. Thus, we discussed lining up, practicing with another student being designated line leader, and having Dora state, "I can't always be line leader, that's okay. I will be line leader another time." Then, just prior to lining up, Dora was reminded that she might not be line leader and she should use her calming skills. The same technique was used to rehearse other difficult situations, such as not earning her points or not having her preferred foods in the cafeteria.

The third hypothesis pertained to problem behavior associated with written work. The antecedent intervention for addressing this issue was to reduce the amount of written work Dora was expected to complete. Dora's teacher found that much of the written work could be completed in alternative formats, such as orally or on the computer. Still, some written work was necessary. Because written work was a trigger for frustration leading to outbursts of aggressive and disruptive behavior, Dora was taught the alternative skill of requesting a brief break when frustrated. To ensure she was learning this skill, whenever written work was assigned, Dora was instructed that she was being given a task that was difficult for her, but she could request a brief 2-minute break whenever she wanted. During the task, staff praised her for persisting and reminded her, approximately every 5 minutes, that she could take a break if the task was becoming difficult and frustrating.

The fourth hypothesis addressed problem behavior that occurred when staff interacted with Dora following minor behavior problems. This hypothesis was addressed by having staff ignore minor problem behaviors. We found that Dora's minor problem behaviors almost always lasted just a few minutes and rarely escalated to more serious problems if she was left alone to compose herself.

The final hypothesis stated that problem behavior occurred following weekend visits with her mother. As a general approach, we offered Dora the opportunity to visit the school counselor, with whom she had established a close relationship, whenever she wanted to talk about something that was bothering her. We also encouraged her to talk with other staff members. As we noted, Dora frequently disembarked from the bus appearing angry and upset. On these occasions, Dora was prompted to visit the school counselor and talk about her weekend visit with her mother.

A few general response strategies were used when problem behavior occurred. First, staff reminded Dora of expected behavior every 5 minutes when her problem behavior began to escalate. This brief reminder was issued from a distance and differed from the immediate and intensive prompting that staff previously delivered following minor problem behavior. In addition, the classroom incentive system was maintained and Dora earned points for following expectations and experienced point losses for engaging in serious problem behavior. Finally, a crisis plan was developed that guided staff in ways to keep Dora, her peers, and the staff safe when dangerous behavior occurred. The plan allowed Dora to remove herself to a safe area in the classroom, rather than having staff physically transport her to another location, a procedure that often proved perilous for Dora's safety as well as the safety of the staff.

In addition to the interventions immediately related to problem behavior, the support team developed interventions that would improve Dora's overall quality of life and also help her develop important lifelong social skills. The team suggested that peer tutoring might give Dora a sense of self-worth and importance, something that she lacked. So, she was assigned to assist students in the kindergarten classroom each day. In addition, we noticed that Dora was in a special education classroom with only boys and never had the opportunity to interact with same age-peers. The team agreed this would be important not only to allow Dora to build friendships, but also to expose her to typically developing students who could serve as role models. Therefore, a lunch bunch was started with three second-grade peers who expressed an interest in meeting Dora and who shared similar interests. The foursome regularly convened at lunchtime. Initially, the girls brought photographs of themselves engaged in activities outside of school to serve as conversation starters. Also, the peers were coached to use questions to engage Dora in conversation. Lunch staff were also encouraged to engage Dora in conversation. In a short period of time, Dora began to build friendships with the girls. Dora's father reported that in the spring Dora was invited to her first birthday party. A final lifestyle intervention, implemented by her father, was joining the YMCA and a soccer team. Dora's preferred activities were sports and she was quite athletically talented. These sports-related activities allowed Dora to show her strengths, meet friends, and learn the cooperation skills required on a sports team.

Dora's Progress

We followed Dora's progress over the course of 3 school years and during the process learned many lessons about what is needed to sustain an intervention over the long haul. First, although we saw a decrease in problem behaviors, it was not as rapid as we had hoped, reminding us that intensive problem behavior that has persisted over a long period of time is quite durable, and that patience and perseverance are needed to meet the goal of reducing it to very low rates. Furthermore, we were reminded of the need to set reasonable (not too ambitious) goals. Dora's aggression decreased to near zero levels across the 3 years we collected direct observation data. However, it took almost a year and a half to attain that goal.

We also found that an intervention may not be carried out as designed across school years in spite of the presence of a support plan. Staff changes mean that teachers may not be familiar with a plan, may not have the skills to implement the plan, or may find that a plan is not aligned with their teaching style and preferences. To address staff unfamiliarity with the plan and lack of skill required to accurately implement the interventions, we conducted regular trainings prior to the start of each school year. As part of the trainings, we used video recordings of teachers correctly implementing the plan to illustrate how it should be implemented. Teachers reported that this video instruction greatly helped them understand the specific procedures necessary for maintaining the alternative behaviors. This experience informed us of the need for systems changes to ensure continuity of plans and training across school years.

Finally, after achieving very low levels of aggression during the second year in which the plan was in place, we saw increases of aggression during the third year. We discovered that aspects of the plan were no longer relevant for Dora and revisions were needed. For instance, the staff found that written work became less problematic for Dora and seldom resulted in problem behaviors. In addition, Dora gradually learned to accept situations when she was not able to get what she wanted, however, a new situation emerged that led to problem behaviors. Dora became increasingly intolerant when she was required to wait for assistance or during transitions. Therefore, an intervention had to be initiated for this new situation. We were reminded that it is critical to regularly review and update each student's support plan at least annually, and often more frequently, to fade or eliminate unnecessary interventions and consider additional interventions when problems emerge in new situations.

Overall, we were pleased with the progress Dora made. Not only did Dora's social behavior improve, but there also was a host of benefits for the school. For example, by the end of the school year one-on-one support was no longer needed. In addition, the design and implementation of an effective behavior plan resulted in the elimination of the need for physical restraint. Finally, we also came to better understand the persistence and patience needed to succeed with students who have engaged in challenging behavior over long periods of time.

SUMMARY

Behavior support plans for chronic and serious problems are built upon information from an FBA. A comprehensive plan includes interventions for setting events (if needed), antecedent strategies, instruction in replacement behaviors or general skills, and ways to respond to problem behavior. For students who engage in dangerous behavior, a crisis plan also should be included. A comprehensive behavior support plan is likely to reduce problem behavior in both the short and long term.

Self-Reflection

1. Many teachers are reluctant to make antecedent modifications because they believe that students should know how to behave and that making such environmental changes means "giving in." What is your philosophy on this issue? After reading this chapter, do you see how antecedent modifications can benefit students?
2. Setting events can be difficult to eliminate. Can you think of a time when you were able to eliminate a setting event for the problem behavior of a student in your classroom or a classroom you have visited? Brainstorm additional ways you could eliminate setting events that a student might experience.
3. There are a number of different antecedent interventions described in this chapter that have been shown to reduce problem behavior. Make a list of the interventions that best fit with your personal philosophy and teaching style, then prioritize the list you have made, beginning with those interventions you are most likely to implement.
4. Perhaps every teacher has used punishment with a student when another intervention would have been more effective (instructional procedure). Recall a time when you have punished (or have observed someone punish) a student for misbehavior. Having read this chapter, can you think of an alternative response you could have used that would have been more effective?
5. Secure the crisis management plan from the school where you work or have visited. Is it well developed and likely to ensure safety, de-escalate the student, and allow him or her to reenter the classroom with little disruption?

REFERENCES

Belfiore, P.J., Lee, D.L., Scheeler, C., & Klein, D. (2002). Implications of behavioral momentum and academic achievement for students with behavior disorders: Theory, application, and practice. *Psychology in the Schools, 39,* 171–179.

Boyajian, A.E., DuPual, G.J., Handler, M.W., Eckert, T.L., & McGoey, K.E. (2001). The use of classroom-based brief functional analysis with preschoolers at-risk for attention deficit hyperactivity disorder. *School Psychology Review, 30,* 278–293.

Dunlap, G., & Kern, L. (1996). Modifying instructional activities to promote desirable behavior: A conceptual and practical framework. *School Psychology Quarterly, 11,* 297–312.

Dunlap, G., Kern, L., dePerczel, M., Clarke, S., Wilson, D., Childs, K.E., & White, R.L. (1993). Functional analysis of classroom variables for students with emotional and behavioral disorders. *Behavioral Disorders, 18,* 275–291.

Hinton, L.M., & Kern, L. (1999). Increasing homework completion by incorporating student interest. *Journal of Positive Behavior Interventions, 1,* 231–241.

Kern, L., Bambara, L., & Fogt, J. (2002). Class-wide curricular modification to improve the behavior of students with emotional or behavioral disorders. *Behavioral Disorders, 27,* 317–326.

Kern, L., Childs, K.E., Dunlap, G., Clarke, S., & Falk, G.D. (1994). Using assessment-based curricular intervention to improve the classroom behavior of a student with emotional and behavioral challenges. *Journal of Applied Behavior Analysis, 27,* 7–19.

Kern, L., & Clemens, N. (2007). Antecedent strategies to promote appropriate classroom behavior. *Psychology in the Schools, 44,* 65–75.

Kern, L., Mantegna, M.E., Vorndran, C.M., Bailin, D., & Hilt, A. (2001). Choice of task sequence to increase engagement and reduce problem behaviors. *Journal of Positive Behavior Interventions, 3,* 3–10.

Moes, D.R. (1998). Integrating choice making opportunities within teacher-assigned academic tasks to facilitate the performance of children with autism. *Journal of the Association for Persons with Severe Handicaps, 23,* 319–328.

National Disability Rights Network. (2009). *School is not supposed to hurt.* Retrieved from http://www.ndrn.org/images/Documents/Resources/Publications/Reports/SR-Report2009.pdf

Salvia, J.S., Ysseldyke, J.E., & Bolt, S. (2010). *Assessment in special and inclusive education* (11th ed.). Boston, MA: Wadsworth/Cengage.

Skinner, C.H. (2002). An empirical analysis of interspersal research: Evidence, implications, and applications of the discrete task completion hypothesis. *Journal of School Psychology, 40,* 347–368.

TASH. (2014). *APRAIS.* Retrieved from http://tash.org/advocacy-issues/restraint-and-seclusion-aprais/

Umbreit, J., Lane, K.L., & Dejud, C. (2004). Improving classroom behavior by modifying task difficulty: Effects of increasing the difficulty of too-easy tasks. *Journal of Positive Behavioral Interventions, 6,* 13–20.

10

Measuring Behavior Change

Throughout this book, we have described a variety of strategies to prevent or reduce behavior problems. Teaching and managing a classroom would be an easy undertaking if teachers could simply implement an intervention and have behavior problems disappear. Unfortunately, this rarely happens. More often, educators see gradual reductions in behavior problems or must try various interventions or combinations of interventions to find just the right one(s). In addition, there is the possibility of the well-known placebo effect, extensively tested in medicine, in which patients show improvement in response to an ineffectual treatment (e.g., sugar pill). In other words, educators sometimes believe an intervention is working when it really is not. For these reasons, along with documentation for reporting purposes and future reference, measuring behavior change is essential. It is important to have a procedure that can accurately and objectively evaluate behavioral improvement. Unbiased information about intervention effects helps educators to avoid believing an intervention is effective when it really is not or too soon discarding an intervention that has the potential to be effective.

There are many different ways to evaluate behavior change. Some methods are more precise than others but can be time consuming. Others may be easy but are not very accurate. It is important to identify a system that 1) measures the behavior of interest, 2) provides a fairly accurate measure of that behavior, and 3) is sensitive to change. That is, some measures of behavior provide a global idea of how a student is doing compared to other students of his or her age (e.g., general level of acting out or externalizing behavior), but may not provide information about a specific behavior (e.g., daily rate of aggression). Furthermore, some measures are not sensitive enough to allow teachers to determine whether an intervention was effective.

In this chapter, we describe different ways to measure behavior. We begin with the preliminary steps that need to be taken prior to measuring behavior. Then we describe several types of measurement strategies along with the strengths and limitations of each. Finally, we provide guidelines for selecting a measurement system, understanding what information it is likely to provide, and determining how it can be best used.

GETTING STARTED

There are a few initial steps to be taken before collecting data on student behavior when preparing to measure student behavior. These include determining the behaviors that will be targeted for intervention (both problem behavior and replacement behavior) and operationally defining those behaviors. Other important preliminary considerations are *who* will collect data and *when* will data be collected. Answering these questions will help determine the type of data collection system to use.

Defining Behavior

The first step for identifying a system for recording behavior is to define the behavior. That is, the teacher (or team) must determine exactly what problem behavior the student engages in that will be the target of intervention. As described in Chapter 8, developing a precise description of the behavior targeted for intervention is the first step in the FBA process and allows for accurate communication among team members. At the same time, replacement skills (described in Chapter 9) also should be defined in a clear and unambiguous manner.

There are several guidelines when defining behavior (Miltenberger, 2005). First, the behavior should be observable, meaning the definition includes actions that can be seen by others. An example of an observable problem behavior is "strikes or attempts to strike other children," and an alternative replacement behavior is "verbally asks a peer to join an activity." Simple labels for behavior, such as *aggressive* or *uncooperative,* are not observable; neither are presumed intentions or states of mind (e.g., James acts angry, Elaine worries, Daniel will have a positive attitude). Teachers should be especially vigilant to avoid highly ambiguous terms that have the potential to stigmatize the student, such as "she likes to manipulate other students."

Second, the behavioral definition should be clear so that there is no ambiguity. For example, teachers may be inclined to characterize behavior using diagnostic labels or classifications, such as *hyperactive* or *depressed.* Such diagnostic labels do not clearly identify the behavior that is problematic and, as mentioned previously, also have the potential to stigmatize children and change teacher and staff behavior toward them. Instead, behaviors suggesting such a diagnosis should be defined. For instance, in the case of depression, a student may show disengagement by not responding to or initiating conversation with peers, keeping his or her head on the desk during class, and failing to turn in assignments. Similarly, hyperactive behavior can be defined as getting out of one's seat during teacher instruction or engaging with a toy for fewer than 10 seconds.

The third characteristic of a strong behavioral definition is that it is thorough. This means that all of the possible dimensions of the behavior are included in the definition. For example, *aggression* may be defined as hitting another student but also might need to include throwing an object at another student or kicking or pushing a student. *Engagement* can be defined as keeping one's eyes on the teacher during a lecture, completing assigned independent work with one's eyes on the paper or book, and raising one's hand and waiting quietly for teacher assistance. With complicated behavior, it is helpful to also describe behaviors that are not included in the definition. For example, a behavioral definition for *self-injury* might be hitting one's own body with an open hand or closed fist, but does not include rubbing or stroking the skin. Similarly, the replacement behavior of raising one's hand to request assistance may be counted if it includes having a hand in the air, followed by asking the teacher for help after being called on, but not counted if it is accompanied by a call out.

When targeted behaviors are defined so that the behavior is observable and the definition is clear and thorough, multiple people should be able to independently observe the student engaging in the behavior, and all should agree that it occurred. A good test is to ask a colleague who does not know the student to read the definition and observe a few occurrences of the target behavior. If both the teacher and colleague are in agreement that the behavior occurred, it is likely that the definition is adequate.

Considerations for Selecting a Measurement System

After the target and replacement behaviors have been defined, there are several considerations that will help determine what type of data collection system will be used (see Table 10.1). The first consideration is who will collect data. If an observer is available who has time allocated specifically for data collection, selecting a data collection system will be easy. That is, just

Table 10.1. Considerations when selecting a data collection system

Considerations	Relevant questions
Who	• Is a person in the school assigned to the task? • How often is the person available?
Competing responsibilities	• Can the person devote all of his or her time to observation? • Does the person have responsibilities that might compete with or interrupt data collection?
Frequency of behavior	• Is the behavior very high frequency, making it difficult to count? • Is the behavior low frequency and easily counted?
Visibility	• Is the behavior covert? • Does the behavior often occur away from the presence of an observer?

about any system can be used, because the individual is able to devote all of his or her attention to the task. This person may be a school psychologist or behavior specialist who has a specific role observing students and developing behavior support plans. As an alternative, during a certain time of the day (e.g., whole group, independent work, play time), a paraprofessional might be assigned the task of observation and data collection. Because data will need to be collected on an ongoing basis to evaluate behavioral change, it is important that this person is carefully trained and can regularly collect data across time (e.g., weekly for 3 or more months, 15 minutes daily during independent work time).

A second consideration is competing responsibilities for the observer. For instance, if the only person available to collect data is the teacher, a data collection system must be identified that allows teaching while simultaneously collecting data. Similarly, if a paraprofessional collecting data may be interrupted to address a student's learning or behavioral challenge, the data collection system must allow for some flexibility. A number of flexible strategies for collecting data are described later in this chapter, including behavior sampling, Direct Behavior Rating (DBR), and permanent product data, that work well for busy school professionals tasked with many responsibilities.

A third consideration is the frequency of problem behavior. Problem behavior that occurs very frequently can be difficult to count accurately. Therefore, a data collection system can be selected that periodically samples how often the behavior occurred during brief periods of time or that simply allows the observer to indicate whether the behavior occurred during a specified time interval. In contrast, behavior that is relatively low in frequency is usually easier to count accurately.

A final consideration is visibility of the behavior. Some behaviors are covert and not easily observable. For instance, stealing, cutting, and bullying are often covert behaviors and may not be easy to see and, therefore, measure via direct observation strategies. In this case, alternative approaches must be identified for determining whether the behavior occurred. For example, checks of injury to the arms or other sites of self-injury can be conducted, a backpack can be examined by a parent for items not belonging to the student, or classmates can be periodically asked to anonymously report incidents of bullying.

When to Collect Data Another decision to be made when planning for data collection is when to observe. First, it is important to collect data at a time when the behavior is likely to occur. For instance, Della engages in inappropriate social exchanges during hallway transitions, gym, and lunchtime, but exhibits few or no social problems during structured class time. Thus, observations must occur when opportunities for social interactions are present.

Second, it is best to select observational periods when problem behaviors occur at a high frequency. This makes it easier to determine whether intervention is effective. For example, Jared engages in property destruction (e.g., ripping up his paper, tipping over his desk, breaking his pencil) during almost every academic subject at least once or twice a week. However, in math, a particularly difficult subject for Jared, property destruction occurs daily, usually several times during the class period. Thus, although it will be easy to tell if an intervention is reducing his property destruction in math within a week or two, it could take several months to evaluate intervention effectiveness in other academic subjects.

Another general rule is that observations should occur at approximately the same time each day. This is because the frequency of behavior can vary tremendously, depending on the activity. In the example regarding property destruction, if Jared's teacher began collecting data during math, then switched to reading after the intervention was implemented, she would believe behavior had decreased and the intervention was effective. Instead, the behavior decrease she observed resulted from the switch in observation time, rather than an actual decrease in behavior problems.

Finally, data need to be collected both before and after intervention is implemented. Data collected before intervention referred to as *baseline* and provide a comparison to evaluate whether intervention was effective. As a general rule, it is important to collect approximately five data points prior to implementing intervention (e.g., across five school days, during five speech sessions) in order to get an accurate measure of behavior occurrences (Shavelson, Webb, & Rowley, 1989). The length of baseline data collection, however, depends on a number of variables. For example, if there is time for only brief observations (e.g., 10 minutes each day), a longer baseline is advised. Similarly, if behavior is highly variable or infrequent, an accurate assessment of behavioral occurrences may take longer.

TYPES OF MEASUREMENT SYSTEMS

There are two general categories of behavioral measurement. Direct systems (i.e., direct observation) code behavior when it is actually occurring. Indirect systems collect data at a time other than that during which the behavior occurred and rely on the memory of the observer. Direct systems of data collection are considered the most accurate for measuring occurrences of a specific behavior because they do not rely on recollection. In recent years, some hybrid systems have been developed that appear to be promising (e.g., DBR; see Chafouleas, 2011). These systems train teachers or observers to rate a target behavior along a certain dimension (e.g., frequency, intensity) after a specified period of time of observation rather than record behaviors when they occur. Thus, they combine features of both direct and indirect assessment. In the following subsections, we describe direct observation strategies, DBR, permanent product (which can be either direct or indirect), and indirect approaches, including schoolwide data collection and standardized measures of behavior. Table 10.2 describes strengths and limitations of data collection methods.

Table 10.2. Strengths and limitations of data collection methods

Method	Strategy	How to use	Target behavior	Strengths and limitations
Direct observation	Frequency	Count each occurrence of behavior	Brief, discrete behavior	Highly accurate and sensitive to change, but time-consuming
Direct observation	Duration	Measure how long a behavior lasts	Behavior that lasts over a period of time	Highly accurate and sensitive to change, but time-consuming
Direct observation	Latency	Record the time it takes to initiate behavior after a cue	Behavior that occurs after some cue	Highly accurate and sensitive to change, but time-consuming
Direct behavior rating	Usually, percentage of intervals	Indicate percentage of time behavior occurred on a scale at the end of a predetermined time interval or activity	Behavior that can be measured in percentage	Requires little time; sensitive to change; accurate with training
Permanent product	Products from behaviors or events	Evaluate objects or outcomes	Behavior that leaves a permanent record	Does not require direct observation; can be used only when behavior leaves product
Standardized assessments	Rating scale or other measure completed by student, parent, and/or teacher	Assess a broad array of indicators of domains of functioning (broadband measures); focus on specific problems (narrowband)	Internalizing and externalizing problems	Compares results to age and gender norms; limited sensitivity to behavioral changes

Direct Observation

There are several different methods for recording behavior using direct observation. Characteristics of the target behavior will primarily guide the selection of a recording method; however, the amount of time the observer is able to spend observing also is a consideration. Event recording requires that every occurrence of a behavior be coded. One method of event recording is to document the frequency of a behavior. This means that the observer codes the number of times a behavior occurs within a prespecified time interval. This method is best to use with behavior that is brief (i.e., occurs for a short period of time) and is discrete (i.e., has a clear beginning and end). Examples of behaviors well suited to frequency counts are hitting, pushing, or saying "no." Figure 10.1 provides an example of an event recording form. As the form illustrates, it is best to break an observational period, such as a 15-minute session or class period, into shorter intervals for accuracy (e.g., 1-minute intervals, 5-minute intervals).

A second method of event recording is to document the duration. When measuring duration, the observer records how long a behavior lasts.

EVENT RECORDING FORM

Name: ______________________ Date: ______________________

Definition of behavior being recorded:

Directions: Determine length of observational interval. Record how often a targeted behavior occurs by marking an X or tally mark in the boxes below each time the target behavior occurred during the observation session.

Initials	**Time**	**1**	**2**	**3**	**4**	**5**	**6**	**7**	**8**	**9**	**10**	**Total**

Figure 10.1. Event Recording Form.

This method is best suited for measuring behavior that spans a period of time. Tantrums, self-stimulation, and engagement or disengagement are well matched to a duration measure. The reason it is particularly important to use duration recording when the goal is to reduce the length of that behavior (as opposed to reducing the number of occurrences) is illustrated in the following example. Almost every day, Alicia engages in two or three tantrums that can last up to 45 minutes. Her teacher introduced an intervention that reduced those two or three tantrums to less than 5 minutes each. By measuring the duration of tantrums, Alicia's teacher was able to determine that the intervention was very effective. Had she used a frequency count, she would have continued to code two to three occurrences each day, resulting in data that indicated the intervention was not effective because the number of tantrums had not changed. Figure 10.2 illustrates a recording form for observing behavior duration. As shown on the form, the start and stop time of each occurrence is noted.

A third way to record events is to measure latency. When measuring latency, the observer records how long it takes to begin a behavior after a particular cue. This method is best used when a teacher wants to shorten the amount of time it takes students to initiate behavior after an instruction or some other cue. For example, a teacher may code the length of time it takes students to get to their seats after the bell rings or the amount of time it takes Jillian to begin writing her story after she is given a story prompt.

The previous paragraphs in this subsection have described direct observation strategies that require observers to continuously observe behavior in order to record frequency, duration, or latency. Behavior sampling is an alternative strategy to record the frequency or duration of a behavior that can be far less time-consuming. As the term suggests, behavior sampling requires observers to record just a sample of behaviors rather than every occurrence. Specifically, a designated time interval is established, such as 1 minute, 5 minutes, 10 minutes, or longer, and the observer codes either 1) whether the behavior occurred during the previous time interval or 2) whether the behavior is occurring at the exact time that the interval ends. This method of recording is best used when behavior is fairly frequent. For instance, India frequently calls out during teacher lecture. Her teacher divided the class lecture into 5-minute intervals, and she codes, at the end of each interval, whether India called out. Similarly, Abel is frequently off task. His teacher, Mr. Zimmer, wanted to collect data on Abel's engagement throughout the day, so he divided the day into 15-minute intervals. He set a vibrating watch to cue him every 15 minutes. When the watch vibrates, Mr. Zimmer looks up at Abel and records whether he is engaged at that exact time. Behavior sampling results in fairly accurate data but does not require constant attention, allowing teachers and observers to teach or engage in other activities while simultaneously collecting direct observation data. Figure 10.3 shows a data collection form for time sampling.

DURATION RECORDING FORM

Name: ____________________ Date: ____________________

Definition of behavior being recorded:

Directions: Record how long each targeted behavior occurred by indicating the start and stop times of each instance.

Initials	Time	Start	Stop	Start	Stop	Start	Stop	Start	Stop	Start	Stop	Total

Figure 10.2. Duration Recording Form.

TIME SAMPLING RECORDING FORM

Name: ______________________ Date: ______________________

Definition of behavior being recorded:

Directions: Record whether the targeted behavior occurred during the interval or was occurring at the exact start of each 5-minute interval.

Initials	Time	1	2	3	4	5	6	7	8	9	10	Total

Figure 10.3. Time Sampling Recording Form.

Direct Behavior Rating DBR (Chafouleas, 2011; Chafouleas, Riley-Tillman, & Christ, 2009) is similar to behavior sampling in that behavior is coded at the end of a specified interval of time, such as the end of a class or particular activity (e.g., independent seatwork). However, behavior is coded on a scale corresponding to the percentage of time it occurred during the interval. To use DBR, the target behavior is first operationally defined, as with other direct observation systems. The developers have created a number of definitions for common behaviors (for specifics, see http://www.directbehaviorratings.org/cms/files%5Cpdf%5CV%201.4%20DBR%20Standard%20Form%20with%203%20Standard%20Behaviors.pdf) that can be used, such as their definition of *engagement:* "Actively or passively participating in the classroom activity. For example: writing, raising his/her hand, answering a question, talking about a lesson, listening to the teacher, reading silently, or looking at instructional materials" (Chafouleas, Riley-Tillman, & Christ, 2009).

In addition to operational definitions, the developers have constructed accompanying scales and associated anchors for behavior. Although various scale gradients have been used (e.g., 6 point, 10 point, 14 point), a 10-point scale appears to be optimal in order to most easily interpret and utilize the data (Briesch, Kilgus, Chafouleas, Riley-Tillman, & Christ, 2012). Figure 10.4 provides an example of a DBR. Using a 10-point scale, engagement may be coded as "never" (1 or 0%), "sometimes" (5 or 50%), "always" (10 or 100%), or anywhere in between. Immediately after the specified interval, the percentage of behavior that occurred is coded on the scale.

Research on DBR is rapidly accumulating, and it appears to be a measure that is quite easy to use (requiring less than 1 minute per student) and also sensitive to change in student behavior. However, an important consideration is that training and practice on the measure increases accuracy of ratings (Chafouleas, Kilgus, Riley-Tillman, Jaffery, & Harrison, 2012), as with any direct observation measure. We recommend that school-based practitioners make sure behavioral definitions are clear and observers practice with the scales prior to actual use.

Permanent Products Permanent products are objects or outcomes of a behavior that offer a record of events that took place. In the context of behavior, inspection of a binder or desk might offer data about a student's organization. Similarly, amount of completed work can indicate how engaged a student was during independent work time. Permanent product data may be used alone to indicate the success of an intervention, as in regularly measuring the amount of classwork a child completes prior to and after intervention. It also can be used in conjunction with other methods of data collection. This may be especially important when students have multiple difficulties, such as problems staying engaged and failure to complete assignments. Although increasing engagement is an important goal, it is not sufficient. It is equally important that the intervention also results in improvements in work completion. Thus, teachers may choose to evaluate intervention effectiveness

DIRECT BEHAVIOR RATING (DBR) FORM

Date: M T W Th F	**Student name:**	**Any changes in the typical classroom routine?** If YES, describe (e.g., fire drill, assembly, field trip):
Observation time: Start: _________ End: _________ ☐ Check if unable to observe	**<u>Behavior descriptions</u>:** **Academically engaged** is actively or passively participating in the classroom activity (e.g., writing, raising hand, answering a question, talking about a lesson, listening to the teacher, reading silently, or looking at instructional materials). **Respectful** is defined as compliant and polite behavior in response to adult direction and/or interactions with peers and adults (e.g., follows teacher direction, engages in prosocial interaction with peers, responds positively to adult request, makes verbal or physical disruption without a negative tone or connotation). **Disruptive** is student action that interrupts regular school or classroom activity (e.g., out of seat, fidgeting, playing with objects, acting aggressively, talking or yelling about things that are unrelated to classroom instruction).	

<u>Directions</u>: Place a mark along the line that best reflects *the percentage of total time* the student exhibited each target behavior. Note that the percentages do not need to total 100% across behaviors since some behaviors may co-occur.

Academically Engaged

% of total time

0 1 2 3 4 5 6 7 8 9 10
0% Never — 50% Sometimes — 100% Always

Respectful

% of total time

0 1 2 3 4 5 6 7 8 9 10
0% Never — 50% Sometimes — 100% Always

Disruptive*

% of total time

0 1 2 3 4 5 6 7 8 9 10
0% Never — 50% Sometimes — 100% Always

*Remember that a lower score for "Disruptive" is more desirable.

From Chafouleas, S.M. (2009). *Direct behavior rating form: Three standard behaviors.* Storrs: University of Connecticut; adapted by permission.

In *Supporting Students with Emotional and Behavioral Problems: Prevention and Intervention Strategies* by Lee Kern, Michael P. George, & Mark D. Weist (2016; Paul H. Brookes Publishing Co., Inc.)

Figure 10.4. Direct Behavior Rating(DBR) Form.

by collecting engagement data using DBR but also collecting permanent product data on the amount of work completed.

The biggest advantage of permanent product data is that the student does not need to be observed directly, making it a feasible data collection approach for teachers with competing responsibilities. One disadvantage is that not all behaviors leave permanent product records (e.g., aggression, talking out). In addition, even when permanent products are available, they do not necessarily provide evidence that the product resulted from the student. For example, a peer or sibling can complete a student's homework assignments. Another disadvantage is that permanent products do not provide contextual information. For instance, an incomplete assignment may be the result of a particularly high number of classroom distractions on a particular day (e.g., guests entering and exiting the classroom, noisy peers), which would not be captured with the product alone.

Schoolwide Data Collection A number of additional types of data are frequently collected in schools for documentation and other purposes (e.g., student attendance, discipline referrals, suspensions). These sources can be useful for determining the need for intervention or to evaluate behavior change. As we described in Chapter 2, school-wide positive behavior support offers an excellent framework for collecting and organizing data, as well as for ongoing analysis and action planning. For example, office disciplinary referrals (ODR) usually are tracked and can serve to flag students with additional support needs. In addition, they can serve as a gross measure of behavior change. However, because ODRs generally are reserved for more serious problem behaviors, they may not be sensitive enough to determine intervention effectiveness. For instance, although the decrease in Morgan's ODRs for aggression from one a month to one every 3 months represents a significant behavioral improvement, this change was not evident for several months. Instead, monitoring the frequency of inappropriate peer interactions would have provided more immediate evidence of intervention effectiveness. Nonetheless, ODRs can serve useful purposes, such as identifying students in need of more intensive intervention, and may be used to supplement other forms of data collection (e.g., DBR, direct observation).

GRAPHING DATA AND INTERPRETING BEHAVIOR CHANGE

After direct observation or school data have been collected, it is critical to organize them in a way that can be easily interpreted. A graphic display of the data provides a clear and easy format for understanding behavior change. Creating a graph is simple (see Figure 10.5). There are two axes, the horizontal (or abscissa) that denotes time and a vertical axis (ordinate) that corresponds to the unit of measure (e.g., frequency, duration, numbers on scale). In order to evaluate responsiveness to intervention, behavior after intervention was implemented must be compared to behavior before it was implemented. Therefore, behavior is graphed both before and

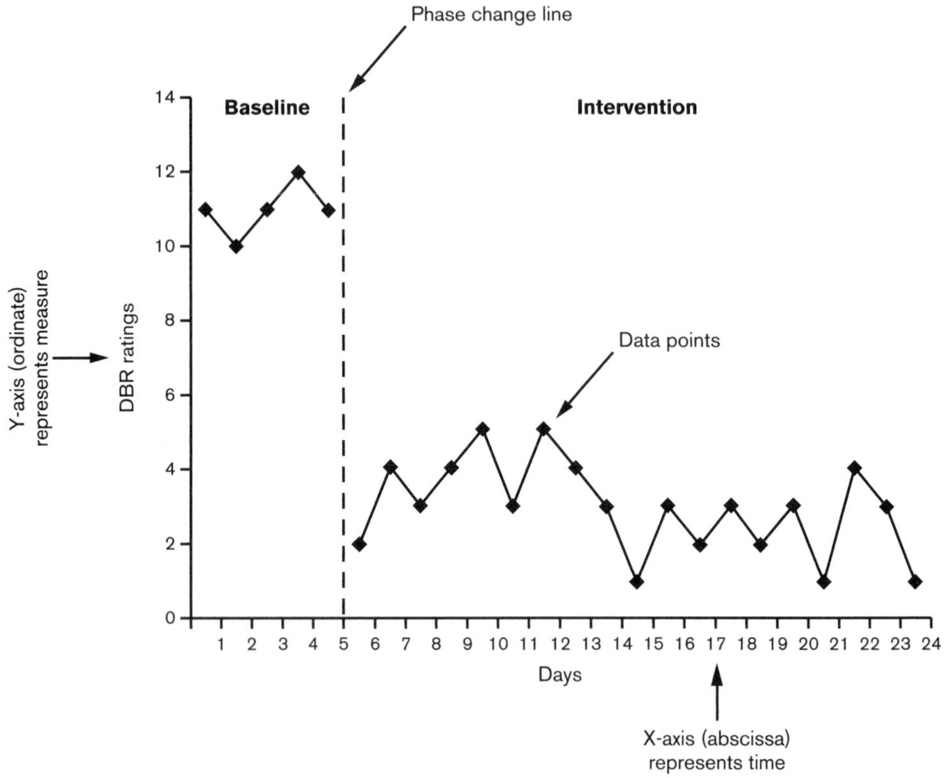

Figure 10.5. Parts of a graph. (*Key:* DBR, direct behavior rating.)

after intervention, separated by a vertical phase change line, as depicted in Figure 10.6. For specific steps on creating graphs using Microsoft Excel, we refer readers to Dixon et al., (2009), http://spreadsheets.about.com/od/excelcharts/ss/line_graph.htm, and http://www.youtube.com/watch?v=FcjV8YODnU4.

After behavioral data have been plotted, behavior change needs to be interpreted. The most common way to evaluate behavior change is by examining level and trend using visual inspection. Level of behavior change refers to how much behavior is occurring (e.g., frequency, duration) during intervention, in comparison to baseline. A large change in level (i.e., decrease for problem behavior and increase for appropriate behavior) generally indicates an effective intervention. At times, however, large changes in behavior are not expected. For example, if a behavior has been occurring over a long period of time or when functionally equivalent replacement behavior is difficult to teach, large changes may not occur. In these situations, intermediate goals might be established. Figure 10.6 shows an example of the level of behavior changing from baseline to intervention. As the graph illustrates, the level of behavior changed substantially after intervention was implemented.

It is very common that behavior does not rapidly change in response to intervention, but instead gradually or slowly improves. This outcome also

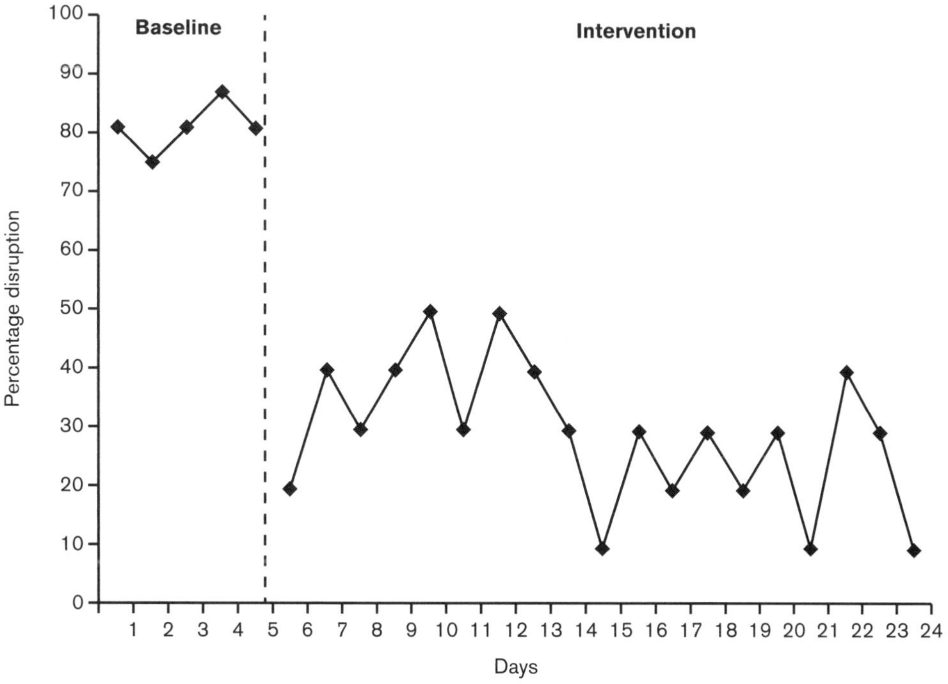

Figure 10.6. Graph showing problem behavior before and after intervention; comparison of baseline and intervention data reveals a change in level of behavior.

is desirable; therefore, graphically displayed data also should be examined for changes in trend. *Trend* refers to the direction in which behavior is moving (i.e., increasing or decreasing) within the baseline and/or intervention phase. When an intervention is effective, the data should show a trend in the desired direction after the intervention is introduced (i.e., decelerating in the case of problem behavior and accelerating in the case of appropriate behavior). One caution is that if behavior is trending in the desired direction during baseline, it is best to hold off on intervention until behavior stabilizes. This provides the opportunity to determine whether intervention actually is needed. In addition, it is possible that behavior will continue to improve without intervention, so waiting for stability will help to determine whether the intervention truly played a role in behavior change. Figure 10.7 shows that the frequency of aggression was trending upward, or accelerating, prior to intervention. Thus, the teacher made a good choice about the need for intervention. Data from the intervention phase shows the opposite trend from baseline, or a decelerating frequency of aggression, indicating that the intervention resulted in a gradual improvement in behavior. As with level of change, school teams must determine the rate of change that is acceptable.

We emphasize the need to keep an eye on how behavior is trending. Teachers often unrealistically expect behavior to rapidly disappear after intervention is implemented, which unfortunately does not often happen.

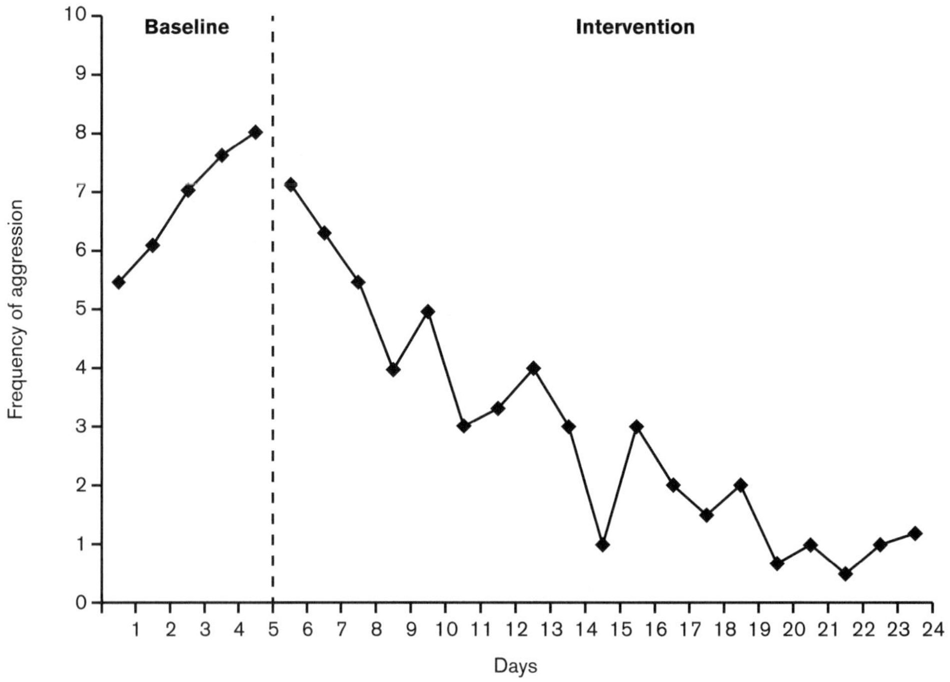

Figure 10.7. Graph showing problem behavior before and after intervention; comparison of baseline and intervention data shows a change in the trend of behavior.

Coupled with this expectation is the tendency to discard an effective intervention because it was not sufficiently "quick acting." Carefully watching the trend of behavior can provide evidence of steady improvement and support the wisdom of sticking with an intervention.

Graphically displayed data should be reviewed frequently. We recommend examining up-to-date graphs at least weekly. Ideally, the graph will reflect an acceptable change in level or trend, indicating the intervention should be maintained. However, if the data indicate that behavior did not change at all in response to an intervention, then the intervention should be discontinued and another intervention developed. If the data indicate the behavior improved, but not to desired levels, the intervention generally should be maintained, but it may be important to consider modifying the intervention or adding additional components. For example, task difficulty might need to be decreased or additional sessions of skill practice added.

OTHER SOURCES OF DATA

Several other sources of data are useful, although they may not provide information about behavior change as immediately and directly as direct observation, permanent products, or school-based data. One example is standardized measures of behavior. Most standardized assessments include norms to compare where the student stands in relation to other students of the same gender and similar age, and many include clinical cut-off scores indicating borderline and clearly clinical levels of problems. These measures can be broadband—assessing a broad array of indicators of functioning across internalizing (e.g., depression, anxiety, social withdrawal) and externalizing (e.g., acting out, noncompliance, attention problems, aggression) domains—or can be narrowband, focusing on specific problems (e.g., measures of depression or anxiety). Information from standardized measures can alert educators of the need for intervention if, for example, a student scores in the at-risk or clinical range. They can also be used to document the impact of emotional and behavioral intervention. However, similar to other broad information, producing change in these assessments often requires a higher dose of evidence-based services (see Fabiano et al., 2014). For example, the Child Behavior Checklist (CBCL) is a measure of student emotional and behavioral problems and strengths (e.g., social skills) that includes subscales measuring internalizing (e.g., depression, anxiety) and externalizing (e.g., aggression, noncompliance) problems in students (Achenbach & Rescorla, 2001). It is one of the most widely used measures of emotional and behavioral functioning for youth ages 8 through 16, and includes parent, teacher, and youth self-report versions, all with strong psychometric properties. However, wording of the measures requires that respondents rate problems that occurred in the "last 6 months," hence limiting the ability to document changes in shorter time frames.

There are several challenges documenting changes in student emotional and behavioral functioning over time using standardized measures (see Greenbaum et al., 1996). As we noted, the measures often are not sensitive to change. An additional concern is that these measures cannot answer the questions "Did the child receive the right evidence-based intervention at the right dose?" or "Were there competing circumstances that may have affected intervention effectiveness (e.g., ongoing or worsening stress at home)?" Furthermore, the timing of the assessment might affect interpretation of the results. The latter point is particularly relevant with school-based interventions that often require conducting a preassessment in the fall (when staff and students are more stressed and weather is not as nice) and then again in the spring (when people may be less stressed, experiencing better weather, and excited about the end of the school year; see Fabiano et al., 2014). These points emphasize the need for careful selection of emotional and behavioral measures and careful planning for how and when they are administered and interpreted.

Standardized measures often have student self-report, parent or caregiver report, and teacher report forms. For a comprehensive assessment, there are advantages to collecting measures from all three sources. Specifically, the likelihood of a valid assessment can be increased through "triangulation" of information. For example, if there are agreements across at least two sources (e.g., self-report and parent report), this increases confidence in the legitimacy of the concern. Self-report measures with children commonly can be used starting at around age 11. Prior to this age, children may not be reliable reporters of their emotional and behavioral functioning. For example, the CBCL measure, one of the most widely used measures of student emotional and behavioral functioning, includes both an adult version and a self-report version, which students can complete at age 11 and older (see Achenbach, 1991). Concerns with self-reports include false reporting (e.g., minimizing problems, exaggerating strengths) and careless responding (e.g., making answers up, skipping questions). There are also concerns with parent reports that include logistical challenges in collecting measures, the need for in-person instruction for accurate use, and disagreements that can occur across parent or caregiver raters. Concerns with teacher reports include ensuring adequate knowledge of students' emotional and behavioral functioning (e.g., familiarity from just one class period may be insufficient) and logistical concerns of teachers completing measures in the context of a very busy schedule.

When using standardized measures, those selected should have adequate psychometric properties, including internal consistency (i.e., the items on the measure assess the same construct or subconstructs), test–retest reliability (i.e., the measures' properties remain generally the same across administrations in time), and validity (i.e., scores on the measure are associated with other phenomena of interest; e.g., ratings of behavior problems correlate with observations of them). This information can be obtained in the publishers' manuals or by directly contacting the publisher. If the measure is in the public domain (or free), a source article is usually referenced (e.g., on the web link to the measure) that includes a review of the measure's psychometric properties. Measures almost always describe internal consistency and usually report on test–retest reliability. Validity data are less common.

In addition, schools are increasingly using measures found in the public domain, given the high cost of many standardized assessments. For example, broadband measures in the public domain include the Pediatric Symptom Checklist (Jellinek et al., 1999) and the Strengths and Difficulties Questionnaire (Goodman, 1997). An example of a narrowband measure is the Mood and Feelings Questionnaire to measure depression in students (Davis et al., 2006). Please note that these public-domain measures have adequate psychometric properties comparable to those that are purchased and, in our experience, they effectively measure student functioning and change over time.

Although there may be time and cost associated with developing the infrastructure needed to collect and score standardized measures, there also is time required to interpret, develop, and refine action plans based on their findings. We draw attention to this concern because assessments are rendered useless when insufficient resources are devoted to interpreting the findings and ensuring that they are used to develop action plans that assist students. School psychologists usually have strong training in psychological assessment and are an excellent resource in navigating issues related to standardized assessments.

At times, rather than administering standardized assessments at school, students are referred to community agencies for more comprehensive assessment of particular problems. Best practice is that evaluators from community agencies have positive working relationships with the school. This means that they avoid language that pathologizes students, are careful in applying diagnostic and other labels, and include recommendations that focus on positive and achievable actions that can be taken to assist the student(s).

SUMMARY

Measuring behavior change is a critical process to objectively determine whether behavior is improving. There are a number of different strategies for directly measuring change. Selecting a data collection method depends on a variety of factors, such as the behavior to be measured, the availability of personnel, competing responsibilities, and personal preference. Once data are collected, they should be graphed and frequently reviewed to determine intervention effectiveness. Although direct observation remains the primary measurement strategy in the field (Lewis, Scott, Wehby, & Wills, 2014), other sources of data can be used to supplement information collected via direct observation, such as permanent products or school-based data. Finally, standardized assessments, such as parent rating scales, teacher rating scales, or student self-report, provide additional sources of important information—particularly, where on the scale students fall in relation to their peers. By combining direct observation data with alternative assessment methods, teams then can be confident in their decision to maintain, discontinue, or add components to an intervention as well as be assured that all parties are satisfied with student progress and the intervention outcome.

Self-Reflection

1. Among the data collection strategies described, which would be easiest for you to use in the context of teaching?
2. List all staff in the school where you work or have visited who might be available to assist with data collection (e.g., school counselor, school psychologist, paraprofessional).
3. You have been told that one of your students regularly engages in problem behavior in the cafeteria (e.g., getting out of his assigned seat, wandering around, and interrupting other students), which is monitored by volunteers. Your first step is to determine how frequently it occurs. What data collection system could you easily teach a volunteer to use that could be completed while he or she is monitoring the behavior of students at multiple lunch tables?
4. List all of the "other" sources of data that are collected in the school where you work or have visited. What type of information can each source of data provide that will assist you in developing a support plan for a student who engages in problem behavior?

5. The number of standardized assessments that schools administer has increased in recent years. School staff (and parents) have raised concerns that testing is taking up too much instructional time and does not provide information that is helpful for instructional decision making. List all of the assessments administered in your school and describe how they are used to inform teaching. If they are not currently used to guide decisions about instruction, describe how they could be used for this purpose.
6. What measures are being collected in your school that are rarely if ever used for decision making? Which measures would you eliminate, and how would you go about convincing school leaders to eliminate them?

REFERENCES

Achenbach, T.M. (1991). *Manual for the Youth Self-Report and 1991 Profile.* Burlington: University of Vermont Department of Psychiatry.

Achenbach, T.M., & Rescorla, L.A. (2001). *Manual for the ASEBA School-Age Forms and Profiles.* Burlington: University of Vermont Research Center for Children, Youth, and Families.

Briesch, A.M., Kilgus, S.P., Chafouleas, S.M., Riley-Tillman, T.C., & Christ, T.J. (2012). The influence of alternative scale formats on the generalizability of data obtained from Direct Behavior Rating Single Item Scales (DBR-SIS). *Assessment for Effective Intervention.* doi:10.1177/1534508412441966

Chafouleas, S.M. (2011). Direct behavior rating: A review of issues and research on its development. *Education and Treatment of Children, 34,* 575–591.

Chafouleas, S.M., Kilgus, S.P., Riley-Tillman, T.C., Jaffery, R., & Harrison, S. (2012). Preliminary evaluation of various training components on accuracy of Direct Behavior Ratings. *Journal of School Psychology, 50*(3), 317–334.

Chafouleas, S.M., Riley-Tillman, T.C., & Christ, T.J. (2009). Direct Behavior Rating (DBR): An emerging method for assessing social behavior within a tiered intervention system. *Assessment for Effective Intervention, 34,* 195–200. doi:10.1177/1534508409340391

Davis, W., Birhamer, B., Melhem, N.A., Axelson, D.A., Michaels, S.M., & Brent, D.A. (2006). Criterion validity of the Mood and Feelings Questionnaire for depressive episodes in clinic and non-clinic subjects. *Journal of Child Psychology and Psychiatry, 47*(9), 927–934.

Dixon, M.R., Jackson, J.W., Small, S.L., Horner-King, M.J., Mui Ker Lik, N., Garcia, Y., & Rosales, R. (2009). Creating single-subject design graphs in Microsoft Excel 2007. *Journal of Applied Behavior Analysis, 42,* 277–293.

Fabiano, G.A., Chafouleas, S.M., Weist, M.D., Sumi, W.C., & Humphrey, N. (2014). Methodology considerations in school mental health research. *School Mental Health, 6*(2), 68–83.

Goodman, R. (1997). The Strengths and Difficulties Questionnaire: A research note. *Journal of Child Psychology and Psychiatry, 38*(5), 581–586.

Greenbaum, P.E., Dedrick, R.F., Friedman, R.M., Kutash, K., Brown, E.C., Lardieri, S.P., & Pugh, A.M. (1996). National Adolescent and Child Treatment Study (NACTS): Outcomes for children with serious emotional and behavioral disturbance. *Journal of Emotional and Behavioral Disorders, 964,* 130–146.

Jellinek, M.S., Murphy, J.M., Little, M., Pagano, M.E., Comer, D.M., & Kelleher, K.J. (1999). Use of the Pediatric Symptom Checklist to screen for psychosocial problems in primary care: A national feasibility study. *Archives of Pediatrics and Adolescent Medicine, 153*(3), 254–260.

Lewis, T.J., Scott, T.M., Wehby, J.H., & Wills, H.P. (2014). Direct observation of teacher and student behavior in school settings: Trends, issues, and future directions. *Behavioral Disorders, 39,* 190–199.

Miltenberger, R.G. (2005). Strategies for measuring behavior change. In L.M. Bambara & L. Kern (Eds.), *Individualized supports for students with problem behaviors* (pp. 107–128). New York, NY: Guilford Press.

Shavelson, R.J., Webb, N.M., & Rowley, G.L. (1989). Generalizability theory. *American Psychologist, 44*(6), 922–932. doi:10.1037/0003-066X.44.6.922

11

Enhancing Student Connectedness to School

Student connectedness to school is a powerful resilience factor that helps to improve both student behavior and academic performance and prevent truancy and dropout. Following a brief description of research that documents its importance, we present practical strategies that school staff can use to increase student connectedness. The strategies are presented in relation to a multi-tiered framework emphasized throughout this book, with Tier 1 strategies used for all students, Tier 2 strategies used to assist students at risk who are showing early signs of disengagement, and Tier 3 strategies used for students who have already disengaged from school and have an enhanced likelihood of dropout. We describe multiple ways of building and improving connections to school in two major dimensions: 1) strategies to enhance student connectedness to school and 2) approaches to increase positive relationships among schools and other youth-serving systems.

THE IMPORTANCE OF STUDENT CONNECTEDNESS

In one of the largest studies on student health, the National Longitudinal Study of Adolescent Health (Resnick et al., 1997), more than 36,000 students from 7th through 12th grades were surveyed on risk, protective, and personal adjustment factors. A range of individual, family, and school factors were found to be associated with positive student adjustment including school connectedness, family–child connectedness, high expectations among parents for school achievement, and student involvement in religious activities. Notably, student connectedness to school was found to be the most powerful factor in protecting male and female students from substance use, early sexual involvement, excessive school absences, and exposure to injury and violence (Resnick et al., 1997). Another large-scale study of more than 11,000 students in Canada also found engagement in school (i.e., being involved in school) to be a critical factor in students staying in school (Archambault, Janosz, Fallu, & Pagani, 2009), illustrating the importance of this construct and its relevance across nations.

An important finding is that when students do not feel connected to school, they disengage, usually before high school, and are at significant risk of later dropout (Orthner et al., 2010). It is important to keep students engaged, because dropout is associated with many other problems in life, including greater unemployment, poorer lifetime wages earned, more health problems, and increased incarceration (Heckman & LaFontaine, 2007; Tyler & Lofstrom, 2009).

GENERAL THEMES IN PROMOTING STUDENT CONNECTEDNESS

Strategies described in this and the following sections are based on the presumption that 1) the school is committed to enhancing student connectedness and 2) there is a team of interdisciplinary staff (e.g., school psychologist, counselor, assistant principal, teachers, nurse, parent[s], school resource officer, others) that is meeting regularly and guiding implementation and ongoing quality improvement of student support, prevention, and intervention in Tiers 1, 2, and 3 (see Barrett, Eber, & Weist, 2013). This team may be the same as the schoolwide positive behavior support (SWPBS) team, or it may be a separate team that is explicitly focused on enhancing school connections and mental health issues. This team should be operating with and using up-to-date literature and strategies to promote student connectedness to school. In this regard, the Centers for Disease Control and Prevention (CDC), in an important summary of the literature (2009), identified four critical themes to enhance student connectedness: 1) support offered to students by adults, 2) student belongingness to a positive peer group, 3) student commitment to education, and 4) a positive school environment. Each of these factors is reviewed in more detail here.

Increasing support from adults. As cited in the CDC (2010) article, students feel more connected to school when school staff are viewed as dedicated, interested, willing to give of their time, and supportive. Similarly, Conner (2011) found that students' perceptions of emotional connections with teachers were directly related to their sense of connection to school. Although intuitive, these findings emphasize the importance of education staff seeking positive relations with all students they encounter. Simple things—such as asking students about their weekend, smiling at them, and wishing them well—can meaningfully increase student engagement and connections with school.

Positive peer relations. The CDC (2010) article emphasized the importance of students having relationships with peers displaying social competence. It is also important that they are involved in other prosocial activities, such as completing homework assignments, having membership in school clubs, and helping others. Consistent with these findings, Ream and Rumberger (2008) found Latino/a students to be more engaged in school and less likely to drop out when they were connected to peers who expressed that school was a priority in their lives.

Commitment to education. The CDC (2010) report stated, "Students who are personally invested in school and believe that a good education is important for reaching their life goals spend more time on homework and in school activities and have an increased sense of connectedness to school" (p. 22). Such investment by students is related to actions of school staff, such as promoting mutual respect among students in classrooms and tailoring strategies to meet the individual needs of students (CDC, 2010).

School environment. A number of environmental characteristics of schools promote student connectedness. These can include aspects of the physical environment (e.g., a clean and pleasant environment that is free from graffiti), elements of school climate (e.g., positive relationships among school staff and students), opportunities for students to participate in decision making, shared positive norms (e.g., social standards agreed upon by faculty and students, such as making eye contact and greeting others when passing them in the hallway), and consistent and positive classroom management strategies used by teachers (CDC, 2010).

Mulloy (2014), in a review on "resilience building" in schools, emphasized the importance of a climate of increased monitoring and individualized attention to promote student connectedness and positive functioning in school. For example, the following questions might be considered by school staff: What systems are in place to monitor students who are frequently absent? What supports are available to teachers to reach out to students or the families of students who frequently miss school or classes or who seem to be struggling to make connections? How are students identified who are experiencing transitions (e.g., new to school, change in family circumstance, new involvement in their life of another youth-serving system such as juvenile justice or child welfare), and what additional supports are available to them?

In addition to these general themes, specific strategies can be embedded within each of the three levels of a multi-tiered system of support, such as SWPBS (see Chapter 2), to promote student connectedness. In the following sections, we describe strategies focused on Tier 1 (increasing connections for all students), Tier 2 (prevention and early intervention for students not responding to Tier 1 programs and supports), and Tier 3 (intervention for students who are already disconnected).

TIER 1 STRATEGIES TO INCREASE STUDENT CONNECTEDNESS

The Wingspread Declaration on School Connectedness (Wingspread, 2004), also described in the CDC report (2010), identified 60 strategies to promote student connectedness that reflect key theme areas. These theme areas include clear and inclusive opportunities for decision making for students and staff, mechanisms for families to provide guidance to schools, increased opportunities for families to be actively involved in their children's schoolwork and achievement, adequate professional development for staff to enable skills in responding to diverse needs of students, and trusting, open, and caring relationships among school administration, staff, students, and their families. These themes reflect guiding principles for Tier 1 programs and strategies to promote school connectedness. The following subsections describe specific strategies that can increase student connections to school.

Parent or Family Involvement in School

In general, the more parents and other family members are involved in school and their child's education, the better the outcomes are for individual students. Parent or family involvement also benefits the school overall, as it helps to improve the climate, which, as discussed in this chapter and others in the book, helps promote positive student behavior and academic performance. Teachers and school leaders should reflect on the style of staff members' interactions with family members. For example, do staff members convey aloofness and communicate with families almost exclusively around a student's problem behaviors, or are staff collaborative, enthused to engage with families, and willing to interact more often about student accomplishments? Of course, the latter is the style that individual staff members should demonstrate.

School staff also need to be cautious about blaming parents for student problems or acting in a way that blames students for their problems. This is a very common behavioral pattern and clearly contributes to families being disconnected from (even angry at) schools. Instead, school leaders, teachers, and other staff should interact with students and families in a respectful, collaborative, and nonjudgmental way. We have found the following four themes to be particularly important: 1) engagement, or purposefully working to build rapport by empathizing with student or family issues and stresses, discussing past experiences with help-seeking (e.g., positive versus negative experiences) while providing assurances that current services will indeed be helpful, and problem solving with the student or family on ways to increase the likelihood of their active involvement; 2) support, or immediately trying to provide assistance to the student or family in the first meeting, connecting them with tangible school and community resources, and helping with strategies that address immediate and pressing problems; 3) collaboration, or working with the student or family as true collaborators, treating them as experts in their own situation who can help develop and implement plans to improve student emotional and behavioral functioning, as well as inviting the student or family into other roles where they can share expertise (e.g., to a planning meeting to improve the school's SWPBS program);

4) empowerment, or conveying to the student or family optimism and hope for positive outcomes, encouraging bold steps toward improvement, and promoting independent problem solving and action. These specific collaborative strategies set the stage for a strong working relationship with the student or family and increase the likelihood of resolving emotional and behavioral problems as well as achieving academic goals (Weist et al., 2009). Teachers can use this framework in interacting with families of students; for example, by asking about past experiences with schools and youth-serving systems and empathizing with past challenging experiences; soliciting and conveying genuine interest in their perspectives, ideas, and recommendations; connecting the family and student to helpful programs and resources in the school and/or community; and displaying a positive, encouraging attitude and hope for positive outcomes.

Enhancing Protective Factors

Consistent with the Wingspread Declaration (Wingspread, 2004) and ideas from the CDC presented earlier, enhancing student connectedness to school relates to a long history of important research on protective factors for positive youth development. Mulloy (2014) proposed that protective factors are "either internal (e.g., self-esteem, problem-solving ability) or external (e.g., positive life events, high levels of social support), and can interact dynamically to promote greater resilience" (pp. 1–8). She described the following specific protective factors that schools can employ to increase student connectedness:

- Supportive and caring teachers
- Consistently high but also achievable school expectations
- Orderly and safe school environments
- Clear and consistently communicated schoolwide expectations for student behavior
- Opportunities for meaningful student engagement
- Specific support for student social-emotional well-being

Improving Classroom Environments

The classroom environment has an important influence on students' feelings of connectedness. For example, Cooper (2013) found that Latina/o students performed better in classrooms that were perceived as safe and affirming, where students are focused on academic engagement and performance. In Chapters 4 and 5, we delineated a number of strategies to improve the classroom environment and increase academic engagement. Classroom teachers may also want to review the Developmental Assets Framework, the Search Institute's research-based list of 40 developmental assets representing positive qualities that help children and youth become caring and responsible people (see http://www.search-institute.org). Table 11.1 lists the 40 developmental assets.

The Developmental Assets Framework has been used widely in the United States and around the world as a strategy to help youth to better understand and increase the operation of protective factors in their lives. In general, research findings emphasize that the more developmental assets children and youth report, the less likely they are to engage in high-risk behaviors and the more likely they are to be thriving. For example, Scales, Benson, Leffert, and Blyth (2000) measured these developmental assets in a sample of 6,000 students in grades 6–12 and found that beyond the contribution of demographic variables, the more developmental assets students reported, the more likely they were to display "thriving indicators," described as school success, leadership, and physical health. Edwards, Mumford, Shillingford, and Serra-Roldan (2007) recommended that school approaches to enhance developmental assets align directly with comprehensive school reform initiatives, and made a number of recommendations for schools and districts to broadly implement programs based on the framework.

Teachers could use the framework presented in Table 11.1 in a number of ways. For example, items have been organized in checklists for students to report on whether the asset is present in their lives. Students could complete the checklists, which then could be used for interactive discussions on external assets (e.g., having a caring neighborhood) that are present or absent in their lives. Similarly, there could be discussion in classes on ways to increase internal assets (e.g., reading for pleasure, providing service to others,

Table 11.1. List of developmental assets

40 Developmental Assets			
1. Family Support	11. Family Boundaries	21. Achievement Motivation	31. Restraint
2. Positive Family Communication	12. School Boundaries	22. School Engagement	32. Planning and Decision Making
3. Other Adult Relationships	13. Neighborhood Boundaries	23. Homework	33. Interpersonal Competence
4. Caring Neighborhood	14. Adult Role Models	24. Bonding to School	34. Cultural Competence
5. Caring School Climate	15. Positive Peer Influence	25. Reading for Pleasure	35. Resistance Skills
6. Parent Involvement in Schooling	16. High Expectations	26. Caring	36. Peaceful Conflict Resolution
7. Community Values Youth	17. Creative Activities	27. Equality and Social Justice	37. Personal Power
8. Youth as Resources	18. Youth Programs	28. Integrity	38. Self-Esteem
9. Service to Others	19. Religious Community	29. Honesty	39. Sense of Purpose
10. Safety	20. Time at Home	30. Responsibility	40. Positive View of Personal Future

The Developmental Assets® are adapted with permission from Search Institute, Minneapolis, MN. More information is available at www.search-institute.org.

resisting negative peer pressure). Such classroom interaction around the developmental assets framework is likely to enhance a positive connection to school among students (Scales, 1999).

Enhancing Student Aspirations

The Quaglia Institute for Student Aspirations (QISA, 2014) focuses on increasing engagement in school by enabling students to pursue their aspirations and feel a sense of empowerment and leadership within the school environment. This differs from the prevailing culture of adults in schools telling students what to do. QISA describes eight conditions that promote student aspirations for academic accomplishment, including 1) belonging, or feeling accepted or a part of a group; 2) heroes, or having others in school who will provide support when needed; 3) sense of accomplishment, or having achievements recognized; 4) fun and excitement in school activities and work; 5) curiosity and creativity, or experiencing encouragement for exploration and out-of-the-box thinking; 6) spirit of adventure, or experiencing encouragement to try new things; 7) leadership and responsibility, or feeling a sense of voice and influence over school functioning; and 8) confidence to take action, or feeling supported in setting and reaching goals. A basic theme in this work is for students to feel in control of their education and to have a voice in helping to shape their lives in school.

A way to put QISA into action is for teachers to consider ways they promote or do not promote student voice and leadership in the multi-tiered framework. Reflective questions, for example, that are relevant to planning at all tiers include the following: Are students active in planning? Are there adequate numbers of students on planning committees? Are students able to speak freely? What is the proportion of student to teacher or staff comments? What happens with follow-up to student questions? Do students believe they are actually shaping school policy and programs? Think of a recent initiative in your school (e.g., to improve school climate) and reflect on those questions and the extent to which student voices were heard. In most cases, such reflection will reveal that students were not or were only minimally involved in school decision making, that adults made most if not all of the decisions, and that decisions were focused on contingencies that improved school life for the teachers and staff as much if not more than improving it for students. We encourage teachers and school staff to explore resources of the Quaglia Institute at http://www.qisa.org.

TIER 2 STRATEGIES TO INCREASE STUDENT CONNECTEDNESS

In addition to the Tier 1 strategies just discussed, ideally used by schools to improve the climate and enhance connectedness to school for all students, there are specific Tier 2 strategies that can be used to increase connectedness to school for students showing early signs of experiencing challenges or living with a condition of risk (e.g., from a high-crime or high-violence neighborhood). In the following subsections, we review general strategies to reduce risk for these students and then present specific strategies, including those focused on mentoring and on reducing conflict.

Reducing the Impact of Risk Factors

The flip side to protective factors presented in the previous section is a range of risk factors that students commonly experience. Risk factors make students more vulnerable and suggest the need for additional supports to reduce their impact. Mulloy (2014) summarized these risk factors, including the following:

- The experience of poverty, a broad and powerful risk factor that is associated with other risk factors presented herein
- Abuse and neglect
- Being exposed to violence in the home, neighborhood, and broader community
- Affiliation with delinquent and drug-using peers
- Having others in the family with mental illness
- Being in a school that is under-resourced and/or overcrowded
- Experiencing frequent school changes
- Being in a family with low expectations for academic achievement
- Being in a family with low levels of emotional and/or social support

Although an understanding of these risk factors should assist in schoolwide Tier 1 strategies that help improve school connectedness (e.g., education and training on the effects of violence and strategies to avoid and reduce violence exposure; see Warner & Weist, 1996), they are most helpful in guiding Tier 2 strategies. That is, students with risk factors should be identified for Tier 2 support. Unfortunately, such screening efforts in schools occur infrequently and/or in a disorganized manner (Dvorsky, Girio-Herrera, & Owens, 2014). Systematic screening for risk factors in schools is a critical need and should be completed regularly (i.e., at least yearly) and whenever a new student enters the school. Specifically, from the list of risk factors presented earlier in this subsection, schools should develop procedures to identify students in school who are within the child welfare system, who have experienced frequent school transfers or moves, or who reside in neighborhoods characterized by high violence.

Teachers are intuitively able to identify students who are struggling or presenting unmet needs. Abraham Maslow's classic hierarchy of needs (Maslow, 1954) is useful in understanding students and enhancing connections with them. The hierarchy emphasizes the foundational importance of lower-level needs; only when these needs are satisfied are people (students) able to focus on higher-level needs. At the base of the triangle are physiological needs (e.g., food, shelter, sleep), followed by feeling safe, being connected to others and experiencing love and belonging, feeling self-worth and esteem, and having abilities and skills. All of these needs are necessary for self-actualization, which occurs when a person is meeting his or her full potential and experiencing a range of positive emotion.

Whether the student is new to the school, has experienced numerous transfers, is in another youth-serving system such as a child welfare agency or juvenile services, has experienced violence, or appears in need of clothing or food, a key factor is for the school to have proactive strategies in place to identify students in need. Foundational to this work, as emphasized throughout this book, is the functioning of teams such as the SWPBS team and its effective use of data to identify students in need. School-employed health staff (e.g., nurses) and mental health staff (e.g., counselors, psychologists, social workers) should be involved in this early identification process and assist in outreach and supportive services that follow. An important strategy is to construct a resource map of programs and services offered within the school building and district and in the surrounding community that would be relevant to addressing student needs. These programs can be organized into a directory that is updated on an annual basis. With an understanding of school and community resources and programs (ideally facilitated by a directory), staff can assist students or families in making connections to these programs. Decision-making teams should then regularly follow up on the status of these connections, reinitiating outreach and assistance to students and families as indicated.

However, a reality that needs to be considered in this work is that when school staff refer students and families to programs offered by community agencies, often these referrals fail. For example, in a study of students referred for mental health services either offered within the school or in a community mental health center (CMHC) located close to the school, Catron, Harris, and Weiss (1998) found that 96% of students referred to the school program received services, as compared to only 13% of students referred to the CMHC. This is related to the many barriers that get in the way of students receiving services in mental health centers, such as poor knowledge of mental health and mental health services, stigma associated with mental health problems, stress in families that impedes a focus on child emotional and behavioral functioning, transportation challenges, and financial or insurance barriers, among others (see Weist, 1997). Unfortunately, in some situations, simply referring a student for services signifies the end of support for some school staff (e.g., checking the "I helped" box), and as suggested by the list of possible barriers, this "support" may be completely unhelpful to the student.

The finding by Catron et al. (1998) underscores the need for the development of a range of supportive services for students in need in school. This can and should include 1) conducting focused assessment of student or family needs (and not emphasizing diagnostic labels); 2) providing helpful strategies to address identified needs or connecting students or family to a school or community program and ensuring this connection actually happens; 3) giving students or families a resource directory, flyers from community-based programs, or phone numbers of helpful programs (e.g., for suicide prevention, emergency assistance in relation to economic needs) and following up with them on the helpfulness of these resources; 4) enhancing parent involvement in schools, including making connections to family advocacy organizations (e.g., the Federation of Families for Children's Mental Health), with representatives of these organizations offering experience and many resources for assisting youth and families in need; and 5) providing focused group and individual support for students on themes such as avoiding and coping with community violence, effectively handling conflict with peers and family members, and building organizational skills for school success (see Mulloy, 2013).

Mentoring Programs

A significant amount of research supports the effectiveness of structured mentoring programs to enhance school engagement (e.g., DuBois, Holloway, Valentine, & Cooper, 2002). A *mentor* can be defined as an adult who makes a commitment to being involved in a consistent relationship with at least one young person who would benefit from mentoring related to some non optimal condition in his or her life (e.g., single-parent status, having a disability, experiencing adverse events in the family or community). The adult should be vetted by an organization (e.g., Big Brothers Big Sisters of America, school system) as not having a criminal background and having positive qualities.

In a review of the mentoring literature, McQuillin, Terry, Strait, and Smith (2013) documented that mentoring programs are particularly popular in schools, but that effects of programs in this setting have not been as strong as programs provided in other settings. This is likely due to the unique barriers to implementing mentoring in schools, such as vetting of mentors, obtaining parental consent and student assent for participation, connecting with students in need in ways that match the way schools operate, and ensuring consistent meeting times. For example, barriers can include navigating the academic schedule and coordinating times for the student and mentor to interact regularly.

To overcome these barriers, McQuillin and colleagues (2013) developed university–school partnerships, involving advanced college students who go into schools to provide focused mentoring (two to three sessions) including motivational interviewing (MI) with students, with findings showing positive impacts on students' academic performance. Generally, MI involves the helping person (e.g., counselor, teacher) assisting the student to explore dimensions of a situation through Socratic questioning (i.e., illuminating relevant choices and suggesting the positive choices so that the student is likely to feel ownership). For example, in working with a ninth grade student who states a desire to apply to college but is not completing homework and is receiving grades of Cs, Ds, and Fs, a script of an interaction using MI principles could proceed as follows: "So, Jimmy, you want to go to college? That is outstanding. Have you considered a major? Which colleges are you most interested in? Have you explored qualifications students need in order to get into those colleges? Hmmm, that is interesting, so in general at the colleges you like the most, students need a GPA of 3.25 to get in. What is your GPA now?" As shown, in this brief example using MI, students are helped in reviewing relevant facets of a particular decision (in this case, going to college) and, rather than the counselor or helper specifically stating what the student needs to do (in this case, improve grades), questioning is organized in ways that will enable the student to arrive at the decision on his or her own, increasing personal motivation and investment to pursue it.

Check & Connect

Check & Connect is a structured mentoring intervention that allows students and an adult in the school to "check in" on behavioral difficulties (e.g., attendance, grades, suspensions) and "connect" by developing a caring relationship, including aspects of psychological engagement (e.g., improving teacher or mentor and student relationship), behavioral engagement (e.g., behavioral monitoring of attendance, suspensions, and other behavioral indicators), and cognitive engagement (e.g., goal setting). Depending on individual student needs, it can also be used to promote academic engagement. For example, the adult can help the student track assignments, learn study skills, and plan for and organize his or her agenda and homework. Interventions using Check & Connect have been shown to decrease dropout rates and mobility (i.e., nonpromotional school transfer during the academic year) and increase attendance rates and enrollment status for ninth-grade students with EBD (Sinclair, Christenson, & Thurlow, 2005). For specific details on implementing Check & Connect, see http://www.checkandconnect.umn.edu.

Addressing and Reducing Student Conflict

Clearly, when students experience conflict with other students, it has great potential to reduce their connectedness to school, and in fact these experiences directly compromise their school performance and achievement (Nansel et al., 2001). Bullying is a major problem that directly affects student connectedness to school. When implemented with fidelity, the SWPBS framework addresses bullying by ensuring an emphasis on clear rules and expectations, positive behavior, monitoring of student behavior, and identifying problematic situations and environments that may lead to increases in problem behaviors and other factors (see Chapter 2). As such, teachers and school leaders are encouraged to ensure adequate functioning of teams focused on Tier 1 SWPBS strategies. These teams may consider implementing specific evidence-based programs such as the Olweus Bullying Prevention Program (OBPP; Olweus, Limber, & Mahalic, 1999). Implementation of programs such as the OBPP is enhanced when this work is done in the context of well-functioning SWPBS (e.g., www.PBIS.org; Barrett, Eber, & Weist, 2013). In addition, please note that a key to reducing bullying and other climate problems is to enhance student voice, as in the ideas presented in the section on Enhancing Student Aspirations (see QISA, 2014).

TIER 3 STRATEGIES TO INCREASE STUDENT CONNECTEDNESS

Students presenting concerning and/or established problems have intensified needs for programming focused on improving their connectedness to school. In fact, these students are the most likely to be poorly engaged in school (Reschly & Christenson, 2006). In addition to comprehensive support plans (Chapter 9), students at Tier 3 may benefit from focused interventions in the form of individual, family, and/or group intervention. Often students and families struggle to receive mental health services in traditional community settings (e.g., specialty "clinics"), and schools themselves are usually under-resourced and unable to effectively address the range of students presenting mental health needs.

These rationales underscore the need for developing "expanded" school mental health (SMH) programs that involve community mental health programs joining with schools to augment the work of school-employed mental health staff and move toward providing a full continuum of effective promotion, prevention, and intervention at Tiers 1, 2, and 3. Increasingly, these SMH programs are joining together with SWPBS to add depth and quality to programs and services at each tier and to promote improved decision making, use of data, implementation of effective practices, and synergistic impacts of programs (i.e., positive impacts may be particularly enhanced when SWPBS and SMH programs work together versus separately; see Barrett, Eber, & Weist, 2013). Teachers are playing a prominent role in the development of these SMH programs (ideally interconnected with SWPBS), which assist in promoting positive behavior in classrooms (see Chapter 4), identifying and assisting youth with more intensive needs so that they receive appropriate intervention more rapidly, and directly helping students gain skills that promote their positive emotional and behavioral functioning (see Chapter 12 for a more detailed review of intervention approaches).

Foundational in identifying and providing effective services for students with more serious emotional and behavioral issues is involving them as partners in care. This approach contrasts with more traditional approaches in mental health service delivery wherein providers take the stance of experts who teach and train the student and his or her family on strategies to help them be more successful. As presented earlier in the chapter, a key to involving the student (and his or her family) in school is to emphasize a collaborative relationship, which includes dimensions of explicitly focusing on engagement (including past negative experiences and ways to make the current experience more helpful), support (tangibly helping the student with a need, such as connection to a mentoring or tutoring program), and empowerment (an overarching theme that results from strong collaboration and a sense of hopefulness to achieve valued outcomes).

INCREASING RELATIONSHIPS AMONG SCHOOLS AND OTHER YOUTH-SERVING SYSTEMS

In any community, schools will be the largest youth-serving system. However, schools are often isolated from other systems, such as juvenile justice, child welfare, health care, and developmental disabilities systems. In addition, schools are very busy places, with teachers and administrators contending with the significant and critically important agenda of educating children and youth while adhering to local and state policies, laws, and federal mandates.

Isolation from other systems and intensive workloads can contribute to a limited focus of schools on the whole child. Strategies that improve student wellness and emotional or behavioral functioning and reduce or remove barriers to learning ultimately increase the likelihood that students will succeed academically and graduate from school. Ideally, these efforts are nested within a philosophy of a "shared agenda" wherein schools and other youth-serving systems work together on mutually recognized goals.

This framework of a "shared agenda" is foundational to expanded school mental health programs and involves community mental health staff joining with schools to augment programs and services at all three tiers (see Weist, 1997). Such partnerships lead to enhanced resources for schools and increased ability to provide high-quality programs and services at Tiers 2 and 3, and, for the mental health systems, lead to significantly improved access to students. Similarly, youth in juvenile justice, child welfare, and other systems usually attend public schools. Without formal connections to these systems, schools often struggle to meet the needs of these youth, who usually experience elevated levels of trauma, emotional and behavioral problems, and challenges in learning.

THE INTERCONNECTED SYSTEMS FRAMEWORK FOR SCHOOLWIDE POSITIVE BEHAVIOR SUPPORT AND SCHOOL MENTAL HEALTH

Unfortunately, in most communities, infrastructure to link various youth-serving initiatives together and with the schools does not exist, nor is there a group that steps forward to organize such a linkage and move the various agencies toward a shared agenda. As mentioned earlier, there are considerable benefits to establishing and enhancing SWPBS and interconnecting this work with SMH to promote depth and quality of services at all three tiers of the multi-tiered system of support. When this is accomplished, as in the Interconnected Systems Framework (ISF; see Barrett et al., 2013), schools begin to become an anchoring point for multisystem collaboration. The ISF provides detail on well-functioning teams, using data to make decisions, choosing interventions based on evidence of positive impact, adjusting interventions to maximize impact, and using evaluation findings for ongoing quality improvement. An example of the added value of the ISF is presented in the following subsection in relation to team functioning.

Critical Role of Teams

As noted throughout this book and in this chapter, the functioning of teams is critical to effectively reduce barriers to student learning and promote student wellness, including positive emotional and behavioral adjustment as well as learning. Ideally, there is at least one well-functioning and inclusive team in a school, with sub-teams focused on planning and implementation of the best practices at each of the three tiers. These sub-teams should be responsible for reaching out to other community agencies to enhance resources and approaches. For example, at Tier 1, school climate enhancement can be assisted through connection to parent–teacher and family advocacy organizations to increase the presence of family members and positive adults in the building. At Tier 2, mentoring programs can be facilitated through connection with communities of faith, recreational programs, and local universities. At Tier 3, services to students with intensive needs can be facilitated by joint planning with agency leaders (e.g., to identify trauma-focused intervention for students with such needs).

In fact, well-functioning school teams are one of the most important processes and quality indicators of programs to assist students in need and promote their academic achievement (Markle, Splett, Maras, & Weston, 2014). However, in most schools, there are multiple teams, such as the individualized education program (IEP) team for students in special education, student assistance teams for students presenting highly challenging problems and/or substance abuse issues, crisis intervention teams, school improvement teams, and so forth. Commonly, many of the same school leaders are on multiple teams and do not have time to participate effectively in all of them. Consequently, teams often lack strong leadership, consistent agendas and processes, and meeting follow-through required to be successful. Thus, a critically important action to improve programs and services for youth contending with emotional and behavioral problems is to engage in resource mapping of teams (see discussion earlier in this chapter), including documenting for all teams 1) the name, 2) members, 3) goals and actions, 4) meeting schedule, and 5) an honest assessment of its impact at student and school-building levels. This information can be used toward potential integration of smaller, less effective teams into a larger, well-functioning team as described in the ISF (Barrett et al., 2013). However, there are a number of strategies for effective team functioning, and in some cases, two or three smaller, effective teams will be an appropriate plan for a school. Resources for effective team functioning in schools can also be found on web sites of national centers for SWPBS (http://www.pbis.org) and SMH (http://csmh.umaryland.edu).

SUMMARY

Student connectedness to school is a powerful protective factor that promotes success in school and beyond. Teachers play a critical role in promoting student connectedness through positive relationships with students, using simple strategies such as making sure every student in the school has at least one positive interaction with a teacher or staff member every day and smiling at and greeting students by name. In addition, there are many strategies that can be integrated in the three-tiered SWPBS framework for enhancing student connectedness, including enhancing protective factors and reducing risk factors (Tier 1), mentoring programs (Tier 2), and improving connections with other youth-serving systems to assist students with more challenging problems (Tier 3).

Self-Reflection

1. Given what was presented in this chapter on enhancing student connectedness to school, think about your own experience in school. What contributed to your feelings of connection? Disconnection? In your current school, identify factors that help students feel connected (i.e., pulling them toward school) versus disconnected (i.e., pushing them away from school). How will you be involved in school teams and decision making to improve strategies for students to feel connected to your school?
2. Think about the concept that every day, every student should have at least one positive interaction with an adult (e.g., teacher, staff member) in the building. What do you do to live out this principle?
3. A reality is that teachers often rapidly form negative impressions of some students related to their behavior, behavior problems, appearance, peers, negative interactions with family, or other factors. When this happens, how does it affect your ability to promote school connectedness among these students? How can you overcome these biased perceptions to positively reach out to these students?
4. Think of an environmental feature in your school that promotes connectedness (e.g., nice lunchroom, consistent and positive rules, outstanding lunchroom monitors) and one that does not (e.g., area of the building that is isolated and not patrolled by teachers, where student misbehavior occurs). How can you be an environmental change agent in your building?
5. Is it possible for you to smile and positively greet all of your students every day, regardless of their past behavior?

REFERENCES

Archambault, I., Janosz, M., Fallu, J., & Pagani, L.S. (2009). Student engagement and its relationship with early high school dropout. *Journal of Adolescence, 32*(3), 651–670. doi:10.1016/j.adolescence.2008.06.007

Barrett, S., Eber, L., & Weist, M.D. (2013). *Advancing education effectiveness: An interconnected systems framework for positive behavioral interventions and supports (PBIS) and school mental health.* Eugene: University of Oregon Press.

Catron, T., Harris, V.S., & Weiss, B. (1998). Posttreatment results after 2 years of services in the Vanderbilt School-Based Counseling project. In M.H. Epstein, K. Kutash, & A. Duchnowski (Eds.), *Outcomes for children and youth with emotional and behavioral disorders and their families: Programs and evaluation best practices* (pp. 633–656). Austin, TX: PRO-ED.

Centers for Disease Control and Prevention. (2009). *School connectedness: Strategies for increasing protective factors among youth.* Atlanta, GA: U.S. Department of Health and Human Services.

Conner, T. (2011). Academic engagement ratings and instructional preferences: Comparing behavioral, cognitive, and emotional engagement among three school-age student cohorts. *Review of Higher Education and Self-Learning, 4*(13), 52–66.

Cooper, K.S. (2013). Safe, affirming, and productive spaces: Classroom engagement among Latina high school students. *Urban Education, 48*(4), 490–528. doi:10.1177/0042085912457164

DuBois, D.L., Holloway, B.E., Valentine, J.C., & Cooper, H. (2002). Effectiveness of mentoring programs for youth: A meta-analytic review. *Journal of Community Psychology, 30*(2), 157–197.

Dvorsky, M.R., Girio-Herrera, E., & Owens, J.S. (2014). School-based screening for mental health in early childhood. In M. Weist, N. Lever, C. Bradshaw, & J. Owens (Eds.), *Handbook of school mental health: Research, training, practice and policy* (pp. 297–310). New York, NY: Springer.

Edwards, O.W., Mumford, V.E., Shillingford, M., & Serra-Roldan, R. (2007). Developmental assets: A prevention framework for students considered at risk. *Children and Schools, 29*(3), 145–153.

Heckman, J. J., & LaFontaine, P. (2007). The American high school graduation rate: Trends and levels. *Review of Economics and Statistics, 92*, 244–262.

Markle, R.S., Splett, J.W., Maras, M.A., & Weston, K.J. (2014). Effective school teams: Benefits, barriers, and best practices. In M. Weist, N. Lever, C. Bradshaw, & J. Owens (Eds.), *Handbook of school mental health: Research, training, practice, and policy* (2nd ed., pp. 59–74). New York, NY: Springer.

Maslow, A. (1954). *Motivation and personality.* New York, NY: Harper.

McQuillin, S.D., Terry, J.D., Strait, G.G., & Smith, B.H. (2013). Innovation in school-based mentoring: Matching the context, structure and goals of mentoring with evidence-based practices. *Advances in School Mental Health Promotion, 6*(4), 280–294. doi:10.1080/1754730X.2013.832009

Mulloy, M.A. (2014). *Resilience-building schools for at-risk youth: Developing the social, emotional, and motivational foundations of academic success.* New York, NY: Civic Research Institute.

Nansel, T.R., Overpeck, M., Pilla, R.S., Ruan, W.J., Simons-Morton, B., & Scheidt, P. (2001). Bullying behaviors among U.S. youth: Prevalence and association with psychosocial adjustment. *Journal of the American Medical Association, 285*, 2094–2100.

Olweus, C., Limber, S.P., & Mahalic, S.F. (1999). *Bullying prevention program.* Boulder: Center for the Study of Prevention of Violence, Institute of Behavioral Science, University of Colorado.

Orthner, D.K., Akos, P., Rose, R., Jones-Sanpei, H., Mercado, M., & Woolley, M.E. (2010). CareerStart: A middle school student engagement and academic achievement program. *Children and Schools, 32*(4), 223–234.

Quaglia Institute for Student Aspirations. (2014). *Aspirations briefs: The aspirations framework.* Retrieved from http://www.qisa.org/dmsView/Aspirations_Framework

Ream, R.K., & Rumberger, R.W. (2008). Student engagement, peer social capital, and school dropout among Mexican American and non-Latino white students. *Sociology of Education, 81*(2), 109–139.

Reschly, A.L., & Christenson, S.L. (2006). Prediction of dropout among students with mild disabilities: A case for the inclusion of student engagement variables. *Remedial and Special Education, 27*(5), 276–292.

Resnick, M.D., Bearman, P.S., Blum, R.W., Bauman, K.E., Harris, K.M., Jones, J., ... Udry, J.R. (1997). Protecting adolescents from harm: Findings from the National Longitudinal Study on Adolescent Health. *Journal of the American Medical Association, 278,* 823–832.

Scales, P.C. (1999). Reducing risks and building developmental assets: Essential actions for promoting adolescent health. *Journal of School Health, 69*(3), 113.

Scales, P.C., Benson, P.L., Leffert, N., & Blyth, D.A. (2000). Contribution of developmental assets to the prediction of thriving among adolescents. *Applied Developmental Science, 4*(1), 27.

Sinclair, M.F., Christenson, S.L., & Thurlow, M.L. (2005). Promoting school completion of urban secondary youth with emotional or behavioral disabilities. *Exceptional Children, 71,* 465–482.

Tyler, J.H., & Lofstrom, M. (2009). Finishing high school: Alternative pathways and dropout recovery. *Future of Children, 19*(1), 77–103.

Warner, B.S., & Weist, M.D. (1996). Urban youth as witnesses to violence: Beginning assessment and treatment efforts. *Journal of Youth and Adolescence, 25,* 361–377.

Weist, M.D. (1997). Expanded school mental health services: A national movement in progress. In T.H. Ollendick & R.J. Prinz (Eds.), *Advances in clinical child psychology* (Vol. 19, pp. 319–352). New York, NY: Plenum Press.

Weist, M.D., Lever, N., Stephan, S., Youngstrom, E., Moore, E., Harrison, B.,...Stiegler, K. (2009). Formative evaluation of a framework for high quality, evidence-based services in school mental health. *School Mental Health, 1*(3), 196–211.

Wingspread. (2004). Wingspread declaration on school connections. *Journal of School Health, 74*(7), 233–234.

12

Interventions to Address Mental Health Needs

In this chapter, we describe the most common mental health problems that children and adolescents experience. We also review the symptoms associated with specific diagnoses and the prevalence of problems. Because it is often difficult to ensure that students receive services to address mental health issues, we present ideas for engaging teachers, students, and families in services and implementing evidence-based interventions. We also discuss ways to assess and maximize the effectiveness of school resources while working with community partners.

COMMON MENTAL DISORDERS AMONG CHILDREN AND ADOLESCENTS

The American Psychiatric Association's (APA) *Diagnostic and Statistical Manual of Mental Disorders, Fifth Edition* (*DSM-5;* APA, 2013) is the most established and accepted system for diagnosing mental health disorders among children and adolescents. In this chapter, we describe common disorders aligned with that system. It should be noted, however, that there is not concordance between the *DSM-5* diagnostic system and the classification system used in education. For example, the educational system may classify a young student with acting-out problems as "emotionally disturbed" and in need of receiving services in special education, whereas the *DSM-5* might use the same symptoms to diagnose the student with Oppositional Defiant Disorder (ODD) or Attention-Deficit/Hyperactivity Disorder (ADHD). This lack of concordance can lead to significant communication problems between schools and other community systems and also underscores the need for collaborative training and immersion in respective cultures for these stakeholder groups.

Moreover, there are a number of cautions regarding diagnosis that we need to emphasize. First, diagnoses are meant to be heuristic, or to help professionals move more rapidly from assessment to designing and implementing an effective intervention that matches the particular disorder. Diagnoses of mental disorders usually are made by licensed mental health professionals, most commonly psychiatrists and psychologists, but also can be made by social workers and licensed professional counselors. However, diagnoses are often unreliable from one mental health professional to the next. In addition, diagnoses tend to accumulate in young people and often have negative connotations for children receiving them, including stigma, avoidance, and even negative treatment by school staff after a student receives a diagnosis (see Rosemond, 2005). Diagnoses also inherently place the locus of causality within the child, when in almost all cases disorders reflect interactions between the child, his or her genetic makeup, and the environment.

The movement toward effective expanded School Mental Health (SMH) services recognizes these problems and believes diagnoses should be used sparingly. In addition, clinicians, teachers, and other people in roles of helping children should be cautious about the labels used with children that may well have a pejorative impact, such as *psychopathology* (i.e., ascribing pathology inside a child) (Weist, 2003), or using educational labels such as *emotional disturbance* or similar state-specific labels. Regarding the latter, a survey conducted with more than 1,100 students and families in Maryland indicated overwhelming rejection of the commonly used educational term *severe emotional disturbance.* Students, as well as families, believed the term was stigmatizing and harmful to them. Instead, students and families recommended the preferred term *emotional challenges* and reported that the term *emotional disabilities* was better than *disturbance.* This consumer feedback contributed to changing a law in Maryland to reflect the new, less stigmatizing term (Walker, Geddes, Leven, Andrews, & Weist, 2010).

With these precautions in mind, we review diagnoses of the most common mental disorders among children and adolescents from the *DSM-5* (APA, 2013). Please note that this system does not contain separate categories for child or adolescent and adult disorders. To receive an official diagnosis, a number of specific symptoms need to be present, along with other criteria such as the duration of symptoms (often for 6 months or longer) and the impact on life functioning. Thus, many students will present symptoms of disorders, but the symptoms may be relatively few in number (or isolated) or not of sufficient duration or functional impact to warrant a formal diagnosis. At times, these "symptoms" should be the focus of intervention (e.g., isolated aggressive behavior), whereas at other times they should not (e.g., quietness that is related to temperament; social withdrawal related to a traumatic event, depression, or anxiety).

Excluding Intellectual Disabilities and Autism Spectrum Disorders, the most common disorders for children and adolescents are related to anxiety, depression, disruptive behavioral disorders (including ADHD), and trauma. Key symptoms of these disorders are presented in the following subsections, with information taken from the *DSM-5*.

Anxiety Disorders

Anxiety disorders affect around twice as many females as males. They often develop in childhood and persist into adulthood if not treated effectively. Anxiety disorders may include high levels of fear (i.e., emotional response to a perceived or genuine threat) and/or anxiety (i.e., worrying or anticipating a future threat). Among school-age children, the most common anxiety disorders are Separation Anxiety Disorder, Specific Phobias, Social Anxiety Disorder, and Generalized Anxiety Disorder.

Separation Anxiety Disorder (SAD) is an inappropriate and excessive anxiety or fear associated with separation from people or a person to whom the child is attached. Symptoms include frequent and excessive distress when anticipating or experiencing separation, frequent and excessive worrying about the loss of attachment figures, frequent refusal to go out or away from the attachment figure(s), nightmares about separation, and complaints of physical symptoms upon or in anticipation of separation. In school settings, SAD symptoms might appear as a child crying excessively, for a number of weeks, after being dropped off at school. SAD is the most common anxiety disorder among children—affecting approximately 4% of the population—is equally common in males and females, and reduces in adolescence.

Specific Phobias reflect significant fear or anxiety about a specific situation (e.g., riding in a car, receiving an injection) or object (e.g., spiders, dogs, particular images). The specific situation or object is avoided, causes distress, and impairs general functioning. Most often, a child's specific phobias occur around more than one situation or object. Teachers might notice a student reporting being afraid of dogs, which might indicate the possibility of a phobia. Around twice as many females experience specific phobias, and prevalence increases from around 5% in childhood to around 16% among teenagers.

Social Anxiety Disorder is significant fear or anxiety about social situations in which the person could be observed or judged by others. Symptoms include distress about and avoidance of these situations, fear of embarrassment and shame, and disruption of functioning. In schools, a student may isolate him- or herself, refuse to answer questions in class, or show a pattern of being absent on days with assignments to speak before the class. Around 7%

of children or adolescents experience Social Anxiety Disorder, and it is about twice as common among girls.

Generalized Anxiety Disorder (GAD) is the experience of excessive worry and anxiety and occurs most days of the week about a number of different events and activities. Individuals experiencing GAD have difficulty controlling worry and often have other symptoms such as tiring easily, having concentration problems, feeling tense, and having disturbed sleep. Teachers may identify a student with GAD by noticing the student seems fidgety, is obviously nervous or tense, or startles easily. The disorder affects about 1% of children or adolescents, with girls twice as likely to experience GAD.

Depressive Disorders

Depressive disorders involve disturbance of mood, including feelings of sadness or irritability, that are associated with changes in physical and cognitive functioning. The most common depressive disorders affecting children and adolescents are Disruptive Mood Regulation Disorder, Major Depressive Disorder, and Persistent Depressive Disorder.

Disruptive Mood Regulation Disorder is characterized by chronic and severe irritability, with frequent temper outbursts manifested verbally or physically that are dramatically out of proportion to the situation. This is a new diagnostic category that attempts to be a less pejorative and more accurate diagnosis than using Bipolar Disorder in children. Symptoms that teachers might observe in students are big mood swings, from compliant, calm, and on-task to agitated and disruptive from one time period, day, or few days to the next. Estimated prevalence is around 2%–5%, with higher rates (level not specified) for males.

Major Depressive Disorder (MDD) reflects significant depressive symptoms, including depressed mood almost every day, and other problems such as reduced activity and interests, notable weight loss or weight gain (without such plans), sleeping problems, loss of energy, feelings of worthlessness, inability to concentrate, frequent thoughts of death, and suicidal thoughts and actions. Symptoms that teachers may see are failure to complete schoolwork, lack of engagement with others, slow movement, tiredness, frequent absences, or flat affect (i.e., a facial expression that seems neutral or sad and does not often change). Prevalence data for MDD for children and adolescents is not well established; for young adults, it is around 7%, with females two to three times more likely to experience it. Children and adolescents with MDD have greater risk for suicide attempts than youth with other disorders, with risk increasing with past attempts, current thoughts of self-harm, plans for self-harm, means to implement these plans, and disregard for negative consequences of attempting suicide.

Persistent Depressive Disorder is also a new diagnostic category concerning long-term depressive symptoms, with symptom severity not reaching the level of MDD. In school, these students may be withdrawn and show symptoms of MDD, but not as intensely, with problems seeming more chronic or trait-like. Prevalence is estimated at around 1%, with no clear data for children and adolescents.

Disruptive Behavioral Disorders

Disruptive Behavioral Disorders (DBDs) are characterized by problems in behavioral or emotional regulation and control and by behaviors that violate the rights of others and/or bring the person into significant conflict with societal norms. DBDs include ODD, Intermittent Explosive Disorder, Conduct Disorder, and ADHD.

ODD is a pattern of angry or irritable mood and vindictiveness or defiant behavior, with symptoms such as frequent loss of temper, being easily annoyed, arguing with authority figures, refusing to follow rules, and blaming others for misbehavior. Teachers may notice behaviors such as a student frequently failing to follow the school or classroom expectations, repeatedly engaging in arguments with school staff, exhibiting frequent temper tantrums, and failing to take responsibility for misbehavior, any of which would suggest ODD. Prevalence of ODD is estimated at 3%–4%, with more common presence in males than females (1.5 to 1).

Intermittent Explosive Disorder (IED) reflects a pattern of frequent behavioral outbursts, including verbal or physical aggression, with aggressive actions clearly out of proportion to circumstances. A student with IED may periodically exhibit periods of rage, including destructive and/or aggressive behaviors that are not responsive to intervention. Prevalence is estimated at around 3%, with no specific data for children and adolescents.

Conduct Disorder (CD) is associated with the concept of juvenile delinquency and represents a repetitive pattern of behavior in which the rights of others and age-appropriate societal norms are violated, with symptoms including bullying, starting fights, using weapons, being cruel to others, stealing, destroying property, and blatantly disregarding parental rules. Students with CD may engage in serious behavior problems at school, such as fighting, bringing a weapon to school, coming to school after using drugs or alcohol, skipping school, violating school rules, and having frequent conflicts with staff and students. Prevalence is estimated at around 4%, with rates higher for males (but not specified how much higher).

ADHD reflects a persistent pattern of hyperactivity and/or inattention that interferes with functioning, with symptoms including failing to pay attention to details, having difficulty sustaining attention, seeming to not listen when spoken to directly, poor follow-through on instructions, difficulty organizing tasks, avoiding tasks that involve sustained mental effort, being easily distracted and forgetful, fidgeting, getting out of seat, having a high level of motor activity, difficulty waiting turns, talking excessively, and blurting out comments. These behaviors are likely to be easily seen in the classroom, particularly during academic demands that require sustained attention. Teachers may also notice difficulties with organization and task completion, and the student may appear to lack self-control, such as being unable to stop blurting out answers. Prevalence is around 5% of children and adolescents, with some elevation (not specified) among males.

Trauma-Related Disorders

Trauma-Related Disorders reflect emotional/behavioral problems that follow the experience of trauma or extreme stress. In children and adolescents, these include Reactive Attachment Disorder, Posttraumatic Stress Disorder, and Acute Stress Disorder.

Reactive Attachment Disorder is a consistent pattern of withdrawn and inhibited behavior toward adult caregivers and others, limited social and emotional responsiveness to others, limited positive affect, or episodes of unexplained irritability or fearfulness without clear reason. Teachers may notice symptoms when they see that students seem stressed about interaction with other students or staff and/or are not interested in interacting. The prevalence is unknown, but may be up to 10% of children who were raised in institutions or environments where they experienced severe neglect.

Posttraumatic Stress Disorder (PTSD) follows extreme trauma such as near or threatened death, serious injury, or sexual violence. Symptoms of the disorder include recurrent and involuntary re-experiencing of intrusive and distressing memories of the trauma(s); distressing dreams; flashbacks or feeling like the event(s) is occurring again; distress and/or physical reactions when faced with cues associated with the event(s); avoidance of people, places, memories, and other stimuli associated with the event(s); altered or missing memories of the event(s); disturbed thinking; and changes in arousal such as being hypervigilant, startling easily, and having sleep problems. These symptoms must occur for 6 months or longer. In schools, signals of PTSD include students appearing "on edge," fidgety, unfocused, disorganized, and startling easily. Prevalence for the general population is around 9%, with no specific prevalence data for children and adolescents.

Acute Stress Disorder includes the symptoms of PTSD described above, but those symptoms occur for fewer than 6 months in duration. Prevalence can be up to 20% of people experiencing extremely stressful events such as severe car accidents, interpersonal assault, or death of a loved one with traumatic aspects. There are no specific prevalence data for children.

According to some experts, the value of the *DSM-5* for educators rests not so much in its classification of the various disorders as in assisting teachers in better understanding and planning interventions for students (Mattison, 2014).

IDENTIFICATION OF STUDENTS SUSPECTED OF HAVING EMOTIONAL AND BEHAVIORAL CHALLENGES

Since the passage of federal special education legislation, schools and school districts have personnel and procedures for initiating school-based referrals for children experiencing problems in school. However, ratios of mental health staff to students are often grossly inadequate in many schools (Weist, Lever, Bradshaw, & Owens, 2014), resulting in barriers to assessment and intervention services. In their work on the prevalence of psychiatric disorders among youth in the United States, Forness, Freeman, Paparella, Kauffman, and Walker (2012) concluded that 12% of the school population might experience at least moderate psychiatric disorders but that only about 1% of these youth are identified for services in special education under the label of EBD, leaving many, many students severely underidentified and underserved. Teachers, particularly in general education, provide a vital link between students experiencing difficulties in school and school-based mental health evaluations and intervention services (Walker & Severson, 1990).

In schools with slow or limited response to students' emotional and behavioral problems, advocacy, along with more information, is usually needed. For example, it is relatively easy for school personnel to identify children who act out and display ODD, CD, ADHD, and substance abuse issues, as they tend to make themselves readily conspicuous among the school population. It is not as easy to identify students suffering from fear, worry, anxiety, depression, and social withdrawal. However, students with both types of difficulties, without intervention, experience poor outcomes in school and later in life. When teachers suspect that students have concerning levels of emotional or behavioral problems, school-employed mental health staff such as psychologists, counselors, and social workers are important resources for securing further evaluation within the school and for making connections with appropriate community providers when necessary.

SCHOOL-BASED INTERVENTION FOR STUDENTS WITH MORE SERIOUS SOCIAL, EMOTIONAL, OR BEHAVIORAL PROBLEMS

As described throughout this book, a multi-tiered system of support, as in SWPBS, is an optimal framework to use in tailoring specific prevention and intervention strategies for promoting improved student functioning in the area of emotions and behavior, wellness, and school success. Tier 1, or schoolwide interventions(described in Chapter 2)—such as having clear and consistent school and expectations that reduce student conflicts and bullying, building positive and nurturing interactions among staff and students, and establishing consistent classroom management and instructional procedures (Chapters 4 and 5)—can help improve student functioning. Tier 2 interventions often involve focused identification and intervention for students without the need to label them (see Chapter 2). For example, students dealing with stressors such as parental divorce or the loss of a loved one might benefit from focused support to help them cope with the circumstances at hand, which may involve two or three sessions with the student and one of his or her parents that are aimed at understanding the stress, providing education about it, reviewing common reactions, and teaching strategies for successful coping. School-employed mental health professionals, such as school psychologists and counselors, often provide this type of focused support. Teachers can be trained to encourage and reinforce the use of these coping skills.

Intervention for more serious emotional or behavioral problems occurs at Tier 3, when teachers and mental health professionals coordinate efforts based on an individualized support plan focused on the unique needs of the student. For example, specific cognitive coping skills assist students in dealing with behavioral problems and problems such as depression and anxiety. To illustrate, goal-oriented thinking (Graziano, Mooney, Huber, & Ignasiak, 1979) is a strategy whereby students, when confronted with a challenging situation or one that has been associated with problems in the past, are trained to pause and ask themselves three questions: 1) What is my goal? (e.g., to do well in math class), 2) Is what I am doing right now helping me to reach my goal? (e.g., being bothered by Jimmy, who is staring at me—no!), 3) If not, what can I do differently? (e.g., ignore Jimmy). Students are then prompted to choose the new or best option. Such training in cognitive coping has been integrated into schoolwide social-emotional learning programs such as Promoting Alternative Thinking Strategies (PATHS; Greenberg, Mihalic, & Kusche, 1998) as a Tier 1 intervention and has also been used in early intervention efforts in Tier 2. This type of intervention can also be used on an individual and more frequent basis for students at Tier 3.

We should also note that in schools, students with externalizing behavioral problems such as defiance, talking back, not obeying rules, and being verbally and physically aggressive often receive attention or some response from school personnel. Common responses to these behaviors are often not helpful. Disciplinary actions such as suspension may inadvertently reinforce the negative behaviors by enabling students to engage in the preferred activity of playing video games at home. Later in this chapter, we discuss effective strategies for responding to these behavioral problems. However, students with internalizing problems—often associated with depression, anxiety, and trauma (e.g., being isolated and not interacting with other students, seeming sad, not participating in class)—seldom receive the same level of attention from school personnel (Weist, Myers, Hastings, Ghuman, & Han, 1999). Although these behaviors do not stand out like externalizing behaviors and are often not as observable, these students' emotional and behavioral concerns are real, interfere with academic performance, and often respond well to evidence-based intervention. In the following sections, we review evidence-based interventions for students with externalizing and internalizing problems. As previously discussed, components of these same interventions will be used by mental health professionals in more intensive interventions with students, but this does not in any way preclude their use by teachers. For each of the skills, we briefly comment on the appropriateness and viability of implementation by teachers.

Modular versus Manualized Intervention

An increasingly prominent theme in school practice is the need to identify *evidence-based interventions,* meaning that a sufficient amount of high-quality research has been conducted on the practice to ensure that it results in the desired student outcome. Child and adolescent SMH practice includes more than 200 evidence-based manualized interventions (see the web site of the National Registry of Evidence-Based Programs and Practices of the Substance Abuse and Mental Health Services Administration, http://www.nrepp.samhsa.gov/). The interventions usually include programs with at least 10 sessions of an hour or more. Unfortunately, the programs prescribe strict adherence to content for each session and are often difficult to use in clinic and school settings (Schaeffer et al., 2005). For example, ACTION is a treatment program used in schools targeting depression in middle school students (Stark, Schnoebelen, Simpson, Hargrave, & Glenn, 2007). It includes 20 group and two individual meetings, and an additional eight-session parent training component (Stark, Simpson, Yancy, & Molnar, 2007). The program has been documented to reduce depression in youth as compared to students receiving "minimal" services for depression in schools (Patel, Stark, Metz, & Banneyer, 2014).

However, consider the significant staff resources, training, and ongoing coaching required to implement such a manualized program in schools. Although programs such as ACTION are critical for informing schools and youth-serving agencies about how to effectively treat emotional or behavioral disorders in children and youth, there are legitimate questions about how feasible they are to implement (Schaeffer et al., 2005). As a result, there has been a move to "modular" interventions, which focus on the top skills associated with improvement among youth diagnosed with particular disorders. This work began in Hawaii at its Department of Health in the early 2000s, led by Bruce Chorpita and Eric Daleiden (2009; also see Chorpita, Daleiden, & Weisz, 2005) and has expanded significantly since then. Chorpita and Daleiden reviewed the literature on effective interventions for children and youth with emotional or behavioral disorders, with the most common being anxiety, depression, trauma-related, and conduct problems. For each disorder area (as well as other areas, such as autism and substance abuse), particular skills that were taught and described in research studies were documented and assigned ratings depending on the extent to which they were associated with effective outcomes. This process led to identification of "winning" or top practice elements with the strongest empirical support.

Targeted skills commonly reflected a cognitive-behavioral therapy (CBT) approach to intervention that emphasizes altering problematic thoughts, feelings, and behaviors that contribute to emotional and behavioral problems. This approach is an objective, data-informed approach based on social learning principles (Bandura, 1963) that emphasizes teaching of skills through modeling, behavioral rehearsal, feedback, ongoing homework for practice of the skill application, and reinforcement of the skills by the therapist. Ongoing collection and analysis of data are used to determine if the interventions lead to desired change.

Chorpita and colleagues developed the PracticeWise system (see https://www.practicewise.com), a user-friendly strategy for clinicians to identify and provide training to students and families on the top skills related to the particular problem or disorder a student experiences. Consistent with the disorders reviewed earlier, a version of PracticeWise is called MATCH-ADTC, describing evidence-based interventions matched to the problems and disorders of anxiety, depression, trauma, and conduct problems. Although the PracticeWise system is copyrighted, specific skills contained within the system fall within common knowledge of effective CBT. In the following section, we describe some of the top evidence-based skills for assisting youth with these four problems or disorders.

EVIDENCE-BASED SKILLS FOR INTERNALIZING DISORDERS (DEPRESSION, ANXIETY, TRAUMA-RELATED)

A number of evidence-based skills are relevant for all internalizing disorders. Some of the more important and frequently trained skills include psychoeducation, cognitive coping, problem solving, and relaxation.

Psychoeducation

Psychoeducation is an evidence-based practice that is effective for all disorders. This approach helps children, adolescents, and family members learn about particular problems, why they occur, and how they can be managed and overcome. For example, the PracticeWise system describes anxiety as a typical reaction that all people experience, working as the body's "natural alarm" to protect them from danger. For students with anxiety problems, the alarm can be too sensitive, going off too easily. Hence, a goal of therapy is to help the individual learn about real versus false alarms.

Cognitive Coping

Many cognitive coping strategies are based on Beck's triangle of thoughts, feelings, and actions and how they interact together (see Beck, Rush, Shaw, & Emery, 1979). For example, an event happens (e.g., name calling), followed by an interpretation of that event (e.g., thinking "that was mean"), which affects feelings (e.g., thinking "that upsets me") and actions (e.g., avoidance of the other child). Students are helped to alter thoughts (e.g., "he does that all the time to many students"), which alter feelings (e.g., neutral) and actions (e.g., business as usual). The emphasis is on thoughts, feelings, and actions being controllable. Cognitive coping strategies cue the individual to identify negative or upsetting events; pause to explore possible thoughts, feelings, and actions in response to the events; use the most adaptive responses; and provide self-encouragement or praise for doing so.

Problem Solving

Problem solving is a version of cognitive coping. It involves helping students to 1) identify when they are in a stressful situation or one that has been a problem for them in the past, 2) pause, ascertaining possible actions to take in the situation, 3) evaluate the costs and benefits of each action, then 4) choose and take the action with the best ratio of benefits to costs. The goal-oriented thinking strategy (Graziano et al., 1979) is an example of a problem-solving strategy. The strategy involves training the student in these four steps, identifying situations in which problem-solving skills are often needed (e.g., on the playground where there are two aggressive peers who commonly engage in mild taunting behavior), and then prompting the student to use these skills in those situations by debriefing with him or her on how it went, in addition to providing encouragement and praise for using the skills and avoiding problems associated with these situations.

Note that, for both cognitive coping and problem solving, students are taught that thoughts, feelings, and behaviors are not automatic, that they have control over them, and that health and wellness are promoted when positive choices are made in difficult circumstances.

Relaxation

Relaxation training focuses on three primary skills: deep breathing, progressive muscle relaxation, and imagery. For deep breathing, the student is taught to get in a comfortable position and slowly breathe in through the nose—breathing deeply so that the stomach pushes out—hold the breath for a second, and exhale through the mouth. During the exhale, the student is taught to focus on feeling the tension leave the body. For progressive muscle relaxation, individuals are taught to progressively tense and then relax muscle groups, beginning in the feet, proceeding up the body (i.e., calves, thighs, stomach, chest, biceps, hands, neck, forehead) and then back down, again focusing on feelings of relaxation and releasing tension. For imagery, students are taught to imagine a favorite place or memory and to let feelings of tension go as they imagine the scene. In a typical scenario, the student is told, "You are at the beach, sitting in a comfortable chair. You can feel the sun on your face, hear the ocean and seagulls. You feel really relaxed and at peace. Imagine that you are in this scene; let feelings of tension slip away from your body. . . ." In teaching these skills, again using social learning principles, the mental health practitioner first demonstrates the skill, has the student practice, gives the individual feedback and asks for his or her feedback, then discusses which approach or combination of approaches the student prefers. Homework is then given to practice the skill(s) every day in the coming week. The advantage of deep breathing is that it can be used anywhere. Students often prefer combined approaches, such as deep breathing and imagery or progressive muscle relaxation together, but this requires being in a private place.

Pleasant Activity Scheduling

For depression, an additional important skill is pleasant activity scheduling. This is related to the downward spiraling of depression. That is, depressed mood contributes to reduced involvement in activities that were previously pleasurable. This reduced involvement makes depressed mood worse, which further decreases the likelihood of involvement in pleasant activities. Negative spiraling often affects academic performance, with poor performance having the same exacerbating effect on mood, which further impairs assignment completion and so on. Using metaphors like Just Do It (from Nike commercials), students are taught about this spiraling, and with the mental health practitioner, generate a list of previously pleasurable activities. The practitioner and student then problem-solve together on a few viable pleasant activities to engage in during the coming week, with assignments to engage in at least one activity per day. As the individual begins to reengage, the number of assigned activities progressively increase. A variation on pleasant activity scheduling is having children and their families problem-solve on ways they can increase involvement in functional behaviors, such as studying and completing homework.

Exposure

For anxiety and fears, an additional evidence-based skill is exposure. Using exposure, the mental health practitioner first has the student make a list or hierarchy of the least threatening to most threatening aspects of a particular event that leads to anxiety and/or fear. For example, if the child is afraid of the neighborhood dog, the hierarchy might include thinking about walking past the dog the night before, waking up in the morning and thinking about it, preparing to leave the house, being 50 feet away, being 20 feet away, being 5 feet away, and being right near the dog while it barks very loudly.

Exposure can be imaginal or in vivo. Using imaginal exposure, the mental health practitioner first trains the individual in relaxation, having him or her give levels of anxiety and/or fear a score (e.g., from 1 "no fear at all" to 10 "more scared than ever before"). The practitioner then guides the student in vividly imagining the scenario at the lowest level of the hierarchy while engaging in a relaxation technique. This step is repeated until the individual rates anxiety after the imaginal exposure at 5 or less (as an example); then the individual and practitioner proceed to the next step on the hierarchy.

Exposure is also an essential element of treating children who have been traumatized. First, the therapist empathizes with the individual in relation to what he or she has been through and provides information on the prevalence of the problem, discussing that many others have experienced it and gone on to overcome the problem and lead successful and happy lives. Then the practitioner encourages the student to tell the whole story (e.g., of abuse that occurred over a year-long period) in summary form, then to break the story down into segments, as described previously, ordering segments from least to most threatening. The individual is then guided in talking and/or writing about segments, proceeding from less threatening to more, again using a rating system of ability to cope with feelings associated with particular events, to guide going on to more threatening steps.

In working with traumatized individuals, metaphors are used such as "If you get a bad cut, and it gets infected, you have to get the infection out. Our talking is like that, helping you to get the pain from what happened to you out and in the open." Students are taught that the memories of what happened will likely not go away, but that they will be able to cope with and accept what happened; for example, being able to say, "Yes, that happened to me, but I know that was not my fault, and many others have experienced it, and I am okay. I can talk about what happened to me" (see an excellent book, *Treating Traumatized Children,* by Beverly James, 1989).

As described earlier in this section, when students experience anxiety, depression, or trauma, mental health professionals can use a variety of specialized interventions to teach students coping skills to alleviate their stress and lead them to successful outcomes. It is important that mental health professionals communicate and collaborate with school staff regarding selected strategies. Communication about selected interventions will increase teachers' knowledge of mental health approaches as well as increase the likelihood that an intervention will be generalized across school settings. For example, when made aware that a student has been taught to use a relaxation strategy or a specific problem-solving strategy, teachers can gently encourage the student to use the strategy when he or she begins to show anxiety in the classroom.

EVIDENCE-BASED SKILLS FOR EXTERNALIZING PROBLEMS

In Chapter 2, we discuss intervention at the schoolwide level to prevent externalizing problems. In addition, we describe more intensive interventions in Chapter 9. In this section, we offer a description of interventions that involve parents. Please note that involving parents and other family members in intervention to improve student emotional or behavioral functioning is commonly the role of mental health professionals such as school psychologists and counselors. In some cases, teachers can assist in making connections between family members and these professionals, and in other cases, teachers may have a more direct role.

In general, involving parents, and in some cases other family members, in treating children with internalizing and externalizing behavioral problems is important. This is especially true for children with externalizing problems, with much of the work to assist them focused on educating family members in strategies to manage their behavior.

Psychoeducation

Psychoeducation is an evidence-based intervention for parents and caregivers of children with acting-out behavior problems. For example, educating parents about positive and negative reinforcement is an important intervention strategy. Also, it is advantageous to talk about instances of "behavioral traps," wherein the child's negative behaviors are positively reinforced (e.g., parent gives in to the yelling and demanding behaviors by permitting the child to play with video games) and the parents' acquiescing behaviors are negatively reinforced (e.g., by the stopping of the yelling and demanding behavior). In addition, some of the skills reviewed in the previous section, such as cognitive coping, problem solving, and relaxation, are also relevant for children with externalizing problems. Mental health staff frequently conduct psychoeducation for parents; however, there may be times where it is appropriate or even indicated for the teacher to provide this training.

Efforts to help parents in the area of child behavior management should emphasize positive or neutral strategies along with a continuum of discipline strategies (that do not cause pain and are not stigmatizing) that can be used if positive or neutral methods are not successful. Positive strategies include communication, fun interaction, praise, and tangible reinforcement and rewards. A neutral strategy is ignoring the problem behavior. Discipline strategies may include time-out or response cost (e.g., removing privileges when a negative behavior occurs). Although mental health professionals often provide training to families in these strategies, they represent common knowledge and common sense strategies for improving child and adolescent behavior. As noted above, teachers may have an indirect or more direct role in these interventions.

Communication

Families with children who have disruptive behavior disorders usually have coexisting communication problems that include yelling by parents and yelling back by children and/or ignoring or engaging in other disrespectful behavior (e.g., laughing, smirking when the parent is attempting to convey something serious). Most often, student–parent interactions are beyond the realm of duties for teacher intervention. However, knowledge of key themes for intervention is helpful. For example, with cases of disordered communication, the therapist works with the family by modeling calm communication and by calmly implementing appropriate consequences when necessary. Teachers can emphasize this approach when they meet with parents.

Fun Interactions

In families with long-term conflict, often the history of conflict has resulted in relationship problems, with parents becoming highly negative about the disruptive child. Prescribing fun interactions between the parent and child helps get the relationship back on track. For example, the family is guided to spend 15 minutes or a half hour each day in recreational activities chosen by the child (e.g., drawing, board games, playing ball) and to let the child lead these activities while the parents refrain from critical comments or providing formal guidance to the child. The key is creating relaxed time that is focused on building the parent–child relationship, not instructing or formally seeking to improve behavior.

Praise

Praise is something that should happen often with children, even those who are presenting very challenging acting-out behaviors. Praise is a behavioral skill referenced throughout this book that teachers and parents should emphasize in their roles as promoters of positive child behavior. Effective praise should specifically reference the valued behavior, be genuine and enthusiastic, and should not be qualified (e.g., "I like the way you cleaned your room, but you need to make your bed better"). Inadvertent praise is especially powerful. With inadvertent praise, the parent (or teacher) praises a behavior or action by the child in conversation with someone else, within hearing range of the child, but in a way that conveys he or she does not know the child is listening.

Other strategies to promote positive behavior, including reinforcement and active ignoring, are reviewed elsewhere in this book (see Chapter 9).

Punitive or disciplinary strategies for children with acting-out behaviors include time-out and response cost (presented in Chapter 9). In general, these strategies should be used after positive strategies have been tried and have not been successful or as successful as expected, and/or if the child is engaging in dangerous behavior. As noted earlier, parents are commonly taught to use these strategies when receiving school or community mental health services for a student's acting-out behaviors. Teachers may be directly or indirectly involved in implementing them as well.

Time-Out

Time-out is an effective strategy for younger children, generally age 8 and younger, wherein children are separated and placed in a quiet place that does not involve stimulation or access to reinforcement following negative behavior such as yelling, hitting, and noncompliance. The child is first told that the negative behavior is not appropriate and that the consequence will be time-out, with a description of the procedure and the place where it will occur. For example, "Hitting others is not okay. Next time you hit someone, you will go to time-out in your room." Usually, when the negative behavior is displayed after this instruction, a warning is given that the next incident will result in time-out. Following the negative behavior, the parent calmly instructs (or escorts, if necessary) the child to the time-out area, with length of time in minutes usually matching the child's age (e.g., 3 minutes for a 3-year-old). If time-out follows noncompliance with a command (e.g., "Please pick up your toys"), then after leaving time-out, the command is reissued, and if the child does not comply he or she goes back into time-out and the cycle continues until completion of the requested behavior, which should be followed by praise.

EFFECTIVE CHILD AND ADOLESCENT THERAPY AND THE ROLE OF TEACHERS

Reforms in child and adolescent therapy have resulted in moving away from approaches that emphasize individual "psychopathology" (a highly pejorative term that, in our view, should no longer be used) to skill-building strategies that recognize the significant influence the environment has on behavior (see Weist et al., 2014). A major theme in this new approach to child and adolescent mental health is that almost all people who interact with children have the potential to be in roles of mental health promoters, and that is most prominently the case with primary care providers and teachers. Effective SMH practitioners learn to select and tailor particular strategies based on each student's needs. Almost all effective therapy with children and adolescents involves working with family members and is skill-focused, as in the modular skills presented earlier in this chapter. Many of the skills trained in therapy with children are skills that teachers are familiar with, and in many cases, teachers can play an important role in teaching the skills and/or promoting their use in the classroom (e.g., cuing relaxation when a student seems stressed, problem-solving a situation with a peer).

As emphasized throughout this book, much of the knowledge regarding child and adolescent therapy is both accessible to and usable by teachers. Skills that address externalizing disorders reflect common sense strategies, and many of the skills for internalizing problems represent problem-solving and coping skills that can benefit all people. Teachers can expand their role in providing mental health support for their students by embracing helping strategies that they have confidence in and seeking additional training as makes sense, including soliciting assistance from school-employed or community-employed mental health professionals when students present more intensive needs. This is not to say that teachers should become counselors or that they should compromise teaching roles to engage in supportive and helping roles with students. Rather, teachers should recognize that they are already a powerful influence in promoting positive emotional and behavioral health in students, and should embrace this role with appropriate training and support.

Use of a team process for communicating among key professionals, coordinating actions, and collecting data for decision making are efficient ways to build comprehensive supports for students with emotional and behavioral disorders (see Barrett, Eber, & Weist, 2013). Teachers should always serve on school-based teams for students receiving intensive or Tier 3 intervention. In addition, there should not be policy barriers that prevent school-employed mental health staff from sharing information with teachers on intervention strategies and the ways teachers can support the intervention. If school-based mental health providers are contracted by community agencies, releases of information should be obtained to enable ongoing collaboration with teachers. Although it is not necessary to share comprehensive background information on the student or family (and sharing may be viewed as a privacy concern), mental health providers should share key parameters of the intervention plan, such as skills that are being taught and ways that the teacher can support the intervention. For example, if a child is working on anxiety management and being taught relaxation strategies, the teacher can be taught the same strategies (e.g., deep breathing) so that he or she is able to subtly prompt the student to use the trained skills upon observing that the child is getting anxious. Teachers also play a critical role in providing feedback to mental health staff on progress the student is making in class (e.g., assignment completion, being on task, following rules), as this progress is a key outcome indicator on the effectiveness of the mental health intervention.

STRENGTHENING SCHOOLWIDE MENTAL HEALTH SUPPORTS

Decision-making teams in schools are essential for students to receive appropriate mental health intervention for emotional and behavioral challenges. Guidance on improving school mental health practices can be found in a monograph on interconnecting SWPBS and school mental health, found on the national technical assistance web site (http://www.pbis.org) and the national Center for School Mental Health Assistance web site (http://csmh.umaryland.edu; also see Barrett, Eber, & Weist, 2013). Guiding questions for teams to consider when seeking to improve mental health practices in the school include the following: Is the principal supportive of enhancing appropriate mental health services for students, and can teachers and school staff set up a meeting with him or her to discuss concerns and advocate for improved mental health response? How are teams focused on student behavior functioning? Are they inclusive? Do they place adequate emphasis on emotional and behavioral concerns as barriers to learning? Are they welcoming and respectful of students and families? Is follow-up to team decision making adequate? Answers to these questions can serve as a blueprint for strengthening mental health practices in the school setting.

An important related theme is that positive emotional or behavioral and school functioning by children and adolescents is a key priority for society, arguably among the most important agendas for any community. Positive functioning connects to academic promotion, graduation, and positive citizenship. Increasingly, leaders in schools and other youth-serving agencies (e.g., mental health, primary care, child welfare, juvenile justice) recognize that the work of improving student functioning and school success reflects a shared agenda, with all agencies and key stakeholder groups (e.g., families, youth, businesses, communities of faith) having a strong vested interest. However, whereas such a shared agenda is aspirational, in many communities, the reality is that each of the systems for youth operates independently. Issues of "turf" continue, so that systems and the professional disciplines working within them are threatened by other systems and disciplines and engage in behaviors that are focused on protecting resources. Many of these challenges are being overcome, and artificial and turf-related boundaries are being broken down; for example, in the SMH field (see Weist et al., 2014), where clear benefits for a shared agenda are being articulated and experienced. This is also being seen in the move to interconnect SMH with positive behavioral interventions and supports (see Barrett et al., 2013), wherein broader school and community efforts are being anchored to an effective multi-tiered framework in the schools. These efforts include inclusive and effective teams, systematic outreach to community agencies by schools and "inreach" by community agencies into the schools, mutual training and collaboration, and moving from multidisciplinary to transdisciplinary approaches wherein staff from different disciplines actually share roles and responsibilities. In addition to consulting references reviewed in this section, teachers can learn more about this collaborative approach to improving emotional or behavioral and school functioning for students through a national community of practice found at http://www.sharedwork.org.

Case Example

Here we present a case example of an eighth grade English teacher, Ms. Macintosh, working with a student, Amanda, who presented more concerning mental health challenges. There was no prior identification of emotional or behavioral concerns for Amanda, who moved into the school system 3 weeks before school started. Review of her academic records revealed that she had been in three different elementary schools and one prior middle school across four states, due to her father's career as a sergeant in the U.S. Army. There was a history of frequent absences, ranging from 12 to 31 missed days in prior school years, with few absences (three) in only 1 year (second grade). Amanda's grades were adequate, with mostly Bs and Cs, an occasional A, and an occasional D. Standardized test scores indicated roughly average performance in most academic areas.

Ms. Macintosh went out of her way to greet Amanda on the first day of school, and each day after would greet her and offer her support (e.g., "I know you are new to the school, Amanda. Please let me know if I can help you in any way."). Amanda seemed very shy and reserved, did not interact much with other students, and by a month into school had already missed 6 days and been late 4 additional days.

Ms. Macintosh organized a conference with Amanda and her parents. Amanda's mother, Ms. Freeman, attended, but not her father (related to being unable to get off from work). Amanda had a younger brother, Brent, who was in fifth grade in the local elementary school. Amanda's mother reported that Amanda's peer relations had been declining for about 2 years and seemed to worsen with the move to the new community this summer. She tended to stay in her room and watch TV, listen to music, or play with her iPad. She had so far not made friends in her neighborhood, nor did she appear interested. Ms. Freeman indicated that Amanda slept poorly and that she often found Amanda in the middle of the night using her iPad, saying she could not sleep, and then being very difficult to rouse in the morning. Amanda's relationships with her family were similarly limited—she rarely initiated conversation or smiled, and responded to family attempts at communication with brief, few-word answers and limited eye contact. Ms. Freeman indicated that Amanda and Brent used to be close, but for at least the past year, Amanda showed no interest in Brent. This was initially upsetting to Brent, but now it appeared that he had moved on. Ms. Freeman also reported problems in her marriage, indicating that she and her husband had received counseling but were now just going through the motions and she was unsure of whether the marriage would make it. Her husband had been deployed three times, had showed some signs of PTSD, and lately seemed to be coping by working a lot and hanging around with his friends. During the meeting with her mother, Amanda said little and seemed distracted and disinterested.

Based on the meeting with Amanda and her mother, Ms. Macintosh became concerned that Amanda might be dealing with depression and/or anxiety. She made a referral to the school psychologist, Dr. Tilman, to express her concern, and Dr. Tilman conducted a focused evaluation documenting that indeed Amanda was presenting noteworthy symptoms of depression, including some thoughts of self-harm. There was no prior history of counseling. Dr. Tilman began seeing Amanda twice per week, focusing on providing CBT to improve her depression. This therapy included working with her mother and Amanda to provide psychoeducation about depression and teaching

Amanda skills including cognitive coping, relaxation, and pleasant activity scheduling. Dr. Tilman worked with Ms. Freeman and Ms. Macintosh to review these skills so they could reinforce Amanda when she used them at home and school. Dr. Tilman also worked on helping Amanda with social skills, including approaching social interaction with peers with more confidence. Ms. Macintosh used the template matching strategy (see Chapter 6) with Amanda, helping her to identify two female classmates, Shannon and Amber, who were doing well in school and who had positive social relations. Amanda observed how Shannon and Amber handled certain situations and began to model these behaviors, and even began to develop a friendship with Shannon.

Dr. Tilman worked with Amanda for 4 months, initially seeing her twice per week, then around once per week, for a total of 17 individual CBT sessions (each lasting around 30 minutes). Ms. Macintosh checked in with Amanda at the end of the class, inquiring how she was doing and providing encouragement for her to use the skills Dr. Tilman was teaching her. They developed a system wherein Ms. Macintosh would wink at her when there was an obviously stressful situation occurring, serving as a prompt for Amanda to use her cognitive coping skills. Over time, Amanda showed progressive improvement in her emotional and behavioral functioning in school, which was also associated with increased social interaction, improved school attendance, improved family functioning (and renewed friendship with her brother), and improved academic performance (from Cs and Ds in Quarter 1 to Bs and one A in Quarter 3). Ms. Macintosh was encouraged by Amanda's improvement. She also felt like she was a key team member, working with Dr. Tilman to help improve Amanda's functioning and school adjustment.

SUMMARY

Emotional or behavioral challenges in children and adolescents include internalizing problems such as depression, anxiety, and trauma-related concerns, and externalizing problems such as oppositional or defiant behaviors, conduct problems, and attention problems. Teachers can provide critical assistance to students and families in helping to identify these disorders in youth, in working with mental health professionals to coordinate and support effective intervention, and in some cases, to directly assist students in need. Many of the modular skills associated with effective practices reflect a cognitive-behavioral perspective as well as practices many teachers are already using. Although teachers are not therapists—and the demands of teaching preclude formal counseling with students—they play a very important role in promoting student mental health and wellness and in addressing their emotional and behavioral challenges, a theme emphasized throughout this book.

Self-Reflection

1. Think about mental health issues you have encountered in your own life, in your family, and/or among your friends (remember that these issues are very common and most people encounter them). What is your view about mental health challenges? How does this view affect your view of students presenting more serious emotional or behavioral challenges?
2. Teachers are very busy professionals. What is your reaction to the idea that teachers are the "de facto" mental health providers, identifying and ideally helping students with emotional or behavioral challenges? What resources and supports would you need to embrace this role? How has this book helped equip you to better address mental health challenges in students?
3. Students with emotional or behavioral problems are commonly stigmatized in schools. Can you think of examples of how this has happened in your school or a school you have visited? What can you do about this stigmatization?
4. The literature strongly indicates that effectively reducing and addressing emotional or behavioral challenges in students helps to remove barriers to their learning and improve their school performance. If you were going to give a 2-minute elevator speech to a school leader (e.g., principal, superintendent, school board member) on the importance of teachers being equipped to address mental health challenges in students, what would you say?
5. Think of a student in your classroom or a classroom you have visited who you know is struggling with emotional or behavioral problems. What are specific ways to provide compassionate and science-based assistance to this student this week?

REFERENCES

American Psychiatric Association. (2013). *Diagnostic and statistical manual of mental disorders* (5th ed.). Arlington, VA: American Psychiatric Association.

Bandura, A. (1963). *Social learning and personality development.* New York, NY: Holt, Rinehart, & Winston.

Barrett, S., Eber, L., & Weist, M.D. (2013). *Advancing education effectiveness: An interconnected systems framework for positive behavioral interventions and supports (PBIS) and school mental health.* Center for Positive Behavioral Interventions and Supports (funded by the Office of Special Education Programs, U.S. Department of Education). Eugene: University of Oregon Press.

Beck, A.T., Rush, A.J., Shaw, B.F., & Emery, G. (1979). *Cognitive therapy of depression.* New York, NY: Guilford.

Chorpita, B.F., & Daleiden, E.L. (2009). *The child and adolescent mental health division biennial report: Effective psychosocial intervention for youth with behavioral and emotional needs.* Retrieved from http://hawaii.gov/health/mentalhealth/camhd/library/pdf/ebs/ebs013.pdf

Chorpita, B.F., Daleiden, E.L., & Weisz, J.R. (2005). Identifying and selecting the common elements of evidence based interventions: A distillation and matching model. *Mental Health Services Research, 7,* 5–20. doi:10.1007/s11020-005-1962-6

Forness, S.R., Freeman, S.F.N., Paparella, T., Kauffman, J.M., & Walker, H.M. (2012). Special education implications of point and cumulative prevalence for children with emotional and behavioral disorders. *Journal of Emotional and Behavioral Disorders, 20,* 4–18.

Graziano, A.M., Mooney, K.C., Huber, C., & Ignasiak, D. (1979). Self-control instructions for children's fear reduction: A multiple case study. *Behavior Therapy & Experimental Psychiatry, 10,* 221–227.

Greenberg, M.T., Mihalic, S.F., & Kusche, C.A. (1998). *Promoting alternative thinking strategies.* Center for the Study and Prevention of Violence, Institute of Behavioral Science, University of Colorado at Boulder.

James, B. (2009). *Treating traumatized children: New insights and creative interventions.* New York, NY: Simon & Schuster.

Mattison, R.E. (2014). The interface between child psychiatry and special education in the treatment of students with emotional/behavioral disorders in school settings. In H.M. Walker & F.M. Gresham (Eds.), *Handbook of evidence-based practices for emotional and behavioral disorders* (pp. 104–126). New York, NY: Guilford Press.

Patel, P.G., Stark, K.D., Metz, K.L., & Banneyer, K.N. (2014). School-based interventions for depression. In M. Weist, N. Lever, C. Bradshaw, & J. Owens (Eds.), *Handbook of school mental health: Research, training, practice and policy* (2nd ed., pp. 369–383). New York, NY: Springer.

Rosemond, J.K. (2005). The diseasing of America's children: The politics of diagnosis. In R.H. Wright & N.A. Cummings (Eds.), *Destructive trends in mental health: The well-intentioned path to harm* (pp. 219–233). New York, NY: Routledge.

Schaeffer, C.M., Bruns, E., Weist, M.D., Stephan, S.H., Goldstein, J., & Simpson, Y. (2005). Overcoming challenges to evidence-based interventions in schools. *Journal of Youth and Adolescence, 34,* 15–22.

Stark, K.D., Schnoebelen, S., Simpson, J., Hargrave, J., & Glenn, R. (2007). *Treating depressed children: Therapist manual for ACTION.* Ardmore, PA: Workbook Publishing.

Stark, K.D., Simpson, J., Yancy, M., & Molnar, J. (2007). *Parents' workbook for ACTION.* Ardmore, PA: Workbook Publishing.

Walker, H.M., & Severson, H.H. (1990). *Systematic screening for behavioral disorders: Technical manual.* Longmont, CO: Sopris West.

Walker, J., Geddes, A., Lever, N., Andrews, C., & Weist, M.D. (2010). Reconsidering the term "emotional disturbance": A report from Maryland. *Advances in School Mental Health Promotion, 3*(2), 46–52.

Weist, M.D. (2003). Promoting paradigmatic change in child and adolescent mental health and schools. *School Psychology Review, 32,* 336–341.

Weist, M.D., Lever, N., Bradshaw, C., & Owens, J. (2014). *Handbook of school mental health: Research, training, practice, and policy* (2nd ed.). New York, NY: Springer.

Weist, M.D., Lever, N., Bradshaw, C., & Owens, J.S. (2014). Further advancing the field of school mental health. In M. Weist, N. Lever, C. Bradshaw, & J. Owens (Eds.), *Handbook of school mental health: Research, training, practice, and policy,* 2nd edition (pp. 1–16). New York: Springer.

Weist, M.D., Myers, C.P., Hastings, E., Ghuman, H., & Han, Y. (1999). Psychosocial functioning of youth receiving mental health services in the schools vs. community mental health centers. *Community Mental Health Journal, 35,* 69–81.

Index

References to tables and figures are indicated with a *t* and *f*, respectively